Hitler's Traitor

HITLER'S TRAITOR

Martin Bormann and the Defeat of the Reich

LOUIS KILZER

PRESIDIO

To Bobbie Gogain and her poetry

Published by Presidio Press, Inc.
505 B San Marin Drive, Suite 160
Novato, CA 94945-1340

Library of Congress Cataloging-in-Publication Data

Kilzer, Louis C.
    Hitler's traitor : Martin Bormann and the defeat of the Reich / Louis Kilzer.
       p. cm.
    Includes bibliographical references and index.
    ISBN 0-89141-710-9
    1. Bormann, Martin, 1900–1945. 2. World War, 1939–1945—Secret service—Soviet Union. 3. Spies—Germany—Biography. 4. World War, 1939–1945—Germany. I. Title.
    DD247.B65 K55 2000
    943.086'092—dc21
  [B]   00-029858

All photos courtesy the National Archives

Printed in the United States of America

CONTENTS

ACKNOWLEDGMENTS

There is no better friend to a World War II researcher than John Taylor. Since 1945, Mr. Taylor has chronicled the records of the war that are housed at the U.S. National Archives. As military archivist there, he helps young undergraduates and grizzled veterans alike with a memory that will never be replaced. He helped this author declassify secret records that made this book possible. Other staff members of the Archives contributed much, including Katherine Nicastro. E. J. McCarthy, editor of this book, put up sagely with some missed deadlines and, otherwise, helped this writer improve his work at every stage. Thank you also to Barbara Feller-Roth for her superb copyediting. In New York, Jane Dystel, my agent, is an invaluable savant and ally. Doug Vaughan, an irrepressible researcher, helped this author both with material and insight. Enoch Needham also helped me through the first chapters, as did Brian Richard Boylan. My wife, Liz Kovacs, helped in innumerable ways, including careful proofreading and general encouragement. Vitaly Konjoukov, a friend and former editor at the Soviet press agency Novosti, helped this author understand better the ways of Stalinist Russia and made several original translations of important Soviet-era articles. And a special thanks is due to my kids, Alex and Xanthe, for enduring a computer hog for a couple of years.

KEY PEOPLE AND ORGANIZATIONS

Abwehr The German military intelligence service.

General Ludwig Beck. Beck would form the core of the army's plotting against Hitler.

Dubendorfer, Rachel Code-named "Sissy." Dubendorfer controlled Rudolf Roessler, known as "Lucy," during the war. Though Dubendorfer refused orders from Stalin to turn over "Lucy" to other Soviet agents, she was allowed not only to live, but to advance in importance in the Soviet intelligence apparatus.

Foote, Alexander Code-naned "Jim," "Granatow," and "Albert Mueller." Foote was a wireless transmitter for the Red Army operation in Switzerland. Before that, he had planned to assassinate Hitler. His book, *Handbook for Spies,* is a classic in "Lucy" literature.

Funkspiel The practice of continuing to use a captured spy's radio transmitter in order to send the enemy often-incorrect intelligence.

Gilbert Code-name for Trepper.

GRU The intelligence arm of the Red Army.

Hamburger, Ursula Last names also are Kucyznski and Beurton. Code-named "Sonia." Hamburger was in charge of sabotage against Germany prior to the German-Soviet pact. She had planned the Alexander Foote assassination of Hitler. Later, she handled the Manhattan Project spy Klaus Fuchs for Soviet intelligence.

Kent Code-name for Sukulov.

Lucy. Code-name for Roessler.

Müller, Heinrich Head of the Gestapo and a creator of the funkspiel.

Moscow Center Also simply known as the Center, this was the short term for the organization that controlled foreign intelligence.

NKVD Soviet secret police and the predecessor of the KGB.

OKH High command of the German army.

OKW High command of the German armed forces.

Oster, Hans High official in the Abwehr who plotted against Hitler.

Pannwitz, Heinz. True name: Heinz Paulsen. He became a controversial figure after he took over the investigation of the assassination of Heydrich. Later commanded the Paris Sondercommando and tried to establish links to the Red Army.

Poliakova, Maria. Code-names: "Gisela," "Mildred," "Vera," and "Meg." Born in 1910, Poliakova headed Red Army penetration of Nazi Germany in 1936 and, at age 27, established Gisela's Family in Switzerland and France in 1937. Later, she became a spymaster for the Red Army 4th Department in Europe during the Second World War.

Rado, Alexander. Code-names: "Dora" and "Albert." Rado was the administrative head of the Rote Drei in Switzerland. Rachel Dubendorfer always challenged his authority.

Rote Kapelle. Also known as the Red Orchestra, this was the term the Germans used to depict Red Army intelligence rings in Europe during the war.

RSHA Reich Main Security Office. This contained the main security organs of the SS, including the Gestapo.

Roessler, Rudolf Code-named "Lucy." A journalist, Roessler developed fantastic sources in the German-Nazi elite, including "Teddy," "Olga," and "Anna." But it was "Werther," an agent in the OKW, who helped Stalin win the war.

Rote Drei Also referred as the Red Three, this was a term the Germans used to depict the Red Army organization in Switzerland. It got its name because the Germans detected that there were three radio transmitters beaming signals to Moscow from Switzerland.

SD Intelligence service within the RSHA.

Sonderkommando A combined German intelligence operation aimed at wiping out Soviet spies, particularly those operating via radio.

Sonia Code-name for Ursula Hamburger.

Sukulov, Victor, also known as Victor Sukolov Code-names "Vincente Sierra." "Kent," "Fritz," "Barcza." His true name is probably Gurevitch. Sukulov was Trepper's number two. He participated in the *funkspiel.*

Trepper, Leopold Code-named "Jean Gilbert," "Adam Mikler," "Ivanowski," "Winter," "Otto," and, most importantly, "Le Grand Chef," and the "Grand Chief." Trepper operated Soviet Intelligence networks in France and the Low Countries. The Germans considered him the number one Soviet spy. He participated in the funkspiel.

"Werther" The name given to the spy that penetrated the Nazi High Command.

INTRODUCTION

CONSPIRACY THEORY

This book describes a conspiracy in search of a theory. It purports to show how the most precious military orders of Adolf Hitler's Third Reich made their way from the Führer's headquarters to Joseph Stalin's within days—sometimes hours—of being issued.

Involved are two beautiful women and another who is a disheveled genius. One of these women is said to have controlled the entire operation from Red Army headquarters in the heart of Moscow. The men include a mapmaker, an adventurist who plotted to assassinate Hitler, and a Red Army spy whose exploits even Ian Fleming could appreciate. The conspiracy involves a far-flung network of couriers, cutouts, and go-betweens. There are dead-letter drops, secret rendezvous, and even invisible ink, all conducted under the nose of the Gestapo. In fact, German secret police helped the conspirators, as did someone standing beside Hitler—welcomed into his secret chambers—a man known as "Werther."

Most of all, the conspiracy produces an astonishing result: Hitler's Germany is demolished while the Soviet Union becomes a world superpower. It is one of the most improbable tales that could be told even in these conspiracy-minded times.

Unfortunately for historians, who must deal with the conspiracy, it is all true. It is well documented in files that historians have already written about and in other secret files that this book addresses. There is no doubt about the conspiracy or, in fact, about almost all of the conspirators. It is the theory that is missing. How did it all work so perfectly well? How did it go undetected by Hitler?

In 1974, F. W. Winterbotham shocked much of the world by revealing that British code breakers at Bletchley Park had cracked the German Enigma cipher early in the war and that the British were often privy to Hitler's secrets. Winterbotham made clear that the full scope of this coup would not be revealed. "It is, however," he said, "the privilege of the victor in war not to disclose just how or how often he broke his enemy's ciphers."[1] And he warned that "if the full British documents are made available for comment, history may change its assessments of some of the generals and personalities of the Second World War."[2]

Historians have yet to grapple fully with Winterbotham's assessment. Is it true that British general Sir Bernard "Monty" Montgomery could seldom handle his German counterpart, Erwin Rommel, even though Montgomery knew most of the German's plans? Was the Battle of the Atlantic won more by subterfuge than by British cheek? The answer to both questions is yes. The breaking of Enigma was decisively important to the British. It even helped give Winston Churchill the spine to stay in the war when much logic said that Britain should have concluded a compromise peace.

Yet all of this, known for more than twenty years, has only slowly made its way into public comprehension. A newsreel mentality of World War II still dominates. Heroes are supposed to remain in place. Churchill often seemed bold and brave, it's true. But he was also well informed.

Yet as great as the Enigma successes undoubtedly were, they do not compare to those that Stalin made of his Red Army conspiracy. Enigma helped Great Britain survive the war. The Red Army conspiracy helped win it. Without the conspiracy, the great Soviet victories at Stalingrad and Kursk may not have—probably would not have—happened. Naturally, in America, this contribution to the war is far less understood than even Enigma's. Events on the eastern front remain largely opaque in the United States. Hitler's traitor and the operation of the Red Army spies are not mentioned in high school history books or even in most English-language narratives of the war's great battles on the Eastern Front. This sad exclusion prevents recognition of some of the most remarkable people of modern history. And it distorts what really happened inside Hitler's Third Reich.

Lucy

One of those remarkable and underrecognized people was Rudolf Rössler, a German journalist and publisher who had been domiciled in Lucerne, Switzerland, since 1933. When Operation Barbarossa—the great German offensive in the East—began, Rössler was forty-four years old.[3] As would befit one of the world's most enigmatic spies, his biography is hard to fill in. Though he was a free man after the war, he never indulged in writing an account of his activities or motives. The Soviets concluded that those motives were purely material, and that is what they preferred. They could understand why a man would take great risks for money. Stalin distrusted idealism.

However, Rössler—code-named "Lucy"—may have been more complicated than that. It is true that he refused to work without substantial compensation: He made seven thousand Swiss francs a month, almost a millionaire's wage in 1942. But it's also true that he later declined to sell his story when it would have earned him even more, and he continued his clandestine life after the war, working for the new Communist government in Czechoslovakia.

How Rössler got involved in intelligence is also shrouded in mystery. It is known that a friend of his, Dr. Xaver Schnieper, invited Rössler in 1939 to work with Swiss intelligence. Rössler was introduced to Capt. Hans Hausamann, head of an unofficial Swiss intelligence organization called the Büro Ha, and to Roger Masson, chief of Swiss military intelligence. This led to some question of whether the neutral Swiss were collecting German intelligence, then relaying it through Rössler to the Soviets. Such a course would have been most dangerous for the Swiss, and out of character. It is far more likely that Rössler was providing the Swiss and the Russians, and perhaps whoever else would pay, with as much information as he could get.

After the war American intelligence concluded that Rössler "was in contact with the Swiss General Staff and thereby gained access to Swiss Military Intelligence. By itself, however, this position does not seem enough to account for the uncommon quality of the Lucy material, which can be described in general terms as a series of accurate and up-to-date reports on the German Order of Battle on the eastern front."[4] *Order of Battle* is the military term for the strength, disposition, and intention of a nation's armed forces. As such, it was as if Lucy had eyes and ears within Hitler's headquarters.

During the war, and under intense pressure from Stalin, Rössler agreed to identify his sources, but by code name only. Werther was the key, a source in the Oberkommando der Wehrmacht (OKW). This was the supreme command where Hitler and Generals Wilhelm Keitel and Alfred Jodl planned out the war. Werther was Hitler's primary traitor. But Lucy had other sources besides Werther, and they, too, presented problems for Hitler. There was "Teddy," a source in the army's High Command (the Oberkommando das Heeres, or OKH), where Generals Franz Halder, Walther von Brauchitsch, Georg Thomas, and later others planned army actions. "Bill" was Lucy's source in the army weapons office, and "Olga" was the source in the replacement army. "Anna" provided information from the foreign office.[5]

The importance of Lucy's agents is not hard to tell. Of approximately 5,500 messages that the Swiss Red Army network sent to Moscow during the war, the Central Intelligence Agency (CIA) was able to decrypt all or some of 332. Werther is the source of sixty-nine of those, or some 21 percent. In all, members of the Lucy group were the source of more than 42 percent of all messages sent to Moscow Center from Switzerland.[6]

All too often in accounts of the Second World War, one event or one action is given credit for turning the tide against Hitler. In the West we often look to the invasion of West Africa or French Normandy as the defining moment. But these moves, however spectacular, did not decide the war. After his victory in France, Hitler placed 3.3 million of his 3.8 million army troops on the Eastern Front.

Most scholars of the war know that Hitler's battle of decision was in the east, at the hands of the Red Army, and in a little-known place called Kursk. This is not to diminish the brave Royal Air Force (RAF) pilots who held out against great odds in their battle with Hitler, or the resoluteness of the British people who endured the Blitz. And certainly the American sacrifice of half a million men and the expenditure of tremendous resources were invaluable contributions. Indeed, if the British had not held out, or if the Americans had refused to enter the war, Hitler could have won. But the Western Allies did what history demanded, allowing the once inept Red Army the chance to deliver the crucial blow.

Together with often underestimating the Red Army's contribution in deciding the war, Americans frequently do not know how close Hitler came to winning, not only in 1940 and 1941 but also in 1942 and even as late as 1943. It is not true that the end was inevitable when the United States declared war. Wars are not won by adding balance sheets. They are won in the field, and that did not happen until Kursk. What is even more hidden in the West is the decisive role played by the three female Red Army spymasters in determining that victory. For these women created and controlled the spy ring that ensnared Werther. Werther, in turn, changed the tide of war against Hitler.

TRAITORS

Who was betraying Hitler? It might surprise many to know that at times it seemed as though everybody in power in Germany had a try at it. It wasn't hard for the upper crust to distrust Hitler, who was seen as an upstart untrained for statesmanship, a man who had only achieved the status of corporal during the Great War. Though they generally liked what he had done with the German economy, which was nothing short of a miracle, they didn't think that the mustachioed little man was anyone who should be taking Germany down a perilous military path. As the 1930s drew to a close, this culture of disdain within Germany's ruling class turned into stark fear, which soon evolved into a culture of treason.

Most people know that on July 20, 1944, a bomb exploded at Hitler's Wolfsschanze (Wolf's Lair) headquarters in East Prussia, which left the Führer shaken but otherwise unharmed. The plotters were caught and most were executed. But most Americans do not realize that this plot was part of an ongoing operation against Hitler that had reached all the important segments of German society except the workers.

It is hard to understand why Hitler—with the resources he had at his disposal, not only from his security services but from his own keen insight into treachery—hadn't crushed his opponents before July 20, and even then either missed or deliberately overlooked many of them. It is true that the tyrant had a contrarian weakness. Whereas Stalin crushed all enemies, real or imagined, Hitler often suffered them. He not only left generals alive after they failed him, he frequently left them in command. Generals Heinz Guderian, Erich von Manstein, and Erwin Rommel—top panzer commanders and theoreticians of the war—frequently disobeyed Hitler. Manstein, told by Hitler in 1943 to hold Kharkov at all costs after Stalingrad fell, agreed in one breath and in the next ordered the city evacuated. Hitler fussed, but that was all. Face-to-face, Hitler tried to charm Manstein into following orders. Indeed, after the war, Guderian told American interrogators that "Hitler was able to convince everybody that his decisions were right through his personal charm, throughout the war."[7] Rommel, connected with the July 20 attempted coup, was given and accepted the offer of suicide. He received a hero's funeral.

For whatever reason, Hitler allowed the culture of treason to surround him until it destroyed him. The list of persons who plotted against him is startling. There were many freelance efforts from the Nazi inner circle to arrange Hitler's demise. Heinrich Himmler, head of the SS, plotted against Hitler from as early as 1942. Only when the Red Army was in Berlin did he give up hope of replacing the Führer.[8] Himmler's head of intelligence, SS general Walter Schellenberg, encouraged Himmler and also made his own separate efforts to betray Hitler.[9] In fact, when Schellenberg went to Switzerland to try to shut down the Red Army spy ring that threatened the Third Reich, he instead spent most of his time trying to stab the Führer in the back. Foreign minister Joachim von Ribbentrop, through an intermediary, inquired of the British whether they might find him as a suitable replacement for Hitler. Even Reichsmarschall Hermann Göring let Western Allies know that he was prepared to step into the Führer's shoes.[10]

These efforts were mostly self-serving and uncoordinated acts of criminals trying to save their skins by hedging their bets. If Hitler lost the war, the Nazi leaders wanted the Allies to know that they were behind-the-scenes advocates of peace. To that end, Himmler brazenly treated certain of the condemned but unexecuted traitors as chattel to be used in bargaining with the British and the Americans. They were witnesses to Himmler's magnanimity.

Though the top Nazi conspirators had selfish motives, they were important to the core conspiracy because they disposed Himmler, Göring, Schellenberg, and others to overlook the true anti-Hitler movement. If the ranking Nazis looked too closely into the movement, they risked exposing themselves.

The core of the "honest" resistance to Hitler formed around former army chief of staff Ludwig Beck, who had resigned in 1938 in protest over Hitler's territorial ambitions. Beck soon wished that he had ordered Hitler's arrest instead of doing the proper Prussian thing in quitting. From the moment that he was out of office, Beck began imploring his successor, Franz Halder, to correct this oversight. From then until he was ousted from power in 1942, Halder was routinely briefed about plots against Hitler, agreeing tentatively to participate in some and rejecting others. Never once did Halder tell Hitler of the whirlwind of treason that surrounded him.

Other army legends conspired against Hitler at one or more times during the war. Field Marshal Günther von Kluge, Field Marshal Rommel, and Field Marshal Fedor von Bock were all compromised. General Georg Thomas, head of the Economics and Armaments Branch of the OKW, was one of the most active players talking openly about the need to replace Hitler. Also involved were Generals Fritz Thiele, chief of communications for the army, and Erich Fellgiebel, his counterpart at OKW.[11]

Sure, there were some toadies who apparently never thought of betraying Hitler, but much of the top echelon in Hitler's army either participated in or willingly ignored plans to depose the Führer.

One branch of the army's conspiracy is most interesting, not because it had the power to actually move against Hitler but because it had power over information. The Abwehr, the army's own intelligence agency, had the means to not only communicate secretly within Germany but also with others outside of Germany. If someone wanted to communicate with Lucy in Switzerland, for instance, an Abwehr ally would be more than useful. And it was in the Abwehr that some of the most audacious traitors arose. At the head of the list was Gen. Hans Oster, the number-two man in the organization. Oster sought almost openly to bring down Hitler.

Oster seemed to talk to anybody who hinted at anti-Hitler sentiment, and he wrote letters in plain language to German generals about the need for anti-Nazi action. Eventually, he urged the generals to assassinate the Führer.

Oster had many assistants. First among them was Hans Bernd Gisevius, originally a Gestapo officer and later an agent of the Abwehr. A freethinking intellectual, Gisevius became Oster's liaison in Switzerland, where Lucy operated. The man who gave Oster, Gisevius, and other anti-Hitler agents cover, though never participating openly in the plotting, was the chief of the Abwehr himself, Adm. Wilhelm Canaris.[12]

Though the military men provided the muscle and communications, civilians and civil servants were also central to the German anti-Hitler movement. They provided the intellectual framework for the conspiracy and were destined to take over civil administration once a coup occurred. None of the generals visualized Germany run as a military dictatorship. Albrecht Haushofer, one of the dark eminences of the war and a foreign office employee, met with many of the conspirators. His titular boss, State Secretary Ernst von Weizsäcker, participated in the treason. Certainly, the fulcrum of the civilian revolt was former Leipzig mayor Dr. Carl Friedrich Goerdeler. An idealist who wanted to save Germany from Hitler and also from the ravages of the Versailles treaty, which ended the Great War, Goerdeler knew almost everyone in the opposition. Like Oster, Goerdeler talked to everyone he could who opposed Hitler, spelling out his agenda on the telephone and in private and public meetings.

Many of these top-level German resisters did not use the tradecraft of trained saboteurs or spies. They used playground tradecraft at best, but until the July 20 debacle, most escaped detection. They formed open societies, met regularly, and exchanged names of confederates from one group with those in another. Yet the Gestapo left them largely alone.

Further, the conspiracy was far more than just a debating club for disgruntled generals and outraged civil servants. There were many plots to jail or assassinate Hitler before Col. Claus von Stauffenberg's bomb ripped apart Hitler's headquarters. Other attempts had been planned and even initiated, but each failed due to schedule foul-ups, Hitler's changing whim, botched maneuvers, or bad luck. The Führer seemed to live a charmed life.

But one of the principal reasons that the conspiracy never reached critical mass, where all the disparate points would have come together, was a palpable sense of dread among many of the conspirators—even those at its core—that replacing Hitler might not be enough to save Germany. That was the Rubicon, the crossing of which caused intense passion and doubt among the generals. The disease had a well-known name: Versailles.

1918
The men who marshaled themselves against Hitler were mostly German nationalists. When they failed to act decisively to join the conspirators at crucial moments, it was because they could get no guarantees from the Western Allies that a move against Hitler's regime would bring peace. Himmler and Göring shared with Oster and Gisevius one thing: the shadow of 1918. It was then that Germany sued for peace, only to find later that peace meant German dissection. No German patriot wanted that. The old-line Prussians, Hitler's National Socialists, and even the

would-be Social Democrats were in an odd confluence of opinion: that after the war, Germany should remain whole.

That did not change much when in 1943 some of the anti-
Hitler Germans began to turn Red. Until then, the movement
had been almost all anti-Bolshevik. The old guard thought that
Hitler's brand of national socialism was far too close to Stalin's for
comfort. When they tried to betray the Nazi regime, they turned
to the West, not because they were believers in democracy but for
the same reason that Hitler turned to the West: The West em-
braced their history and culture. Himmler, Göring, Schellenberg,
Beck, and most of the others are known to have offered their services only to the West. All evidence suggests they felt, probably
correctly, that a fate worse than Hitler would be Stalin.

Gisevius, one of the most ardent members of the conspiracy,
said that the fall of Stalingrad changed this among several of the
latecomers. The conspiracy became politically more complicated. With the West shunning the opposition's anti-Nazi offers,
some German officers discovered socialist roots. They began to
look at Beck, Gisevius, and Goerdeler as "rightist" has-beens in a
fast-evolving world. More and more of the oppositionists "came
to the conclusion that the war simply must not—not any
longer—be lost to the Russians. At worst it must be won together
with them."[13]

These forces, Gisevius said, "discovered that, fundamentally,
they had always been against the plutocracies, against the
unimaginative, aged Western powers. And they concluded that
the only way to evolve away from the Nazi regime was along totalitarian and collectivist lines. Paint the brown gray again and
let the gray be merged with the old revolutionary red."[14]

So by the time conspirators actually ignited a bomb in Hitler's
presence, their goal was to cause rapprochement with the Russians against the West, not the other way around.

Yet even these men who late in the war turned to socialist politics did not wish the destruction of Germany or her armies. The
one common denominator of members of the conspiracy
against Hitler was the ideal of a united Germany, whatever the
political color.

But the omnipresent culture of treason permeating the top reaches of the Third Reich could only help the real penetration of the high command by agents faithful to Stalin—agents who wanted Germany, not just Hitler, destroyed. With the top officials in the SS, army intelligence, and the Wehrmacht High Command together with the intelligentsia and the foreign ministry, all either participating in or consciously overlooking many acts of treason, who would notice just another line of information leaving the Reich, particularly one emanating from Hitler's headquarters? And who would dare say anything even if a traitor was suspected?

WERTHER

Beginning in 1941,[15] such an agent appeared. Werther was the product of the remarkable Red Army operation in Switzerland. General Halder complained after the war that the Red Army knew German orders even before the Wehrmacht. That was probably only slightly exaggerated, if at all.[16] Werther sent his messages to Lucy, who in turn sent them through a series of agents controlled by two of the least known but most important people of the war—the extraordinary women whom you will soon meet. Through this route, long, delicate, and complicated messages streamed daily from Hitler's center of power to Stalin's.

Who was the traitor who transcended all the others?

On the surface the answer is simple: Hitler betrayed himself. It began after the Munich conference of 1938 when Hitler so embarrassed British prime minister Neville Chamberlain that he froze out any hope of a nonmilitary resolution of British-German affairs. Hitler did not fully comprehend this until his invasion of Poland in September 1939 prompted a British declaration of war, followed soon by one from Paris. But even after this, Hitler retained the deadly illusion that an understanding with Britain could be had—if not easily, at least eventually.

In the months that followed the start of the Second World War, Hitler showed that he had little heart for defeating the British by a crushing annihilation. He held out for something less, a compromise. Although the Battle of France was swift and hard, Hitler did not follow up with an immediate invasion of Great Britain. "Invasion," Winterbotham later wrote, "however incompetently mounted and carried out, would have been invincible . . ."[17] Hitler's generals thought so, too. Instead, Hitler went for half measures on the battlefield and aggressive covert measures in the shadow war.

Hitler was a man of immense contradictions. One of the most dominant was this paradoxical and self-defeating attitude toward the British. Hitler dreamed of a Germany in racial kinship with the Britons, indeed even in a military alliance. This drove Hitler's foreign policy, even as Germany built a military machine that could threaten Britain's empire. All of Hitler's early plans were based upon Great Britain agreeing with this geopolitical vision: Britain would let the German Reich be the major power on continental Europe in return for all the assistance that Germany could offer to keep Britain at the head of the world's greatest maritime empire. It would be Great Britain, with Germany as her stalwart economic ally, that would prevail against the Americans and the Japanese. To Hitler, only the shortsightedness of politicians on both sides prevented the two countries from reaching this union of common interests. This is one of the fundamental chords of the Second World War.[18]

When Hitler finally attacked the Soviet Union—the most dangerous strategic move he ever made—he explained that it was intended as a way to win over the British to his side as much as to defeat the hated Russians. It was an insane strategy that came within a breath of succeeding. Despite all the treason that surrounded him, Hitler came very close to proving that naked will could prevail. Only American general Robert E. Lee had been as audacious in modern war. And he, too, almost won.

TRUST

As Hitler rolled through the Soviet Union, abiding by a strategic vision that became known to his enemies as folly incarnate, Stalin lost his armies one after another until it seemed that he had no more to lose. In extremis, Stalin had only one hope. He could surrender vast amounts of Russia to the Germans, or he could trust an unknown stranger. Stalin, a man who trusted no one, who even once said that the lack of evidence of a conspiracy was proof that a conspiracy existed, decided in 1942 that trust was all he had. At the moment of extreme peril, Stalin stuffed his suspicions into his pocket and chose, for a while, to believe the stranger.

Werther would become Stalin's prehensile grip on the Third Reich's throat. Day after day, Werther told Stalin exactly where the German panzers were, where they were heading, and how many reserves remained in the rear. And day after day, Stalin countered the German moves, although clumsily at first with the loss of legions of men. But Stalin learned in time that he didn't have to counterattack until counterattack actually meant something. And he learned that he did not have to fear giving up land. In Russia, land was cheap. What he needed to do was draw the Germans into a trap. Werther would tell him how.

Stalin ended up fighting the Second World War largely on the basis of intelligence from a spy he could not even identify with a real name. His own agent, an exasperating but brilliant woman in Switzerland, refused to disclose either Werther's or Lucy's identity even when ordered to do so by Stalin himself. Stalin did not order the renegade agent back to Moscow and a certain death in the Lubyanka. Instead, he buried any offense he suffered and let the agent live, because she was too important for retribution. Her secrets continued to stream into Moscow until near the end of the war, because Stalin needed her and her treasured spy Werther more than he needed anything else. Loss of face he could hide.

Who was Werther? This book seeks him out. There are only a few possibilities, all seemingly improbable, but when compared to the full length of the conspiracy against Hitler, maybe they weren't so improbable after all. At the very least, what might seem improbable happened. Someone at the highest level of the Third Reich sent to Moscow Center messages of ultimate importance—information that Stalin used to win the war.

Whoever Werther was, he was the greatest conspirator in the twentieth century's greatest conspiracy. He deserves, at least, an effort at a good theory to explain him. The few who have tried have produced meager and unconvincing results.

Any start at the theory of Werther must begin with several dashing Red Army agents, who themselves were as improbable as they were real. Many didn't know one another. Many knew only parts of what the others did. One agent, though, knew and controlled everything. Maria Poliakova was the orchestra leader. In January 1945, the Second World War having been decided but not yet ended, Maria was waiting near a Moscow runway for the return of some of her prized agents.

They were the ones who had made Werther possible.

Notes

1 F. W. Winterbotham, *The Ultra Secret* (New York: Dell, 1974), p. 15.

2 Ibid., p. 18.

3 CIA, *The Rote Kapelle: The CIA's History of Soviet Intelligence and Espionage Networks in Western Europe, 1936–1945* (Washington, D.C.: University Publications of America, Inc., 1979), p. 344.

4 Red Orchestra files, RG 319, Box 60, National Archives, p. 795.

5 According to the CIA, Lucy had known connections with three of the now-known members of the conspiracy against Hitler: At the Abwehr, the German army's counterintelligence office, there was Gen. Hans Oster; in Switzerland there was the Abwehr's liaison, Hans Bernd Gisevius; and in Leipzig, former mayor Carl Goerdeler had contacts with Lucy.

6 CIA, *Rote Kapelle*, p. 185.

7 RG 165, Entry 179, Box 721A, "Observation on Armoured Tactics."

8 See "Report on the Case of Walter Friedrich Schellenberg," Captured German Records Division, National Archives.

9 Ibid.

10 Louis C. Kilzer, *Churchill's Deception* (New York: Simon and Schuster, 1994), p. 183.

11 CIA, *Rote Kapelle*, p. 187.

12 Hans Bernd Gisevius, *To the Bitter End* (Boston: Houghton-Mifflin, 1947), p. 439.

13 Ibid., p. 461.

14 Ibid.

15 The CIA has argued, based on certain intercepted cables, that the most important messages from the spy ring did not begin until the summer of 1942. This position overlooks statements by some of those involved in the ring and also doesn't give enough note to the disarray in Soviet intelligence during the war.

16 Students of the secret war who recognize this spy ring might be confused. Most accounts have given credit to three or

four men, not three women. This is because of many things. Most important is that the men were allowed to tell their stories after the war and the women either chose not to or were killed for their efforts. The men who wrote about themselves were Alexander Foote, a mere encoder and transmitter of messages who wrote in 1949 a *Handbook for Spies;* Alexander Rado, the group's chief bureaucrat who was considered by Moscow as a cutout but who wrote *Codename Dora;* and Leopold Trepper, a truly important spy but not in the Swiss network. Trepper wrote *Le Grand Jeu.* The fourth man in the operation—who was never known to Stalin—was Rudolf Rössler, code-named Lucy. Not even Rado, who supposedly was the chief administrator of the spy ring, knew who Rössler was.

17 Winterbotham, p. 47.

18 Kilzer, *Churchill's Deception,* pp. 99–109.

Chapter One

Spy Stories

PARIS

On a runway outside of liberated Paris on the morning of January 6, 1945, a plane belonging to Joseph Stalin's Red Army stood ready for takeoff. A cold front had blown in. The sky was gray, the temperature freezing. Inside the plane—the press had been told—were the first Soviet troops to be repatriated by Russia's victorious allies. In reality, there were no army troops inside, only spies.

Alexander Foote, Alexander Rado, and Leopold Trepper were veterans of the secret war against Hitler's Third Reich. Each one was a hero to the Soviet cause. But each also bore battle scars that could condemn him in Moscow. As the plane idled, Foote, Rado, and Trepper looked out to the drizzle on the runway and wondered what exactly they had won.

FOOTE

As a spy, Foote was the most improbable. American intelligence files described the thirty-nine-year-old Liverpool native as being six feet tall, "broad shouldered, well-built; sandy hair, thinning and receding; clean-shaven, deep-set eyes, high forehead, full lower lip, large ears. Badly dressed, uneducated, speaks English with a North-country accent. Speaks good German, some French and very little Russian. Chain-smoker. Fond of women. Adventurous and restless."[1]

Foote joined the British RAF in 1935 but deserted the next year to join the 15th (British) International Brigade fighting Franco in Spain. He ended his career there as an ambulance driver. Red Army agents had tagged him as a probable courier, but before he could do any of their business, Franco defeated the Republicans and Foote fled.

Back in England, a Red Army agent offered Foote a chance at "secret and dangerous" work abroad.[2] Foote accepted, not knowing what he would be doing, how he would be paid, or who his employer was. It was crazy in Europe, and even such a crazy plan made certain sense. Foote left Great Britain with only a rendezvous point and a password.

In October 1938, on a park bench in Geneva, Foote met his spymaster, "Sonia." Foote was smitten. He described Sonia as a stunningly beautiful woman, slim, black haired, someone who stood out from the crowd. She held out a green parcel and an orange, the prearranged signs. Foote in turn said, "Excuse me, but where did you buy that belt?"[3]

Sonia saw Foote's rough edges but also his intelligence and sense of daring. There was room in her network for such a man. She sent her new agent to Munich to learn about the enemy and pick up some German. Foote soon picked up more than that. Looking for a cheap place to have lunch, Foote found the Osteria Bavaria, a small, undistinguished eatery with a working-class clientele. After having settled down for a meal one afternoon, Foote noted that patrons and waiters stiffened and looked furtively about.

Suddenly into the cheap cafe walked Adolf Hitler.

The proprietor of the restaurant, it happened, was an old comrade of Hitler's from the Great War. The old guard was a sentimental weakness that Hitler had never overcome. If he could help the proprietor by his patronage, he would.

Foote learned that Hitler had been doing just that for the last fifteen years, sometimes several times a week. Now, even as leader of the Third Reich, he was accompanied by what seemed to be a tiny band of followers, including his adjutant and photographer.[4] Foote reported all this back to Sonia.

Sonia, in charge of sabotage operations against Germany, saw a rare chance to commit the ultimate sabotage. She sent Foote a collaborator, Leon Beurton,[5] and a new mission: Assassinate Adolf Hitler at the Osteria Bavaria.[6]

Foote was not overjoyed with the news, and neither was his new companion. "We were neither of us very willing actors, as neither of us really fancied a martyr's crown," said Foote.[7] Still, Foote, now code-named "Jim," had already accepted Moscow Center's money. He reasoned that he had to at least see if assassination was possible. On Sonia's orders, Foote and Beurton watched Hitler come and go, amazed at how easy it would be to place a bomb next to the thin partition that separated the Führer's small, private dining room from the rest of the cafe. Thinking that there must surely be SS agents lurking in disguise, Beurton decided to try to smoke them out. As Hitler walked in one day, Beurton made a sudden reach into his breast pocket, as though to draw a gun, then pulled out a cigarette case. If the SS men were present, they would surely act. Beurton hoped that they would not act too decisively. Instead, as Beurton pulled out the case, absolutely nothing happened. Evidently there were no agents around. Assassinating the Führer would be easy.

While Foote waited for the Center to provide the briefcase of explosives that could end Hitler's life, international events overtook matters. The Nazis and the Bolshevists were secretly talking. On August 24, 1939, came word of the Russo-German pact.

Foote would not be bombing Adolf Hitler, nor would anyone else in Sonia's stable. Instead, Stalin ordered an end to all operations against Germany.[8] American intelligence after the war said that the assassination plot by Foote and Beurton was not amateurish. Concluded one such report: "The choice of two rolling stones [Foote and Beurton] from the International Brigade, Englishmen with good campaigning records but without formal Communist Party connections, may have both been deliberate and sound. Moreover, as we know from his own testimony, Foote, had he been caught as a saboteur, could not have named the organization for which he was working."[9] A perfect patsy.

In lieu of assassinating Adolf Hitler, Sonia was instructed by Moscow to teach Foote and others in her cell the art of the wireless operator.[10] Foote learned to code and decode secret messages based on an elaborate Soviet enciphering system. And he learned Morse code, which he would use to contact the Center.

Sonia's Soviet wireless cell became the only one in Switzerland and thus the only one to have direct contact with the center at the start of the war. Soon Jim's transmissions would take on special importance in Moscow. From his transmitter came the most important information that Stalin would receive after the Soviet dictator's dalliance with Hitler turned sour. Foote would be tasked with transmitting intelligence from a spy code-named Werther, a traitor in Hitler's High Command.

Now, as he waited in the spy plane on a cold Paris runway, Foote was not as courageous as he had been six years before when he contemplated assassinating Adolf Hitler. He knew the stories. People ordered to Moscow often did not live happily, if they lived at all. There was a certain madness, an aberration on the road to a socialist utopia, in the land. Yet Foote told himself that the Center knew his accomplishments. If anyone, he was a hero of the Soviet Union. He would go.

RADO

Next to Foote in the Soviet plane sat Alexander Rado. Code-named "Dora," Rado had been the chief administrator of the Red Army's Swiss spy ring. A skilled cartographer and the man who first coined the term *Soviet Union*, Rado was morally challenged. His handling of Red Army funds in Switzerland was not in order, and his fortitude was in question. Rado had occasionally taken credit for recruiting spies and garnering intelligence when others had contributed some or most of the effort. But the most important problem that Rado faced was explaining exactly why he had fled his Swiss post in late 1943. The Gestapo's Sonderkommando[11]—made up of members of the Gestapo, military intelligence, and other security services and charged with wiping out Soviet networks in the west—had already shut down Red Army operations in Germany, France, and Belgium and was pressuring the Swiss to do the same on Switzerland's supposedly neutral turf.

Rado had no taste for arrest. As Swiss police closed in on him, he slipped underground and eventually made his way to Paris. Foote and most of the others in the net were not so lucky. They spent several months in Swiss jails, until their captors felt that an Allied victory was assured and it was better all around to let the Soviet agents out on parole.

As a young man, Rado had been a Red radical in his native Hungary and was appointed in 1918 as commissar to the Soviet government that briefly existed there. It was a bloody time, and the commissar of the Red Terror surely had some of that blood on his hands. Rado knew firsthand the terror that Foote could only imagine.

In the Soviet plane, Rado was anxious and withdrawn. If he made it back to Moscow, he did not think it would be as a hero of the Soviet Union. His network had helped win the war, but Rado knew that that would mean little to Stalin. Stalin cared nothing at all about heroes. Almost every foreign resident spy chief who had been called back to Moscow before the war had been shot. Why wouldn't this be so for Rado?

TREPPER

Close to Rado sat Leopold Trepper, one of the most flamboyant, resourceful, and devious spies the world has ever known. Unlike Foote and Rado, Trepper had operated from Belgium and France, sending the center often vital information about German industry, logistics, and plans. In December 1942, Hitler's Gestapo finally tracked down Trepper in Paris, at his dentist's office. But although many in his network were subjected to fierce torture, then execution, Trepper was treated as a special prisoner.

The Sonderkommando wanted Trepper to play a game that on the surface was a simple one. He was to hide his capture from Moscow Center and continue reporting as if nothing had happened. The Gestapo would be the real supplier of information. In other words, Trepper was to become a double agent.

That was a typical enough event during the Second World War. And all spies knew the rules: You either doubled or you were killed. But this was no ordinary double. Trepper was told that important German generals were prepared to rebel against Hitler and wanted to show their bona fides to Stalin by giving up important secrets. Once these generals were established as true representatives of the German High Command, they would help arrange a separate peace.

At first, Trepper thought that this was a cover story meant only to gain his cooperation. Soon, though, he knew that a most complicated game was under way. An ordinary playback double-cross was conducted at relatively low levels in the command. This one was not. Someone unknown and at the highest level was playing a game that was opaque and bewildering. Trepper did not understand.

If the game, called a *funkspiel* by the Germans, was simply meant to gain Russian confidence, only to betray the enemy when it was convenient, no Nazi leader would have been involved. And such matters typically lasted only a week or two, or until Moscow caught on. And Moscow always caught on.

This *funkspiel* was different. It involved not only military but political matters. Trepper came to believe that someone on the German side might actually be planning to replace Hitler or perhaps even help Russia defeat Germany.

This thought occurred to Trepper in 1942. Now, in January 1945, on a plane bound for Moscow, Trepper betrayed no such suspicion. His concern was more immediate. He looked around the cabin and saw the drawn faces of his fellow passengers. Were they returning as heroes, as Foote believed? Or would they soon be facing a bullet in the brain in the basement of the Lubyanka, as Rado feared? Trepper held out hope that the war had ended the terrible purges. He made himself look forward to seeing his wife and children, who were in Moscow. Trepper had survived the Gestapo, after all. Life in Moscow had to be better.

DEFECTION

At a stopover in Cairo, where he shared a room with Foote, Rado's mood darkened even further. He confided to his subordinate that he was unsure about his future. The Center, he said, might view him as a captain who had lost his ship. Moscow would not be happy that the Swiss operation had died while he was still its leader.

Nonsense, said the often naive Foote. The network had operated from the first days of the German attack on Russia and had
done an essential job. Besides, he said, the ship had not sunk.
The most important spy in the network, Werther, was still ready
to work. In fact, when Foote left Switzerland for Paris in late
1944, he had been able to bring with him some fresh information from Werther.[12] Foote said he had relayed that information
to a Soviet diplomatic representative in Paris.

Rado was startled. He had told the Center that the Swiss and
the Gestapo had crushed his network. Now Foote was telling him
that the most important spy of all had been and was still willing
and able to work. This would make Rado's dispatches to the Center seem at least in error. Worse, and perhaps more certainly,
Stalin could find that severing ties with Werther was criminal.
Rado sat in silence for a moment, tapping his fingers on a table.
Then he rose and walked out the door.

The next day as the Soviet plane readied to complete its flight
to Teheran, Baku, then Moscow, there was no sign of Rado. He
had bolted.

The mission would continue without him. Once airborne,
Trepper became obsessed by Rado's decision to defect. He had
respected Rado and his keen survival instincts. That he would
take off meant only one thing: "He did not care for the prospect
of ending his life in one of Stalin's jails; hence he disappeared
in Cairo after making sure that his wife and children were safe
in Paris."[13] But Trepper did not believe that he himself had that
option. His family was in Moscow, not safe in Paris. And he knew
that Stalin often punished the families of those who disap-
pointed him. Trepper would continue on. Perhaps, he convinced himself, he was seeing ghosts.

GISELA'S FAMILY

Outside a small airport near Moscow, Maria Poliakova waited for
the spy plane from France. It was 4 P.M. on January 14, 1945, and
already Moscow's winter sky was dark. Maria was the most important spy of all, for she had established and controlled the
networks in France and Switzerland. She was the spymaster who

controlled Rado, Foote, and—indirectly—Trepper. Her networks had contributed as much as anything to the now certain
defeat of Adolf Hitler.

Maria had never looked like a spy, according to standards of
the trade. She did not blend into the crowd. Even now, at thirty-
six years of age, dressed in the uniform of a major of the Red
Army, she was stunning. American counterintelligence agents after the war described her as a five-foot-six Russian Jewess with a
"striking, masculine appearance; black hair, good-looking Mon-
gol face with high cheekbones." Foote simply called her "a
beauty." But her physical appearance wouldn't have mattered at
all were it not for her "exceptional intelligence and phenomenal
memory."[14] She was fluent in French, German, English, and Russian and had traveled extensively with her father, a representative
of the Soviet Foreign Trade Commissariat, on missions to Germany, France, and Switzerland. She easily passed for a westerner.

With such rare talent, it is no wonder that she was recruited
early in life by the Central Committee of the Young Communists.
She had wanted to become a doctor, but her master in the Kom-
somol, Alexander Kosarev, saw her potential as a spy. "We have
enough doctors," Kosarev said. What the new Soviet republic
needed were secret agents, especially young, intelligent women.[15]
Maria was not convinced, but she accepted an invitation to meet
with Jan Karlovich Berzin, head of Red Army intelligence, also
known as the Fourth Department. As would so many, she immediately fell under Berzin's spell.[16] He asked Maria, only twenty-
four, to become a "fighter for the Red Army" but also a fighter
who would be a "thinking comrade."[17]

Maria was already the mother of a child, but the identity of the
father has never been released by the KGB or its successor agencies. She worried about leaving the baby behind. Berzin told her
not to be concerned; the state would take care of the child.

After Hitler came to power in 1933, Poliakova traveled to Germany on a secret mission. What exactly she did as the Soviet
Union's top illegal agent inside Germany is not known. In remi-
niscences nearly half a century later, Poliakova refused to disclose what the mission was, saying only that she had been instructed "to find Germans sympathizing with our country and to

make them our friends." She said that this mission had been "successful."[18]

Poliakova returned as a star in the Red Army, but she still yearned to become a doctor and to raise her child. Berzin shamed her about this supposedly selfish request. "We cannot afford to ignore your experience," he said, promising that a secretary named Natasha in the Fourth Department would make sure that the child was cared for. In the meantime, Maria would go to a new and special school to learn more about the art of intelligence.

A year later, Maria was again posted to Western Europe in a new assignment. Former top-secret American intelligence reports say that in 1936, Poliakova became head of the Fourth Department's Swiss operation, with wide authority over other groupings in Western Europe.[19] American counterintelligence officers said that Poliakova was chief of Red Army intelligence in Nazi Germany itself.[20] The Americans also said that Poliakova helped Soviet penetration in Great Britain and France through the control of one of Trepper's associates, Henri Robinson.[21]

On this second mission, based primarily in Switzerland, Maria Poliakova's code name was "Gisela," and the expansive network that she developed there became known as "Gisela's family."

In late 1937, Poliakova's life and work were suddenly at risk. As with Stalin's other top foreign agents, Poliakova received an urgent notice from Moscow to return. She did not hesitate long. But before she could leave, she had to hand over her operation to others. Part of her "family" went to Rado, who inherited most of the spies whom Poliakova herself had recruited. But there were two other parallel organizations in Switzerland, also parts of Gisela's family, that would play key roles in handling the penetration agent Werther. One organization was headed by Ursula Maria Hamburger, the spy whom Foote knew as Sonia. The other one was run by Rachel Dübendorfer, code-named "Sissy."*

---

*In other works, she is called "Cissie" or "Sissi." Several secret agents were known by different and often closely related code names. To keep things clear, this book uses what I believe are the most common ones.

Maria herself returned to an emotionally barren country where her father figure, Berzin, had been liquidated. For a time it seemed that her networks in Germany and Switzerland were destined to be ignored by new replacements in the Fourth Department who knew almost nothing about the operations of foreign spies. Though Maria walked into the Kremlin itself to receive an award for her accomplishments, her new bosses gave her the duties of a clerk.[22] Berzin's masterpiece of intelligence in the West rotted until few in Moscow knew anything about it. The new bosses seemed unaware of their potential resources in the West. Maria later wrote: "The essentials—communications, radio transmitters, financial resources, extra equipment and ciphers—all this was almost lost in all directions."[23]

Maria's father and brother, were all shot as enemies of the people.[24] Yet somehow—Maria does not mention how in her brief official memoirs—she lived. After the war, the Americans said that she managed to live by using "her ability, her memory and the width of her experience."[25]

How Maria Poliakova managed to outlast Stalin may never be known. But it is clear that after Germany attacked the Soviet Union, Poliakova's special family—Gisela's family in Switzerland—became indispensable to Joseph Stalin. Suddenly Maria's agents were the most crucial in the world. She became chief of Section I of the Fourth Department of the GRU, Russia's spymaster for the European theater of the Second World War.[26]

Sonia

Ursula Hamburger had spent her youth for the cause. She was thirty-two years old and a twelve-year Red Army intelligence veteran when the Russo-German pact was announced. The news seemed to devastate her. "She had worked for many years on the most orthodox 'anti-Fascist' basis and she spoke with bitterness to both Beurton and Foote about Russia's volte-face," said an American intelligence report.[27] Foote wrote: "The German-Russian Pact hit us like a thunder-bolt out of a clear sky . . . Its effect on Sonia . . . was of course shattering."[28]

This was a lie perpetrated on her own agents. Sonia was the

perfect field agent. People knew her only as she wanted to be known. Foote lamented for her emotional devastation, never suspecting that it was an act.

Hamburger was much like Poliakova. She stood out in a crowd, whereas a more perfect spy would have been nondescript. But, also like Poliakova, it didn't seem to matter. Hamburger was born in 1907 and began her professional life as a Berlin journalist. But soon she was recruited into the Soviet cause, an agent of the Red Army's Fourth Department. As had Poliakova, Hamburger won world experience traveling with her father, a lecturer at the London School of Economics. Beginning in 1930, Sonia and her husband, Rudolf Hamburger, ran a Soviet intelligence service in Shanghai.[29] Exposed in 1935 by the Chinese government as foreign agents, Sonia and Rudolf made daring escapes. Sonia managed to slip onto a Soviet ship. In 1936 she ended up in London. Her husband later got out via the United States.[30] The two reconnected in Warsaw, where they established wireless contact with the Center. Rudolf returned to China but was eventually captured by the Americans. He confessed his role as a Soviet spy and was sent back to Russia to an unknown but probably certain fate. He has not been heard from since.[31]

After her husband disappeared, Ursula married one of her first recruits, Leon Beurton, the Englishman who had accompanied Foote on his mission to assassinate Hitler. It seemed to be a marriage of passion, not connivance, though Sonia surely found it handy to be the wife of a British citizen.[32]

She was master of an organization of many spies in Switzerland, but she was going to leave the most important components to Rado. In May 1940, Moscow ordered Rado to meet with Sonia.[33]

"My code-name is Sonia," Hamburger told Rado. "The Director told me to get in touch with you . . ."[34] She asked Rado what he most needed to continue his effort. Rado said he needed a secure line to the Center—if possible, one established through wireless transmitters. This Sonia could provide.

Not only were Foote and Beurton available, but they could train others. Those others, husband and wife Edmond and Olga

Hamel, were nearly perfect. Edmond had an excellent cover; he was a radio mechanic.[35] Once, Swiss police found a transmitter hidden under Edmond's floor. He told them that it was an ordinary radio that he thought looked so much like a transmitter that he believed it best to conceal it. The police officers shrugged their shoulders and left.

Sonia traveled to Great Britain in the summer of 1940. Beurton stayed behind until 1942. According to American intelligence after the war, Sonia, devastated by Stalin's dalliance with Hitler, retired from the Red Army, her idealistic images dashed. "There is no evidence that [Sonia] did any intelligence work in the British Isles between 1941 and 1949,"[36] the CIA first thought.

It was not true. Sonia continued to be one of Stalin's most important spies. In England she was known as Ursula Kuczynski, her maiden name. Whatever malaise she suffered from the Nazi-Soviet agreements in 1939 was quickly resolved. In England, far from becoming the peaceful retired ex-spy that the Americans thought, she became, for a time, the controller of Klaus Fuchs. A brilliant German physicist, Fuchs had escaped to Britain, where he became a major theoretician on nuclear fission. With Sonia's help, Fuchs was able to travel to America, where he became the main Soviet spy who penetrated the Manhattan Project, the American secret program to develop the atomic bomb.[37] Sonia went from plans for blowing up Hitler to plans for blowing up America, or to at least abscond with America's secrets in time for Stalin to deal with them. As Fuchs's controller, she was for a time one of the world's most important spies.

SISSY

The title of the world's most important spy would have to be shared by another of Gisela's family. Her code name was "Sissy."

Sonia left the Swiss operation when most others in the Red Army network were following Stalin's orders to cut down or eliminate their anti-Hitler activities. Sissy never cared much about Stalin or his orders. She kept her organization working despite a poverty of funds and the myopia of the Kremlin. Rachel Dübendorfer ran her Swiss operation independently of Sonia and Rado and, at times, of almost anyone.

Whereas her master, Poliakova, was sophisticated, young, and beautiful, Rachel Dübendorfer was a decade older, somewhat disheveled, and clearly neurotic. American intelligence described her as "untidy in appearance and habits."[38] Some men in the Russian intelligence services did not like Rachel, were jealous of her superb contacts, and constantly, but without success, tried to bring her to heel.

Sissy was born in Warsaw in 1901 and married German attorney Kurt Caspary around 1921.[39] Out of that union came a daughter named Tamara. After Rachel divorced Caspary, she arranged a marriage of convenience to Henri Dübendorfer in 1932 in order to gain citizenship in neutral Switzerland. She left Dübendorfer almost immediately and began living with a plump, German-born journalist named Paul Boettcher. Her cover was employment in the International Labor Organization of the League of Nations.

Whatever Dübendorfer's faults, they were mere shadows compared to her successes. As one of Poliakova's spies, Dübendorfer would develop a network of sources, including the fabled Werther, that would help determine the outcome of the Second World War. Werther sent his messages to Dübendorfer's sub-agent Lucy, who sent the messages to Dübendorfer via another cutout named "Taylor." The operation became known in the annals of espionage as the "Lucy spy ring."

But it was Dübendorfer—the harried malcontent—who made it work. Stalin wanted to remove Dübendorfer from the ring and replace her with someone more malleable who would at least tell him the true identity of Werther. But Dübendorfer crossed swords with Stalin. She would not tell him anything about Werther except that he worked in the OKW and had access to all of Hitler's secrets. Perhaps Sissy herself did not know the true source of the Werther material. But Dübendorfer was resolved on one thing: As long as she lived, she would not allow any of Stalin's minions to get a single independent word to Werther, or to Lucy. Rachel Dübendorfer stood up to Stalin, as no man or woman had ever done before, and lived.

Her instincts were probably right. Had one of Stalin's hacks gotten his hands on this delicate operation, it could have easily been blundered. As it was, Stalin continued to receive the price-less information and made good use of it at important times. Dübendorfer and Lucy continued to live and prosper, and Werther continued to bring defeat upon Hitler. The machine worked.

In fact, even as Rado was complaining about Rachel to the Center, the Center was deciding that her information was some-times even too hot for the resident agent to see. In 1942, in a grievous blow to Rado's stature, Poliakova sent him a message to relay to Rachel. She told Rachel, "You must learn a code and receive additional instruction."[40] This meant that Rachel could use her own code, unknown to Rado, to pass her messages to Moscow. Worse, from Rado's perspective, Rachel could send back messages through Rado's own radio operators that neither the operators nor Rado could decipher. She could say anything, including making comments about Rado himself. This was a privilege allowed no other spy in Rado's net. It was certainly not standard tradecraft for the station chief to be circumvented by a field agent. Judging from Rado's subsequent missives to Moscow, this indignity hurt his feelings greatly.

In the end, many of the most important messages on specific topics went to Rachel directly. Rado was kept in the dark as Stalin dealt more directly with Werther.

Rado's only meaning for Rachel was that he had key radio transmitters, notably Foote, and without them her information would mean nothing. So she was forced to tolerate her boss, al-though she never socialized with him or had a kind word to throw in his direction.

NIGHT AND FOG

Stalin had another machine with a more barbaric purpose.

As the spy plane carrying Trepper and Foote finally landed at the small airport, Maria Poliakova, bundled in a full-length fur coat, waited in the distance. When Trepper stepped off, he did not notice her. Instead, he tried to get a glimpse of his family. It was dusk, and he could not see clearly, but he was able to discern enough to know that his family was not there. There were only officers. He was directed to get into a car, where he recognized one of the passengers. "Where are my wife and children?" he asked. "Don't worry," came the reply. "They're doing very well. Your wife's taking a cure in a rest home. We didn't have time to inform her . . ."[41]

From there, Trepper descended deep into a Soviet night and fog.[42] For ten years he would languish in Stalin's punishment cells. First, at the Lubyanka, he was considered a prisoner of some rank and distinction. Later his condition deteriorated as his interrogators lost track of who he was or why he was imprisoned. The Center had cut him loose, and all his interrogators knew for sure was that he was in prison, was Jewish, and was, therefore, guilty. They set about trying to find out exactly what crime he had committed.

At the Lefortovo prison, one of the most notorious in the world, Trepper's interrogator asked: "Will you tell me how you, a Polish citizen, were able to enter the Soviet Union?" When given the answer, the interrogator laughed and did not bother to write it down. Except for a few days after his return to Moscow, Trepper was never asked about his work for the Soviet Union during the war, only about unnamed crimes that he had supposedly committed against the state.[43]

From the loud torture rooms of Lefortovo, Trepper was sent to a Soviet isolator cell outside of Moscow, where the only talk, and that was rare, came in whispers. No sounds, no clanging cell doors, no guards pacing outside, no screams. The walls were thickly padded. There was no way to tell day from night, season from season. Human contact was almost nonexistent. It was Stalin's rendition of Dante's cold center of hell, and it almost always broke men who had somehow survived the Lubyanka and Lefortovo.

THE DIRECTOR

Alexander Foote stepped from the same Soviet spy plane that Trepper had departed. Certainly, he could have gone to the same cold hell, though he did not know it at the time. As he reached the tarmac, Foote noticed that the gray Soviet buildings

were unadorned and "shabby." And he felt the bitter cold of
Moscow.[44] From a distance, he saw a man and a woman approach—Poliakova and an aide.

Foote did not know Poliakova or her role in his own spy ring.
But he sensed that she was the power here.

Poliakova and the aide, who was never to appear again, took
Foote to a two-room flat in central Moscow in a complex hous-
ing wives and families of Russian generals away at the front. They
were met by Olga, Foote's new housekeeper, and Ivan, his "interpreter." Olga had prepared a banquet for Foote and Poliakova, and during it Foote and Poliakova began some casual
talk.[45] No business was discussed. That, she said, would begin in
the morning.

Sure enough, Maria returned the next day with a list of questions "as long as your arm."[46] She sat down and began talking. It
was now all business. She asked questions about Rado's disappearance, then began to reveal herself. Foote was astonished.
Not only did he discover that Poliakova had been Rado's predecessor in Switzerland, but she had controlled the entire operation during the war. In fact, Maria Poliakova knew far more
about the spy ring than did Foote.

After she left, a stunned Foote looked at the question list composed by the Center. He was not pleased.

It was obvious to him that he was under suspicion as an agent
provocateur of the British. The Center noted that his reports
about the status of the Swiss ring differed markedly from Rado's.
Besides, he had been arrested by Swiss authorities in November
1943 and released ten months later. More than anyone, the Soviets knew how an arrest could change a person. They suspected
that information Foote had sent after his release was directed by
British secret agents trying to thwart the Red Army. Moreover,
Foote was British. Stalin distrusted the British more than any
other nationality.

But unlike Trepper, who had quickly become indignant at his
interrogation—and suffered the consequences—Foote remained calm. His sole purpose now was to save his life. He understood the system and was later to write: "It was entirely ruthless, with no sense of honor, obligation, or decency towards its

servants. They were used as long as they were of any value and then cast aside with no compunction and no compensation."[47] Foote also knew that the British conspiracy notion "could only have been bred in brains to whom treachery, double-crossing, and betrayal were second nature."[48] He knew that if he made one mistake in the days that followed, one tiny contradiction, he would not be housed in what in 1945 Moscow stood as luxury, but most likely in the Center's special prison at the Lubyanka. And his questioner would not be the gentle Poliakova but one of the brutal specialists of the People's Commissariat of Internal Affairs (NKVD).[49] Foote decided that the only thing that could save him, and even that had the slimmest of chances, was to tell the truth, blemishes and all. He would not try to burnish anything.

He soon knew that he had made the right decision. The questions were constant and interwoven. Foote saw them as forming a grand tapestry. Questions asked one day appeared on another in a slightly different form, then were asked again days later, changed a bit further. Everything was being examined until the whole Swiss operation, as Foote knew it, was laid bare.

No direct physical or emotional pressure was applied. Poliakova told Foote that he was free to walk anywhere in Moscow, provided that Ivan, his interpreter, was beside him. He was free to, and did, attend various theater performances. He was even taken for a stroll past the British embassy, across the languid Moscow River from the Kremlin.[50]

But Foote still felt the pressure, and part of it he could not control. Hanging over everything was Rado, whose apparent defection in Egypt fueled Russian suspicions. The Russians seemed to think that Rado was in British hands or had been killed by British agents to prevent him from contradicting Foote.

Relief finally came weeks later when the Egyptians told the Russians that they had arrested Rado. A Soviet agent was sent to Cairo to speak with him. Whatever Rado told the agent eased Foote's situation. Rado had, in fact, tried to defect to the British, but the British wouldn't have him, forcing him into Stalin's arms, where he promptly disappeared.[51]

Finally, six weeks after Foote arrived in Moscow, his most critical time arrived. Maria told him that the director himself—

Foote assumed him to be head of Red Army intelligence—
wanted to meet him. Olga would prepare a feast, and Poliakova
would attend. They had a few more questions they wanted to ask
Foote in person. The director wouldn't be sure that he was dealing with an honest man, Foote decided, unless he could look
into his eyes.

The director and Poliakova arrived in a large limousine, followed by cars carrying guards. "The Director was a charming individual," Foote later recalled. "In his early forties, he was intelligent and intellectual, and looked it. He spoke fluent, almost
faultless English . . . He had a heavy responsibility to bear, as he
was, I believe, directly responsible to Stalin himself, and, according to [Poliakova], was one of the few people in the Soviet Union
who could see Stalin without an appointment."[52]

The meal began at 6 P.M., and the group continued talking until two the next morning. Although the gathering seemed con-
vivial, it was clear to Foote that there was an issue of great concern to the director as well as to his masters. First, the director
wanted to know Foote's theory about how Werther sent his information so quickly to Lucy and thus to Dübendorfer. Foote
said he didn't know, but he offered a guess: Someone in the
Third Reich commanded not only top-secret information but
also a wireless transmitter. It was one of the most improbable
things he could imagine, yet that was the logical explanation. In
the end, even the director had no better theory.[53]

Next, the director turned to the heart of the matter. Out of
thousands of radio transmissions that Foote had sent to Moscow,
a single one became the focus of the interview: In May 1942,
Foote had sent a message to Moscow Center concerning the po-
sitioning of German troops just before a Russian offensive to recapture Kharkov.

"Usually 'Lucy's' information had been correct," the director
said, "but once it had proved disastrous." He pulled out the cryp-
togram from Foote's dossier and handed it to him. "Do you remember sending that?" he asked.[54] Foote, who knew nothing
about the consequences of this thin piece of yellowing paper,
said that he could not distinguish the message from the many
others he had sent. It was, he allowed, in his code, so it certainly

came from his transmitter. And it was information from Werther. Other than that, the message seemed routine to Foote.

It was not routine, countered the director. "That message cost us 100,000 men at Kharkov and resulted in the Germans reaching Stalingrad. It was sent over your transmitter." Suddenly Foote knew the meaning of the game that the Center had been playing with him for the past few weeks. One of the messages from Werther had backfired, and the Center wanted scapegoats. Foote was the nearest one at hand.

The director continued: "After we received this and saw the damage that it wrought we could only assume that 'Lucy' was a double agent and all his information was false and supplied by the *Abwehr*."[55]

For weeks after the Kharkov debacle, the Center tried to ignore the Lucy material, the director told Foote. But after checking all the information from Lucy, the Center decided that "as all the other information from that source was correct and could be proved correct, the source was after all reliable." Then came the director's potentially deadly conclusion: "The information must have been falsified after it left Germany. Perhaps, my dear 'Jim,' you can throw some light on this?"[56]

Foote was being accused, indirectly, of three crimes: He was an Abwehr agent, he caused the deaths of 100,000 Russians, and he allowed the German advance on Stalingrad. Foote immediately understood the gravity of the charges. He knew that he could not dissemble in any way. The alleged crimes were immeasurable.

If he was to survive, he must depend only on the truth. He told the director that the message had come to him not from Rachel Dübendorfer but through Alexander Rado. Foote had merely been the "pianist" who played the message on the wireless back to the Center. The information had always come to him in a sealed envelope, and he never left such messages lying around, so there was no chance that someone could have substituted a phony message for a real one after it had reached him.

If there was any changing, Foote implied, it had to have been Rado, not Foote, who did it.

The director, Poliakova, and two others asked Foote to step into his bedroom so that they could evaluate his answers. It was about 2 A.M. After eight hours of questioning, Foote was spent. He was alone in his room and naturally beset with anxiety that bordered on panic. It lasted for half an hour. He felt as though he was a prisoner and the Russians were his jury. Then came a knock on his door. Foote was asked to return.

The inquisition was over. The director, Foote later reported, "appeared to be in an extremely good humor and slapped me jovially on the back." The whole Lucy matter could not be solved until after the war, the director told Foote, but as far as the May 1942 incident was concerned, he was "entirely exonerated." In arriving at this judgment, the director said that Foote's simple acceptance of the "Bear's embrace" was evidence of his innocence. If he had been a double-cross agent in 1942, he would have had no incentive to board the Russian spy plane in Paris in 1945.[57]

Meanwhile, the Soviets would question Rado, the man who had bolted from that same spy plane during its stopover in Cairo. The director said: "Very soon there will be no place in the world where it will be possible to hide from the Center."[58]

Notes

1 RG 319, Box 60, Vol. 6.

2 Ibid.

3 Alexander Foote, *Handbook for Spies* (London: Museum Press Limited, 1964), p. 24.

4 Ibid., pp. 26–27.

5 In his book *Handbook for Spies,* Foote used the name Bill Philips to identify Leon Beurton.

6 Foote, p. 31.

7 Ibid.

8 RG 319, Box 60, p. 778.

9 Ibid., p. 779.

10 Ibid.

11 Leopold Trepper, *The Great Game* (New York: McGraw-Hill, 1977), p. 266.

12 Foote, p. 146.

13 Trepper, p. 332.

14 RG 319, Box 60, Vol. 6.

15 *Military Historical Journal,* 1990, p. 58.

16 Ibid.

17 Ibid.

18 Ibid., p. 60.

19 RG 319, Box 60.

20 Ibid., p. 763.

21 Ibid., p. 1,087.

22 *Military Historical Journal,* 1990, No. 3, p. 61.

23 Ibid., p. 62.

24 CIA, p. 174.

25 RG 319, Box 60, p. 769.

26 CIA, p. 328.

27 RG 319, Box 60, p. 787.

28 Foote, p. 35.

29 CIA, p. 287.

30 RG 319, Box 60, p.775.

31 Sandor Rado, *Codename Dora* (London: Abelard-Schuman, Ltd., 1976), p. 33.

32 RG 319, Box 60, p. 786.

33 Rado recalled the first meeting with Sonia taking place in December 1939; the effects of the Phony War itself were enough to hamper communications with Paris. American intelligence in the Red Orchestra files of the National Archives put the move about five months later. Foote recalled that his service with Rado began in August 1940.

34 Rado, p. 32.

35 Foote, p. 44.

36 RG 319, Box 60, p. 787.

37 Pavel Sudoplatov and Anatoli Sudoplatov, *Special Tasks* (Boston: Little, Brown and Company, 1994), p. 138.

38 RG 319, Box 60, p. 904.

39 CIA, p. 274.

40 Ibid., p. 176.

41 Trepper, p. 334.

42 Ibid.

43 Ibid., pp. 349–50.

44 Foote, p. 149.

45 Ibid., pp. 149–50.

46 Ibid., p. 150.

47 Ibid., p. 142.

48 Ibid., p. 151.

49 Ibid.

50 Ibid., p. 152.

51 CIA, pp. 152–53. Rado was not killed. He was imprisoned for a decade and released only after Stalin died.

52 Foote, p. 153.

53 Ibid., p. 154.

54 Ibid.

55 Ibid.

56 Ibid.

57 Ibid.

58 Ibid.

Chapter Two
Intuition Warfare

The Beginning

Long before Maria Poliakova guided her network to a victory over Nazi Germany, before Werther even existed by name, Adolf Hitler started a war that he hoped he would never have to fight. The Führer had stepped through the looking glass. His British enemies were the people he most respected; his Russian partners he had sworn to defeat. To begin the war on these terms was a vast miscalculation. Not only would the Allies fight, however hesitantly, the war would also galvanize Hitler's enemies from within. The culture of treason was born.

In the end, those internal enemies combined with the Russians to destroy the Third Reich. They made Werther possible.

Break

Hitler had gambled as no other European since Napoleon—occupying the Ruhr, annexing Austria and the Sudetenland, taking Czechoslovakia—and in doing so had transformed Germany from a near-vassal state to a major power. Hitler seemed ready to quit after one last correction in the geopolitical map: Western Poland and its corridor through Danzig to East Prussia was, he had convinced himself, his final territorial goal. Most in the West believe that he would never have stopped on his own. Maybe so; but it is clear that at this point, Hitler did not want another world war.

The trouble with this plan was simple: Great Britain and France had guaranteed Poland's borders, which caused Hitler no end of self-doubt during the summer of 1939. The British could not be ignored.

Hitler had stared down a British bluff before. After he and Neville Chamberlain had decided the limits of German territorial ambitions at Munich, Hitler found a lawyer's reasoning to change things. The British protested mightily, indignantly, and in the end worthlessly. They did nothing. To Hitler, that was a confirmation. Britain had a world empire to try to save. What did she care about subtle events in Central Europe?

Still Hitler hesitated.

Earlier in his life, Hitler had sought to be an artist and an architect. He was somewhat talented at both. Now, as a politician, it was an artist's reasoning that guided him in matters of state and war. One of his greatest generals, Heinz Guderian, said that Hitler conducted "intuition warfare,"[1] and he meant it as a compliment. But most of Hitler's generals did not understand his intuition and did not like it. They wanted logic and reason to prevail, and they didn't see it in the little former corporal. On the eve of war with Poland and maybe with France and Britain, too, the Führer's intuition seemed to be failing him.

Everything Hitler had done so far to tear up the Treaty of Versailles had worked. Surely, his assault on Poland would not cause war. But Chamberlain was being an obstructionist, making up for his past sorry performance, and Hitler could get no clear reading that his latest intuition was correct. In early August 1939, he appeared to want to rush headlong into the confrontation. With the Russo-German nonaggression pact of August 23, Hitler had so isolated Poland that not even the West would be stupid enough to think that there was any use to their little understandings with Poland.

Sure France and Great Britain might protest, but once it was clear that Poland no longer existed and that Russia, too, was claiming Polish territory, the Western Allies would be reasonable. "I would have to be an idiot if, on account of the measly Corridor question, I should slide into a war like the incapable nitwits did in 1914," Hitler told army chief of staff Franz Halder.[2] To Rudolf Hess, his deputy, he simply declared: "I will not attack England. Why should England attack me?"[3]

But even after the Soviet pact, Hitler waffled. He pushed back the date of the invasion, he worried, he gathered around him his most trusted aides. Yet in the end it was his responsibility alone. He offered to negotiate with Poland, then did not let his foreign secretary do so in any real fashion. He seemed to want British mediation and not want it at the same time. Finally, he decided to risk it all, perhaps join company with those he described as the 1914 "nitwits." On September 1, 1939, German tanks crashed through the Polish borders.

Two days later, the British ambassador marched into the foreign ministry with what everyone suspected was unwelcome news. Foreign minister Joachim von Ribbentrop made sure that he was nowhere around. Paul Schmidt, only a translator, was there to meet Ambassador Sir Neville Henderson. It was the ultimatum that Hitler had gambled would never arrive. Schmidt took the news to the Reichschancellery. Rudolf Hess, Hermann Göring, and Ribbentrop were there with the Führer.

"Hitler was sitting at his desk and Ribbentrop stood by the window," Schmidt later wrote. "Both looked up expectantly as I came in. I stopped at some distance from Hitler's desk, and then slowly translated the British Government's ultimatum."

When Schmidt finished, no one in the room seemed able to inhale, the blow had been so severe. Hitler, Schmidt recalled, "sat immobile, gazing before him. He was at a loss . . .

"After an interval which seemed an age, he turned to Ribbentrop, who had remained standing by the window. 'What now?' asked Hitler." Ribbentrop's answer was simple: "I assume that the French will hand in a similar ultimatum within the hour." Göring looked at Schmidt and said softly: "If we lose this war, then God have mercy on us."[4]

Hitler turned to Hess, his closest friend, to whom he had dictated *Mein Kampf*. "Now, all my work crumbles," he said. "I wrote my book for nothing." Ribbentrop told interrogators after the war that on the morning of September 3, 1939, Hitler felt "his life's work collapsed when Britain declared war on Germany."[5]

SECRET PROTOCOLS
Though jolted by the British declaration of war, Hitler regained

his optimism within days, buoyed as much by what didn't happen
as by what did. As the autumn of 1939 advanced, the Allies' declarations stood, although the Allies themselves seemed not at all
ready to do any real fighting. It was a war of peace feelers, not
bullets, a phony war in which both sides postured and both sides
were perplexed.

Neville Chamberlain had had his fill of the German leader,
had been embarrassed by his duplicity, and was in no mood to
make peace on any terms that Hitler might find acceptable. But
Chamberlain didn't appear to be in any mood to make war, either, in large part because England was in no position to do so.
Great Britain's problem was compounded further when the Soviet Union, citing the necessity of rebalancing power, invaded
Poland seventeen days after Hitler did, thus making good on
one of the "secret protocols" of the Nazi-Soviet pact. Stalin was
able to claim the nearly defenseless eastern Poland with the expenditure of only seven hundred Soviet lives.

Sir Alexander Cadogan, permanent undersecretary in
Britain's foreign office, wrote in his diary on September 23,
1939, that Foreign Secretary "H.[alifax] asked me about our
'War Aims.' I told him I saw awful difficulties. We can no longer
say 'evacuate Poland' without going to war with Russia, which we
don't want to do! I suppose the cry is 'Abolish Hitlerism' . . .
What if Germany now sits tight? [French general Maurice]
Gamelin doesn't look to me like flinging himself on the
Siegfried line. What do we do? Build up our armaments? What
for?"[6]

While the British sought to clarify their war aims, Hitler
sought out the role of statesman. He would find a way to make
peace, to prove that his intuition warfare had not failed him. On
October 1, he invited Benito Mussolini's son-in-law, Italian foreign minister Count Galeazzo Ciano, to the Reichschancellery
and assured him that the war in the west was unnecessary. If the
Allies somehow thought that Poland was worth it, he would endeavor to do what he could to create a residual Polish state.[7] General Wilhelm Keitel, chief of staff of the Wehrmacht, said that
Hitler believed that "the whole thing was a rattling of sabers for

the benefit of the rest of the world, certainly nothing worth taking too seriously. . . . Despite our grave doubts, it did seem almost as though even now Hitler's intuition was to prove right again, for the daily reports from the west brought only news of minor skirmishing with outlying French units in the zone between the Maginot Line and our West Wall."[8]

Meanwhile, the Germans sent peace feelers throughout Europe and, in the person of Swedish businessman Birger Dahlerus, directly to Whitehall itself. Holland, Belgium, Spain, Norway, Finland, and others offered to mediate. No one, it seemed, wanted the war that had been declared. Hitler certainly didn't, but he at least was preparing to fight if need be. He assured his generals that his offers of peace were sincere. But he warned that if Britain remained obstinate, he would be ready for war. "When we get to the Channel, the English may then change their minds," he said.[9]

Though anyone reading *Mein Kampf* or familiar with Hitler's private and public talks would know that Hitler desperately sought a rapprochement with England—indeed, he had always prophesied a kind of principled German-British confederation—the British knew mostly that Hitler had stabbed them in the back in Czechoslovakia and was not to be trusted.

On September 26, Dahlerus met with Hitler and Reichsmarschall Hermann Göring. In a memorandum summarizing the discussion, Hitler is said to have explained: "Germany had won a victory in Poland which was without precedent in history. In 14 days he [Hitler] had completely destroyed a country of 36 million inhabitants which had an army of 45 divisions, in part well equipped, and whose soldiers had fought bravely." Simply put, the Führer had "no intention of allowing anyone to interfere in the solution of the Polish question."

However, Hitler at the same time allowed that "if the British still wanted to salvage something of Poland he could only advise them to hasten the peace discussions. Beyond this [Hitler] was entirely prepared to join in guaranteeing the status quo of the rest of Europe. . . . If the British desired peace in Europe they should make it clearly understood."

Hitler asked Dahlerus to tell the British that Germany was prepared to end the war, "for she needed peace in order to cultivate
the newly acquired areas in the East that had formerly belonged
to the German cultural sphere. This would require at least 50
years."

Germany was going to resettle its dense population to the east,
something that might actually take as long as a hundred years.
Hitler said that the Jews could be consigned to a redesigned Polish state.[10]

But the British were unimpressed. "He [Dahlerus] spent most
of Tuesday with Göring and Hitler, but their terms are as to be
expected: give us a free hand in Central and E. Europe and we
will guarantee the British Empire," Cadogan wrote.[11]

By October 6, Hitler took his peace offensive public with his
famous Reichstag speech, again offering a rump Polish state and
saying that "it would be more sensible to tackle the solution before millions of men are first uselessly sent to their death, and
milliards in property destroyed."

If not, he continued, "Then the French artillery will fire at
Freiburg, and the German at Kolmar or Schlettstadt. Long range
guns will then be set up, and from both sides destruction will
strike deeper and deeper, and whatever cannot be reached by
the long distance guns, will be destroyed from the air. And that
will be very interesting for certain international journalists, and
very profitable for the aeroplane, arms and munition manufac-
tures, etc., but appalling for the victims."[12]

That said, Hitler told his generals in private: "If it should become apparent in the near future that England and, under England's leadership, also France, are not willing to make an end
of the war, I am determined to act vigorously and aggressively
without great delay."[13]

What the British were ready to do was made clear by Cadogan
the next day. In his diary he wrote: "Called to War Cabinet 12.30
for discussion on reply to Hitler. I had talked to H.[alifax] about
this: the line, according to me, is to say frankly (and the P.M. hes-
itates to say this) that *we won't make peace with Hitler* [italics in
orig.]. Get rid of Hitler: that is our war aim—not peace aim. Do

that first: then you win the war. Remove him and there will be such disunity in Germany that they can't win. But it's right. And it *should* [italics in orig.] work, *if* [italics in orig.] we couple it with an assurance that we don't want to *dictate* [italics in orig.] a peace."[14]

So the idea developed in the British War Cabinet that getting rid of Hitler was the fastest way of getting rid of Germany—not completely, of course, but enough to eliminate her as a continental power. This latter caveat would not be made public until long after the war, but it was the guiding principle of British policy.

Chamberlain soon publicly answered Hitler's Reichstag speech by laying out the first tenet of British policy but not the caveat. Said the prime minister: "The peace which we are determined to secure, however, must be a real and settled peace, not an uneasy truce interrupted by constant alarms and repeated threats. What stands in the way of such a peace? It is the German Government, and the German Government alone."[15]

With that, Hitler began preparing in earnest to fight the war that he had started on September 1. His generals had drawn up an old-fashioned assault that they code-named "Case Yellow." It envisioned a main thrust running through Holland toward the Channel, then bending toward Belgium. When General Halder presented his plan, Hitler was unusually silent. But after Halder left the room, the Führer turned to General Keitel and said, "That is just the old Schlieffen plan, with a strong right flank along the Atlantic coast. You don't get away with an operation like that twice running." Then Hitler mysteriously intoned: "I have quite a different idea and I'll tell you about it in a day or two."[16]

What Halder had proposed was a plan similar in almost all major respects to the one that Germany had used in the First World War. A veteran of that war, Hitler had no intention of repeating its mistakes. That he actually knew how to go about changing the plan wasn't known in October 1939 to Hitler's generals, or likely to Hitler himself. Hitler's intuition had not yet spoken clearly about what he must do, but it had told him what he must not do.

What Hitler did see clearly, and what his generals should have seen after the successful Polish campaign, was that airpower and tanks, not infantry alone, would shape the new war. Whatever Hitler conjured up would at least take advantage of these. Hitler soon asked his generals if attacking France directly might be better than the drive through Belgium. At first, the suggestion seemed mad. France, after all, had built the Maginot line to stop Germans from ever thinking seriously about this option. But if Hitler wanted this studied, it would be studied.

To his rebellious generals, Hitler's determination to act shaped their determination to react. To them, Hitler's plans were mad, promising only ruin. The plotting against the Führer, always simmering from below, bubbled up.

EARLY TREASON

Even on the first day of the war, the culture of treason that pervaded the Third Reich was evident. State Secretary Weizsäcker spoke with Carl Jacob Burckhardt, then the League of Nations high commissioner for Danzig, about the need to send Hitler a strong message. He did not mean a Chamberlain-like warning. He meant a military message. Weizsäcker told Burckhardt about his willingness to deal with Britain on the side, "to be a traitor to his country for peace."[17]

Others had joined in. While dining at the Continental in Munich, Ulrich von Hassell, former German ambassador to Rome, and Carl Goerdeler, former mayor of Leipzig, exchanged viewpoints. The West, they reasoned, should be willing to deal with a "healthy, vigorous Germany" denuded of a government that had fraternized with communism. Get rid of Hitler, put in a responsible and traditional German regime, and the West would have accomplished what it wanted and the war could end. Surely, Britain and France would jump at the chance; after all, the Nazis were "half or three quarters bolshevist,"[18] and most felt that bolshevism was the ultimate threat. It had always been that element—the socialistic tendency of Hitlerism—as well as his recklessness that until now had so appalled most of those in the conspiracy.

One of the conspirators' plans called for a number of divisions to stop in Berlin "in transit from west to east. Then [Field Marshal Erwin von] Witzleben would appear in Berlin and dissolve the SS . . ."

Hassell continued: "A doctor would declare Hitler incapable of continuing in office, whereupon he would be taken into custody. Then an appeal would be made to the people along these lines: prevention of further SS atrocities, restoration of decency and Christian morality, continuation of the war, but readiness for peace on a reasonable basis."[19] Hassell said that Grand Admiral Erich Raeder was willing to cooperate if the army acted.[20]

The key, though, was the army, and that meant Halder. The general was always prone to a patrician's view toward Hitler and a patriot's view toward Germany. In 1938, as the little despot brought Germany closer and closer to a confrontation with the West, Halder urged his then superior—Chief of Staff Ludwig Beck—to take action, remove Hitler, and prevent a bloodbath. Being an honorable soldier, Beck could not see himself doing this. Instead, he resigned in protest of the Führer's bellicosity. Yet in leaving his position, Beck became the pivot of the many conspiracies that swirled around Hitler. As he turned over his command to Halder, Beck knew that he should have taken a different course. "I now realize that you were right," he told Halder. "Now all depends on you."[21]

Halder, though, found it far more difficult to take action when he actually had the power of army chief of staff than when he was merely the chief's assistant. Beck came calling with advice for Halder to do what Beck wouldn't do when he had a chance. Goerdeler came with the same advice, as did Hassell: Hitler must be removed and the war ended. But Halder now saw that the two issues might not be separable. He assured the conspirators that "the German Army will do its duty for the Fatherland, even against the Hitler government, if and when the situation calls for it."[22]

The problem was that, as Halder later explained, times had changed. When Beck had the opportunity to replace Hitler, Germany was at peace. Now she was at war with France and Great Britain, and a coup was possible only if those countries agreed to go along. If not, Germany could face a foreign and a civil war simultaneously, a situation from which there could come only defeat.

A coup by Halder and the army would have to include more than just the arrest of the head of state. Hermann Göring, though he might go along with a coup if he emerged the new leader, would certainly resist a plan that put someone else in charge. The coup plotters had not yet settled on Göring's fate; they believed that he may be the best one to hold the nation together, but they worried whether he would be acceptable to the West. Himmler and the SS would certainly be enemies of the plan; if there was anybody the generals hated more than Hitler, it was Himmler. So Himmler and the strong SS corps would have to be dealt with at uncertain cost. Certainly the German people were still behind their leader, though enthusiasm for the war was nowhere to be found. No, if Halder were to move, he had to have clear signs that France and Britain would not use the opportunity to continue and certainly win a war against a divided Germany.

Even such stalwart anti-Hitler leaders as Gen. Georg Thomas agreed in full. The Western powers would have to agree to "a Germany that is intact, and above all, an intact Army so that our enemies would run a considerable risk if they persisted in continuing the war."[23] Every one of the conspirators understood the problem: the Abwehr's Hans Oster, Beck, Thomas, Halder, Goerdeler, Gisevius, and all the others. What they desired was a unified and strong but peaceful Germany. Ironically, on those points, the conspirators were not at all different from the man against whom they conspired. These were, after all, patriots who liked a great deal of what Hitler had been able to accomplish. No one, for instance, wanted to see Poland restored in such a way as to have East Prussia separated from Germany. And they supported the other territorial augmentations of Germany that Hitler's cunning had accomplished. They supported the Anschluss and the reuniting of the Sudetenland with Germany. Like the Führer, these men were enemies of the Versailles treaty. What they objected to was the way that Hitler went about getting this real estate, how cavalier he seemed when facing the over-whelming might of the Allies. The conspirators did not object to the real estate itself.

So, with great naïveté, the conspirators went through a dozen channels to get an agreement with the British for a peaceful change of power in Germany and a conclusion of the war. The war cry was, after all, that the fight was against Hitler, not Germany. That's what the BBC said. Certainly there must be reasonable ways to get out of this mess without Germany having to go back to the powerless state in which it found itself in 1918.

As Germans fanned out to contact the British, it was clear what their demands were. Hassell wrote them down as such: "(1) moderate demands (German parts of Poland to us, the remainder to be independent, a new arrangement in Czechoslovakia); (2) the restitution of the rule of law in Germany; (3) general disarmament, with specific guarantees in the case of Germany (control of airplane and submarine production); and (4) the restoration of world commerce."[24]

Halder approved the approaches to the British—some of the most delicate through the offices of the Pope—while continuing his planning to destroy France and Great Britain through a military strike. Oster, the Abwehr man, arranged for the Vatican meetings. He recruited an attorney named Josef Müller to negotiate with Father Robert Leiber at the Vatican.

Months passed. One deadline after another for war against the west was issued by Hitler, then called off—more than twenty in all. Hitler couldn't bring himself to pull the trigger. Besides, he was not comfortable with the battle plan, Case Yellow. Something was wrong here. His intuition told him so.

X REPORT

As Hitler's patience narrowed, Müller and Leiber continued to meet, the German side being eager and the British reticent. There were some verbal assurances from the British, but verbal assurances meant almost nothing in this through-the-looking-glass world. The whole point was to convince the German generals that they could act decisively against the Third Reich.

Eventually, and much too late, these negotiations did produce a report, and it was written. The trouble was that it was written by the Germans and signed by no one on the British side. But it was a report of what the British representative had verbalized. The British supported this procedure; the Germans didn't. It left the door open for British denials. The German generals were serious men. Although they respected the Pope, they could not blindly accept his assurances that this agreement would stick.

The written report that Müller composed from memory, the X Report, apparently no longer exists, and memories of what it contained vary. But it is clear that even when reading it in a light most favorable to Germany, it had a fatal flaw. In describing the future of Europe, the British representative had used the phrase *decentralization of Germany*. Those three words were damning for an early resolution of the Second World War. The Peace of Westphalia and the Versailles treaty had aimed at the same thing. No German patriot, particularly in a country whose army had known only success, could agree to this. A victory in arms should not leave Germany destitute.

Another report came back that the Chamberlain government would agree to "status quo prior Munich,"[25] which was about the same and equally unacceptable.

Halder knew that there was almost no chance now to avoid whatever plan the Führer was intuiting. Yet he felt compelled to give a copy of the X Report to the commander of the army, Walther von Brauchitsch. Brauchitsch was repelled. "What we have here is pure national treason," he told Halder. "We are at war . . . That one in time of peace establishes contact with a foreign power may be considered. In war this is impossible for a soldier."[26]

But such were times in Germany that even the supreme commander of the OKH let the treason go unpunished. Not a hint of what had happened made its way to the Führer, at least not that is known. The conspirators saved their lives, but the actions of the British and the reluctance of Halder to act alone probably irreversibly condemned the Continent to a long and bloody siege.

But not all lost hope completely. After Brauchitsch rejected the X Report, the others in the conspiracy continued seeking ways to bring the British around. Halder, though, knew that he had to prepare for Hitler's war. Embittered after the war, Halder recalled the whole conspiracy in 1939 and 1940 and how the negotiators failed to get the needed assurances from Great Britain. "The peace assurances of England were all bluff," he said. "None of them were [sic] serious." The real British policy was simple: "At bottom, England want[ed] to destroy us anyway."[27]

Some of the conspirators simply could not believe that millions of lives might be shed because the British were pigheaded about their approach.[28] "How tactically wrong it is to demand a change of regime from outside," Hassell wrote. "This frightens the generals who remember 1918."[29]

The conspirators were not alone in failing to understand the British position. Hitler and his government couldn't either. The ambassador from Italy, a country that truly did not want the war, tried in January to convince Ribbentrop that the Western Allies could settle the war if the Germans came up with a face-saving restoration of part of Poland. Ribbentrop did not understand. "This opinion, however, seemed to me to conflict to a certain extent with the fact that the Führer had offered such a peace to the Western Powers in October, but they had scornfully rejected it. The most varied statements by British and French statesmen, the most recent of which was yesterday's speech by Chamberlain, constantly demanded the elimination of the 'tyrant,' that is, of the Führer, and consequently of the German people."[30]

Hitler had no clearer insight than his foreign minister. On November 1, 1939, Alfred Rosenberg, the Nazi ideology chief, wrote in his diary: "The Führer mentioned several times that he still considered a German-English understanding to be desirable, particularly in the longer term . . . He couldn't grasp what they [the British] were really after. Even if England secured a victory, the real winners would be the United States, Japan and Russia. England would come out of a war shattered in any case, let alone if it suffered a military *defeat* [italics in orig.]"[31]

It was a sapient observation, but it did not prevent Hitler from planning the defeat of his long-sought-after Nordic cousins. What is in part remarkable about Hitler and his conspirators was how obsessed they were with the British, who had but ten divisions with 310 tanks on the Continent, and how little they concerned themselves with the French, who had 104 divisions and 3,063 tanks.[32] But Hitler, who commanded merely 2,445 tanks, discounted the French and planned instead to win over or beat down the British. But of all the enemies Hitler ever faced, he never showed hatred or even much anger toward the British, at least not as a people. It is to this day debatable whether he even showed resolve.

During one meeting with his generals, after calculating the best way of defeating England, Hitler said that "the great successes of the first month of war could, in the event of an immediate peace, serve to strengthen the Reich both psychologically and materially to such an extent that, from a German point of view, there could be no objection to concluding the war, provided the success won by our armies was not jeopardized by the peace treaty . . ."[33]

The British did not see or appreciate the dangers in the Blitzkrieg, although it was a British expert—B. H. Liddell Hart—who best outlined its theoretical parameters. Instead, Chamberlain remained inflexible, perhaps because that was politically the only way he could remain. Hitler's Czech betrayal—which he thought of as a minor correction in course and could not understand the British position at all—had made any further concession to the German leader impossible. Sumner Welles, representing President Franklin Roosevelt, found this out in March 1940, when he asked the British prime minister whether England would accept peace if Europe were restored. Chamberlain said no, never. Hitler "personified a system with which the British Government had learned from bitter experience it was impossible to make terms . . . We could not be satisfied with any settlement from which it did not clearly emerge that Hitler's policy had been a failure."[34] In other words, not only did Britain want Hitler gone and Europe restored, it wanted any successful policy of Hitler's to be wiped out. Germany might not have to re-turn all the way to its Weimar past, but it would have to go much of the distance.

Hitler was not the only German who rejected these terms. They were unacceptable to the conspirators, who could have brought him down.

Hitler lamented that the British were dreamers "still living in the Victorian era, when all they had to do was send out cruisers to restore order in the world." Now, America was a bigger factor, as were Japan and the Soviet Union. Even "Germany considered herself today to be a stronger power than England."[35] Could not the British see that the world had changed?

It is true that there were crosscurrents in the British leader-ship. Anthony Eden, Lord Halifax, Lord Beaverbrook, and many others, some left over from the appeasement days, occasionally thought of ways to prevent the war. The Duke of Windsor, of course, was leading everyone. But if it was at this juncture desir-able to prevent a war, and most historians think that the war was a necessary evil, it was altogether too late.

It wasn't until March 12, 1940, that British hard-liner Sir Robert Vansittart hit upon the obvious: Encourage the German generals, regardless. As Cadogan had earlier seen, the British could tell the generals what they wanted to hear, let Germany de-volve into whatever chaos would follow, and then see. The British could suffer sudden memory loss at any juncture. They could ask, what agreement? At any rate, they could hardly be worse off if they intrigued with the generals than if they did not. Were it not for his stupid wounded pride, Chamberlain would have come to this conclusion earlier.

At this point, however, Vansittart had little chance of succeed-ing with the German generals even if he had sat down and con-ferred face-to-face with Halder himself. Chamberlain's bunglers chose to deal with former German chancellor Josef Wirth, a con-firmed anti-Hitlerite living in Lucerne, Switzerland. A left-winger,[36] Wirth had no direct contact with the generals, and lit-tle prestige. Yet it was through Wirth that Vansittart sent word that the British would not attack while the generals seized power.

Vansittart also promised economic assistance and even a military "diversion" if the generals needed one.[37] The contact led to nothing. If the British had earlier said this clearly through Pope Pius XII—and committed it to something better than Müller's memory—the war could have taken a much different course. But now there seemed only one way.

ACTION

Hitler had little alternative now but to strike in the west. Eight months had passed since he had invaded Poland. He had publicly asked for a settlement, and Western leaders had publicly rejected his moves. Hitler's covert overtures had met similar fates.[38] Though the moral onus of the war was clearly on his side, the West shared some of the responsibility by declaring war, then avoiding peace. Perhaps the drift to real war was never reversible, but the record is clear that Hitler and his German opponents originally thought otherwise.

Time was working against Germany. Great Britain could tap resources from around the world, whereas Germany's formidable industrial strength depended upon raw materials that were susceptible to interdiction by sea power, in the case of Scandinavian iron, and by air, in the case of Romanian oil.

Between oil and iron, oil was the larger concern. Germany had almost none of its own and was dependent on Romania's Ploesti oil fields, which were dangerously close to British forces in North Africa and Russian forces to the east. If the Ploesti complex was wiped out, German tanks could not move and German politicians could not rule.

After the war started, Germany tried to find new sources of oil with little initial success. Two weeks into the war, von Ribbentrop was in Moscow asking Stalin if he would relinquish some oil fields in captured lands because Russia already had enough oil for her own needs. Stalin said no.[39]

Hitler understood the calculus. By November 23, 1939, he framed everything by its equations. Addressing two hundred of his commanders, Hitler said: "Treaties, however, are only kept as long as they serve their purpose. Russia will hold herself to it only so long as Russia herself considers it to be to her benefit. Bismarck thought so too. . . . We can oppose Russia only when we are free in the west. Further, Russia is seeking to increase her influence in the Balkans and is pressing toward the Persian Gulf. That is also the goal of our foreign policy."[40]

Hitler returned to his theme of driving the main thrust of the Wehrmacht into France, not Belgium. In this, he had found a younger general who agreed and had worked out some details. Erich von Manstein, who was to play a preeminent role in the Russian campaign, said that German armor should move through the Ardennes forest in Luxembourg and into France at Sedan. He and Hitler felt that a strong feint in Belgium would draw off the cream of the Allied divisions and lead them into a terrible trap.

After the war, as Keitel awaited the hangman, he described well Hitler's (and Manstein's) ideas: "Because I have not much time left, I will not go in detail into the strategic questions arising from all this, as they will be dealt with by others anyway; I will only go so far as to make it quite plain that it was Hitler himself who saw the armored break-through at Sedan, striking up to the Atlantic coast at Abbeville, as the solution; we would then swing round [northward] into the rear of the motorized Anglo-French army, which would most probably be advancing across the Franco-Belgian frontier into Belgium, and cut them off.

"I had some misgivings, as this stroke of genius could go awry if the French tank army did not do us the favor of automatically driving through Belgium towards our northern flank . . ."[41]

The generals resisted this daring idea until fate intervened. On January 10, a German plane carrying a copy of the old Case Yellow plan made a forced landing behind enemy lines. From then on, the generals had to assume that Case Yellow was compromised. The Hitler-Manstein alternative looked more and more promising.

What is generally not known is the degree to which Hitler went in accommodating his generals at this time. Historian Brian Fugate noted: "Hitler had previously shown himself inclined to defer important decisions if they appeared likely to cause disagreements among his advisors, and it was this weakness in his character that Halder could use to his advantage."[42] Whether Hitler would have insisted on the Hitler-Manstein plan had it not been for the downed plane may never be known. But with their plans exposed, Halder and his staff had to take a new look at Hitler's conception and were surprised to find that it just might work. They detested gambles, which surely this was, but they also liked victories, which this one seemed to offer. So they began the long logistical planning that would prove to some that the Führer was either a genius or a fool. Yet to a few of the generals, if Hitler's plan worked, it would prove only that he was lucky. They knew that already, just as they knew that luck had a habit of running out.

Stalin was pleased. His only military rival in the West was about to go to war with the capitalist democracies. Earlier in the year, Nikolai Yezhov, who under Stalin's tutelage had killed millions as head of the secret internal police, was removed and soon shot. In his place came Lavrenti Beria. Stalin and Beria saw no need to irritate Hitler. The art of war insists that one should never disturb an enemy who is in the process of committing suicide. Stalin thought that this applied to Hitler.

Stalin reaffirmed his orders that his secret agents, including Gisela's family, should remain inactive in matters concerning Germany.

Notes

1 RG 165, Entry 179, Box 721.

2 Testimony of Franz Halder taken by Col. John Amen at Nuremberg, October 1945. National Archives.

3 Wulf Schwarzwaller, *Rudolf Hess: The Last Nazi* (Bethesda, Md.: National Press and Star Agency, 1988), p. 180.

4 Paul Schmidt, *Hitler's Interpreter* (London: William Heinemann, 1951), p. 157.

5 XE000887, Box 8.

6 Alexander Cadogan, *The Diaries of Sir Alexander Cadogan* (New York: Putnam, 1971), p. 219.

7 DGFP, Vol. 8, p. 188.

8 Wilhelm Keitel, *Memoirs of Field Marshal Keitel* (London: William Kimber, 1965), pp. 93–94.

9 John Lukacs, *The Duel: 10 May–31 July 1940, The Eighty-Day Struggle Between Churchill and Hitler* (New York: Ticknor & Fields, 1991), p. 81.

10 DGFP, Vol. 8, No. 138.

11 Cadogan, p. 220.

12 Raoul de Roussy de Sales, ed., *My New Order: A Collection of Speeches by Adolf Hitler* (New York: Reynal & Hitchcock, 1941), pp. 755–56.

13 DGFP, Vol. 8, No. 224.

14 Cadogan, p. 221.

15 Ibid., p. 223.

16 Keitel, p. 102.

17 Klemens von Klemperer, *German Resistance Against Hitler* (Oxford: Clarendon Press, 1992), p. 101.

18 Ulrich von Hassell, *The von Hassell Diaries* (Garden City, N.Y.: Doubleday, 1947), p. 74.

19 Ibid., p. 101.

20 Ibid., p. 103.

21 Harold Deutsch, *Conspiracy Against Hitler in the Twilight War* (Minneapolis: University of Minnesota Press, 1968), p. 31.

22 Klemperer, p. 176.

23 Hassell, pp. 127–28.

24 Ibid., p. 76.

25 Anthony Cave Brown, *"C": The Secret Life of Sir Stewart Menzies* (New York: Macmillan Publishing Company, 1987), p. 215.

26 Deutsch, p. 133.

27 Ibid., p. 269.

28 Hassell had been involved in an extensive effort outside the Vatican framework to negotiate with Lord Halifax. That effort, too, failed to provide a satisfactory answer to the general's concern over foreign hostilities during a German army coup.

29 Hassell, p. 108.

30 DGFP, Vol. 8, No. 518.

31 NAZ, p. 758.

32 Ibid., p. 764.

33 Ibid.

34 Cadogan, p. 261.

35 DGFP, Vol. 7, No. 591.

36 CIA, p. 207.

37 Klemperer, p. 165.

38 Perhaps the most unusual approach was Walter Schellenberg's romancing of British agents Best and Stevens at Venlo. Schellenberg, operating with Himmler's blessing, was negotiating the end of Hitler's reign. This was probably with Hitler's knowledge, but whether or not the negotiations were serious may never be known. The negotiations ended abruptly after an assassination attempt on Hitler on November 8, 1939. Hitler ordered Schellenberg to arrest Best and Stevens, which he did in an audacious raid across the Dutch border the next day.

39 DGFP, Vol. 8, No. 152.

40 NAZ, p. 764.

41 Keitel, pp. 102–3.

42 Brian Fugate, *Operation Barbarossa* (Novato, Calif.: Presidio Press, 1984), p. 124.

Chapter Three

MIRACLE

UNLIMITED POWER

When the Wehrmacht launched its attack on May 10, 1940, the plan worked with near perfection. As Hitler had guessed, the Allies took the bait and headed to meet the German feint in Belgium. Soon General Guderian's tanks thundered out of the Ardennes and by May 11 were near Sedan. Erwin Rommel crossed the Muse River on May 13, and by the next day France and Great Britain knew that they had been had. All Germany needed to do was race its armor toward the Channel and cut the enemy in half.

But Hitler, with sure knowledge that his plan had outfoxed the enemy's high command, became hesitant and seemingly embarrassed by his good fortune. On May 17, for the first time in the Western campaign, Hitler told his generals that an advance toward the Channel was not the most important matter. "It may even have to be slowed down temporarily," he said to his generals, who planned to do no such thing.[1]

Hitler was looking at things differently than his generals were. Roles had reversed. Hitler's gamble now looked like a sure thing. The generals wanted to press ahead when Hitler did not. Halder complained that Hitler was "nervous" and so "frightened by his own success, he is afraid to take any chance and so would rather pull the reins on us. Puts forward the excuse that it is all because of his concern for the left flank!"[2] Try as he might, though, Hitler was having almost no effect on his generals, who had detected the clear scent of blood and were charging on.

Hitler became alarmed. Halder wrote that the Führer "rages and screams" at the westward advance and "won't have any part of continuing the operation."[3]

By May 21 Hitler's army had accomplished what four years of the First World War had not. Despite Hitler's warnings to Halder, German forces were at the Channel. The French and British were separated.

Across the Channel there was panic. Winston Churchill, who had taken over as prime minister on May 10—before the depth of the calamity could have been predicted—was now trying anything he could to stem the tide. He wrote desperately to Mussolini, in words he never before would have used:

"Having taken over the Office of the Prime Minister I feel strongly impelled to send you, the leader of the Italian nation, a message of goodwill across that gap which seems to be widening so rapidly.

"Is it too late to prevent the shedding of blood between the British and Italian peoples? Of course, we could annihilate each other and redden the Mediterranean with our blood. If this should be your will, then it must be, but I wish to say that I have never been an enemy of the Italian people, nor have I in my heart ever been opposed to the man who rules Italy."[4]

He assured Mussolini that his entreaty did not come from weakness, but the Italian dictator surely viewed it as such and made the text available to the Germans, who also shared his interpretation.

The British grew more desperate. In a note to Gen. Hastings Ismay, Churchill said: "One must always be prepared for the fact that the French may be offered very advantageous terms of peace, and the whole weight be thrown on us."[5]

One of the empire's most enduring hopes was to bring the United States into the war. That long-term plan now took on immediate gravity. To President Franklin Roosevelt, Churchill painted a chilling picture. If American help was not available soon, he told the president, "you must not be blind to the fact that the whole remaining bargaining counter with Germany would be the fleet, and if this country was left by the United States to its fate no one would have the right to blame those then responsible if they made the best terms they could for the surviving inhabitants. Excuse me, Mr. President, [for] putting this

nightmare bluntly. Evidently I could not answer for my succes-
sors who in utter despair and helplessness might well have to accommodate themselves to the German will."[6]

While Churchill scrambled to influence the Americans, someone in Britain was apparently trying to influence the Germans.
On May 21, Halder wrote in his diary one of the most cryptic ref-
erences of the war: "We are seeking to arrive at an understanding with Britain on the basis of a division of the world."[7] Exactly
who was involved in this massive real estate negotiation is unknown to this day, and many of the possibly relevant documents
in Great Britain are still sealed.

While Churchill tried to stem the German tide, a grim melan-
choly spread over London. The war, everybody was beginning to
sense, was being lost as the German war machine taught the
British a new type of warfare, more impersonal and deadly than
ever before. It was a warfare that favored a quick offensive over
any defensive scheme so far devised. This was not a rerun of the
Great War. The spearhead from the Ardennes had reached the
Channel, having met with scant resistance on the killing fields of
the First World War. And now there was little the British could do
about it.

By May 22 the British decided that the situation was so severe
they had to grant the prime minister, in his own words, "practically unlimited power over the life, liberty, and property of all
His Majesty's subjects in Great Britain. In general terms of law
the powers granted by Parliament were absolute."[8] Churchill
now had powers that on paper were equal to those of his opponent. And he had one asset that Hitler couldn't match—
the British Secret Intelligence Service (SIS). Churchill had said
that in times of war, truth was so valuable that it must be surrounded by a "bodyguard of lies." If he were to worm his way out
of this calamity, that SIS bodyguard would have to work as never
before.

And time was a British enemy that even the SIS could not now
tame. The British Expeditionary Force was squeezed into a
pocket by the Channel port of Dunkirk, and there was no practical way to save that force or its equipment. If the Germans be-

haved like Germans, sending in their bombers and tanks and men, the British army would be wiped out.

Hitler was not pleased with that prospect. He later explained to close associates: "The army is England's backbone . . . if we destroy it, there goes the British Empire. We would not, nor could not, inherit it . . . My generals did not understand this."[9]

On May 24, Hitler made his move. Field Marshal Gerd von Rundstedt had the day before ordered the march on Dunkirk stopped so he could straighten up his line. Now Hitler ordered that the halt continue until he said otherwise. He demanded that his generals actually heed this order. The most remarkable thing about the order, except that it was given at all, was the way it was given. Churchill revealed in his writings: "We intercepted a German message sent in the clear at 11:42 A.M. on May 24, to the effect that the attack on the line Dunkirk-Hazebrouck-Merville was to be discontinued for the present."[10] It was a Führerorder sent without coding, "in the clear," so that no one could mistake its meaning. Hitler himself had halted the German advance.

Halder certainly knew part of what was happening, and it was he who now was raging. "Now political command has formed the fixed idea that the battle of decision must not be fought on Flemish soil, but rather in northern France. To camouflage this political move, the assertion is made that Flanders, crisscrossed by a multitude of waterways, is unsuited for tank warfare."[11] But at this point it is unclear whether Halder or Churchill realized the full message that Hitler was giving.

On May 26, Halifax asked Churchill to consider making terms with the Germans. Churchill responded that he "would be thankful to get out of our present difficulties on such terms, provided we retained the essentials and the elements of our vital strength, even at the loss of some territory."[12] Churchill told his counterpart in France, "It would indeed be a tragedy if by too hasty an acceptance of defeat we threw away a chance that was almost within our grasp of securing an honourable issue from the struggle."[13]

On the afternoon of the next day, Hitler authorized a resumption of the attack. Records from the British cabinet meeting that morning are to this day sealed. By the afternoon, Churchill said that nothing firm could be decided until the evacuations under way at Dunkirk could be evaluated. Halifax stated the situation bluntly: "If we got to the point of discussing terms of a general settlement and found that we could obtain terms which did not postulate the destruction of our independence, we should be foolish if we did not accept them."[14]

Churchill posed a leading question to his chiefs of staff: "In the event of terms being offered to Britain which would place her entirely at the mercy of Germany through disarmament, cession of naval bases in the Orkneys, etc.; what are the prospects of our continuing the war alone against Germany and probably Italy?"[15]

In a discussion with Lord Halifax, Churchill continued in the same vein, explaining: "If Herr Hitler was prepared to make peace on the terms of the restoration of the German colonies and the overlordship of Central Europe, that was one thing. But it was quite unlikely that he would make such an offer."[16]

That this was precisely what Hitler would have offered, Churchill perhaps did not yet know. But it is clear that Britain and its prime minister were ready to seek a peace on any halfway reasonable terms. On May 28 Churchill asked Lloyd George, the British prime minister during the First World War and the Briton whom Hitler most respected, to join the cabinet. It was a signal that the hard-liners were wavering in London.

These documents about the late May cabinet meetings, released well after the war, contrast significantly with Churchill's 1949 book entitled *Finest Hour.* In it, Churchill says, "I was sure that every Minister was ready to be killed quite soon, and have all his family and possessions destroyed, rather than give in."[17] In reality, Churchill wanted to save Great Britain, and if he had to deal with the Devil to do it, he would. But unlike some of his colleagues, he was not convinced that the time was right.

Across the Channel, many in the German officer corps were still trying to figure out what exactly the Führer was doing. General Hans Jeschonnek overheard Hitler explaining his halt before Dunkirk: "The Führer wants to spare the British a humiliating defeat."[18] Hitler later explained to a close friend, "The blood of every single Englishman is too valuable to shed. Our two people belong together, racially and traditionally—that is and always has been my aim even if our generals can't grasp it."[19]

In some table talk during the war, Hitler complained that "Churchill was quite unable to appreciate the sporting spirit of which I had given proof by refraining from creating an irreparable breach between the British and ourselves. We did, indeed, refrain from annihilating them at Dunkirk. We ought to have been able to make them realize that their acceptance of the German hegemony in Europe, a state of affairs to the implementation of which they had always been opposed, but which I had implemented without any trouble, would bring them inestimable advantages."[20]

Hitler's pause had saved the British Expeditionary Force, but in name only. Some 338,000 British and French troops got away—at a terrible cost. The campaign, which was to continue in France for a few more weeks, had cost the West 170,000 dead, compared to Germany's 27,000. But the materiel costs for the British were of more strategic importance than those of the lives ended. The equipment of the entire army was lost: 7,000 tons of ammunition, 90,000 rifles, 2,300 guns, and 120,000 vehicles were all now in German hands.[21] Many months would be needed before the losses could be repaired.

The conspirator Hassell marveled at the success, saying that it resulted from "excellent leadership, along with criminal negligence and bad leadership on the other side. . . .

"The skepticism of most of the generals, above all Beck's, is proved wrong; the swaggering Fromm has been proved right. The credit due Hitler and Göring for producing these weapons and Hitler's personal success in directing the campaign are undeniable facts. . . . One must now reckon with a new structure for Europe, in Hitler's image, achieved through a peace supporting his wide aims. They are preparing to wipe out the peace of Westphalia . . .

"Domestically, the new forms will become evident through the ascendancy of Hitler's brand of socialism, the destruction of the upper class, the transformation of the churches into meaningless sects, et cetera.

"Since National Socialism, as it had now developed, is completely soulless, its intrinsic creed being power, we shall get a godless nature, a dehumanized, cultureless Germany, and perhaps a Europe, conscienceless and brutal.

"Weizsäcker thought there was some consolation in the knowledge that very often in history great transformations have been wrought by criminals."[22]

But Hassell was a bit premature. At this point, any rational person—and those in the British cabinet were quite rational—would agree that the situation appeared to be final. Great Britain possessed a disarmed army, and an army without weapons would not be worth much against the Wehrmacht. There were still the Royal Navy and Royal Air Force, but the German generals did not doubt for a second what should be done.

Immediately after Dunkirk, Gen. Erhard Milch said: "I strongly advise the immediate transfer to the Channel coast of all available Luftwaffe forces . . . The invasion of Great Britain should begin without delay."[23]

But would a man who had just allowed more than 300,000 enemy soldiers to escape unharmed be expected to order an air and sea invasion, only to humiliate the country he wanted least to humiliate?

Keitel described the situation like this: "Nobody was in the dark about the risk we would be running; everybody was well aware that its success would demand a maximum effort by army, navy and air force, but everybody realized that the longer the invasion was postponed, the stronger the British defenses would become . . .

"Nobody feared the British Army since its collapse and its enormous material losses at Dunkirk; but the Royal Air Force and the vastly superior Royal Navy were factors which could not be ignored. The War Office was accordingly strongly in favour of risking the operation and made every possible effort to promote its execution: for the first time, Hitler found himself under considerable pressure from that quarter, a circumstance to which he was totally unaccustomed. The air force was also ready, and confident of its ability to provide an umbrella over the naval and landing operations, but they rightly insisted on a period of good weather as being a pre-condition for the success of the whole operation."[24]

But Keitel at least had a glimpse of insight into Hitler's thinking. He said that Hitler resisted the pressure of his generals because "he was reluctant to countenance the inevitable loss of his last chance of settling the war with Britain by diplomatic means, something which I am convinced he was at that time still hoping to achieve."[25]

By ignoring his generals, Hitler lost his best chance for ending the European war before it became a world war. "Invasion, however incompetently mounted and carried out, would have been invincible, . . ." wrote British spymaster F. W. Winterbotham. "It is perhaps difficult for those younger generations to realize that in 1940 we were totally defeated in France, and that all that stood between us and total surrender was the disarmed remains of the British Army evacuated from Dunkirk, and the Royal Air Force, pitifully small compared with the vast air fleets of the Luftwaffe."[26]

INSIGHT

At this point, Great Britain could have made peace with Hitler on terms that might have served her interests. She would not have lost territory, because Hitler was demanding none. Hitler, according to his conversations with his deputies, would have given her concessions that would have left the Royal Navy stronger, not weaker. Hitler offered to restore Western Europe, which to Britain was at least an even proposition. General Günther Blumentritt visited Hitler's headquarters and was surprised to find the Führer in good spirits.

"He then astonished us by speaking with admiration of the British Empire, of the necessity for its existence, and of the civilization that Britain had brought to the world . . . He concluded by saying that his aim was to make peace with Britain on a basis that she would regard as compatible with her honor to accept."[27]

Had she accepted, Britain could have escaped, mostly unharmed, the miscalculations of her leaders, Hitler thought. Her real enemies, Hitler said, were maritime—the United States and

Japan. How could fighting Germany now help her compete against those foes? "The British," Hitler told Jodl, "have lost the war, but they don't know it. One must give them time and they will come round."[28]

Once that happened, Hitler had always thought he would turn his attention to the Soviet Union. But now he was expressing some doubt. "There will remain," Hitler told associates, "our settling of our accounts with the East. But that is a task that opens global problems . . . perhaps I shall have to leave that to my successor. Now we'll have our hands full for years, to digest and consolidate what we have achieved in Europe."[29]

Italian foreign minister Count Galeazzo Ciano detected the change in Hitler's aggressiveness. "Hitler is now the gambler," Ciano wrote in his diary, "who has made a big scoop and would like to get up from the table risking nothing more."[30]

With a disarmed home army and tenuous positions around the globe that could become only more tenuous if the battle continued, why didn't Great Britain accept the offer? There are two probable reasons: It didn't understand the offer, or it already knew that Hitler would not press the advantage. The third possible reason—that Great Britain wanted to fight to the death against the evil of the Nazis—is romantic but contradicted by the desperate cabinet minutes of late May and June.

Fighting Hitlerism, the standard line of pre-Dunkirk British propagandizing, was hardly considered by the British Cabinet in the four weeks following Dunkirk. Hitler had won. No serious person falls on his sword over a lost cause.

By June 17, Hitler heard that his bet at Dunkirk was paying off. When R. A. Butler, the undersecretary of state for foreign affairs, met Björn Prytz, Swedish minister to London, Butler told Prytz that "no opportunity would be neglected for concluding a compromise peace if the chance [were] offered on reasonable conditions . . ." Butler then left Prytz in his office and talked to Halifax. Halifax, in turn, sent in a message: "Common sense and not bravado would dictate the British government's policy."[31]

What Churchill had, and in slim measure, was hope. Not for

military reasons, because by any calculation Britain was on that score impotent. The hope stood in the German Führer.

John Lukacs, a historian of this period, says that Churchill had a certain insight that Hitler did not mean to bring Great Britain to ruin, and if the British could hold out during this, the bleakest period, perhaps America could change the balance of power, or perhaps even Hitler would turn his attention to the east, or by some other combination of luck England could survive.

Each day that passed with Hitler doing nothing but touring Paris was a day of hope. Besides, on May 22, the British had succeeded in breaking into the Luftwaffe's Enigma codes, an enciphering method that the Germans thought was ironclad but Churchill's mathematicians at Bletchly Park thought was fair game. And with every passing day, the mathematicians seemed to get better at cracking into Hitler's plans. To the public, it seemed only that Churchill was omniscient. Somehow, the prime minister seemed to know that German paratroopers were not soon to darken British skies.

Churchill, in fact, was not omniscient, despite Bletchly. Enigma was not fully broken. And even if every order from the high command was known, there was no guarantee that Hitler might not change his mind.

Churchill gambled on a simple proposition: The messages from Germany were encouraging. No invasion was imminent. Why not wait? Send out a peace feeler now and then in Switzerland, Sweden, and Spain, but in general why not play for time? The U.S. president wanted in the war, somehow. And Russia's dictator surely had no less a territorial ambition than Hitler. The two countries would clash sometime.

It was a gambler's act for sure. The deal that Hitler offered would not stay on the table for long. In mid-June, Churchill intensified his work on the American side of the equation, painting for Roosevelt a picture even gloomier than his previous message:

"A point may be reached in the struggle where the present ministers no longer have control of affairs and when very easy terms could be obtained for the British islands by their becoming a vassal state of the Hitler empire. A pro-German government would certainly be called into being to make peace and might present to a shattered or a starving nation an almost irresistible case for entire submission to the Nazi will. The fate of the British fleet as I have already mentioned to you would be decisive on the future of the United States because if it were joined to the fleets of Japan, France and Italy and the great resources of German industry, overwhelming sea power would be in Hitler's hands."[32]

This specter never ceased to rouse the president, and Churchill knew it. Even when the prime minister knew that the Nazis were headed east, he didn't let the president know. The idea of the British fleet falling into the hands of Hitler was a nightmare that the president must feel. Neither he nor the State Department, it seems, had taken time to analyze Hitler's copious comments about how preserving the British fleet for the British was one of the goals of German foreign policy.

Hitler's generals wanted to press Britain at all costs. The Führer didn't; he was sure that the war was over. After the French surrendered on June 21, Hitler confidently decommissioned thirty-five divisions, a cut of some 22 percent in German armed strength.[33] That was not the action of a man anticipating a continued struggle with Great Britain, much less a war with Russia.

Ciano wrote, "Hitler makes many reservations on the desirability of demolishing the British Empire, which he considers, even today, to be an important factor in world equilibrium. I ask von Ribbentrop a clear-cut question: 'Do you prefer the continuation of the war, or peace?' He does not hesitate a moment. 'Peace.'"[34]

On June 24, Rudolf Hess told his physician Felix Kersten, "The Führer spoke again of how important the British Empire is for world order. Germany and France, along with England, must jointly resist Bolshevism, which is Europe's real enemy. That was also the reason why the Führer allowed the British Expeditionary Force to escape Dunkirk . . . I can't imagine that the cool, pragmatic English would rather put their heads in the Soviet's noose than to come to an agreement with us."[35]

But as days passed without word that the British government was ready to settle the war, Hitler grew worried. Halder wrote in his diary, "The Führer is most concerned about the question of why Britain will not yet make peace. He sees the answer, as we do, in the fact that Britain still has hopes of Russia. He reckons therefore that England will have to be compelled to make peace by force. But he does not like doing this. The reason is that if we crush England's military power the British Empire will collapse. That is of no use to Germany. German blood would be shed to accomplish something that would benefit only Japan, America and others."[36]

Hitler decided to press his peace offensive. On June 26, the British received "a flash to the effect that Hitler is going to offer us sensationally generous terms." The War Cabinet met, but the records of that meeting were never photographed or made public.[37]

On July 19, 1940, Hitler took the podium in the Reichstag. Never before had military men been present in such numbers and in such prominence. Raeder, Brauchitsch, and Keitel were on the government benches, behind the Cabinet ministers. Göring was seated as Reichstag president. Hitler wanted to deliver a symbolic message as well as a verbal one: His generals were behind him. That this was not true he either didn't know or didn't presently care.

In all, Hitler sounded much the way he did in his October 6 speech, but now a battle had been won, whereas in October it had not yet begun. That was the startling part. Hitler was speaking about peace from unquestionable strength. He told a supportive audience that, should the war continue, "a great world empire will be destroyed. A world empire that I never intended to destroy or even damage. . . . As victor, I am speaking in the name of reason. I can see no reason why this war should go on."[38]

Afterward, peace feelers darted throughout Europe, some in official cloaks and some not. But for the record, the British rejected Hitler's entreaty on July 22.

This prompted Hitler to do two things that were contradictory. They can, in fact, be understood only through Hitler's long-term hatred of Bolshevism and his disinclination to destroy the British. All the themes that were spelled out in his book, his table talk, and his public statements now came into play. Hitler could not bring himself to do what his generals knew had to be done.

On the last day of July, Hitler told Halder and Brauchitsch that the air war against Great Britain would begin, but it was clear that he did not have much faith in it. He told his generals pessimistically that "if results of the air war are not satisfactory, [invasion] preparations will be halted." And he gave the generals a short timetable to complete their task. Then he revealed his real reasoning and the actual strategic plan for conducting the war. Said the Führer: "Russia is the factor on which England is mainly betting. Something has happened in London! The English were already quite 'down,' now they are a bit up again. We have tapped their telephone conversations . . . However: should Russia be smashed, then England's last hope is extinguished."[39]

Halder wrote in his diary: "Britain's hope lies in Russia and the United States. If Russia drops out of the picture, America, too, is lost for Britain, because elimination of Russia would tremendously increase *Japan's power* [italics in orig.] in the Far East."[40] Halder wrote that the first German thrust would be toward Kiev and securing flank protection of the river Dnieper; the second thrust would be toward the Baltic States. Finally there would be a drive on Moscow.

With Enigma deciphering German codes, Churchill knew that the real Battle of Britain had been won before the first Luftwaffe plane arrived. Even before Hitler announced his decision to his generals, Churchill confidently told a colleague: "If Hitler fails to beat us here, he will probably recoil eastward. Indeed, he may do this even without trying an invasion."[41]

Swiss Connection

Before the shooting war began, Rachel Dübendorfer, codenamed Sissy, would send intelligence gathered from at least seventeen sources to Henri Robinson, Maria Poliakova's French agent. Robinson was able to transport the packet to the Soviet military attaché at the Russian embassy, who then would deliver it via diplomatic pouch to Moscow. After the invasion, this method was impossible and Dübendorfer was cut off from the center for six months.

In December 1940, Robinson sent a courier to Dübendorfer to check up on her network.[42] In January 1941 came the reply: Rachel's network was teetering from lack of contact and funds. Rachel could not understand the seeming indifference that the Center had developed toward Germany after the consummation of the Russo-German nonaggression pact. However, through means unknown, she had survived this period and kept her network operating, regardless of Stalin's wishes. In fact, Rachel did most things in spite of Stalin.

Rachel handed a packet of intelligence to Robinson's courier to take back to France. When he opened the packet, Robinson could not believe what was there: seemingly flawless intelligence from inside Hitler's Third Reich. Robinson sent Sissy's intelligence immediately to Moscow and, judging the situation to be critical, sent her two thousand American dollars, a substantial sum at the time and more than Robinson's own cash-strapped operation could afford. The expenditure had not been authorized by the Center, but Robinson could not believe that the masters in the Kremlin would be upset. The intelligence was of the highest value. When the Center saw Sissy's information, it had no complaints.

In March, Robinson was able to tell Moscow of the receipt of more priceless information from Sissy. But whatever was in these packets, it could not compare to the information that Sissy would soon be supplying the center. She would make her greatest contribution during the Russo-German war, which was coming sooner than Joseph Stalin ever imagined.

Soon, Werther himself would enter the equation. Once that happened, the English would have a great and intrepid ally.

Notes

1 Lukacs, p. 66.

2 Franz Halder, *The Halder War Diary: 1939–1942*. Charles Burdick and Hans-Adolf Jacobsen, eds. (Novato, Calif.: Presidio Press, 1988), p. 149.

3 Ibid.

4 Ibid., p. 160. Churchill's account is almost identical; see Winston S. Churchill, *Their Finest Hour* (Cambridge, Mass.: Houghton-Mifflin Company, 1949), p. 120.

5 Churchill, p. 56.

6 Message C-11x from Churchill to Roosevelt. Numbering system introduced by Warren F. Kimball, ed. *Churchill and Roosevelt: The Complete Correspondence*, Vol. 1 (Princeton, N.J.: Princeton University Press, 1984).

7 Halder, p. 156.

8 Churchill, p. 63.

9 Lukacs, p. 86.

10 Churchill, p. 76.

11 Halder, p. 165.

12 Lukacs, p. 93.

13 Churchill, p. 126.

14 Lukacs, p. 94.

15 Churchill, p. 88.

16 Lukacs, p. 97.

17 Churchill, p. 100.

18 Lukacs, p. 86.

19 John Toland, *Adolf Hitler* (Garden City, N.Y.: Doubleday, 1976), p. 611.

20 Martin Bormann, *Hitler's Secret Conversations* (New York: Farrar, Straus and Young, 1953), p. 90.

21 Churchill, p. 141.

22 Hassell, p. 139.

23 Robert Smith Thompson, *A Time for War* (New York: Prentice Hall, 1991), p. 250.

24 Keitel, p. 116.

25 Ibid., p. 118.

26 Winterbotham, p. 47.

27 B. H. Liddell Hart, *History of the Second World War* (London: Cassell & Company, 1970), p. 83.

28 Robert Goralski, ed., *World War II Almanac: 1931–1945* (New York: G. P. Putnam's Sons, 1981), p. 122.

29 Lukacs, p. 149.

30 NAZ, p. 778.

31 Lukacs, p. 132.

32 C-17x Vol. 1.

33 NAZ, p. 782.

34 Ibid., p. 777.

35 Felix Kersten, *The Kersten Memoirs: 1940–1945.* Constantine Fitzgibbon and James Oliver, trans. (New York: Macmillan, 1957), p. 88.

36 NAZ, p. 783.

37 Lukacs, p. 1400.

38 NAZ, p. 786.

39 Lukacs, p.198.

40 Halder, p. 224.

41 Lukacs, p. 200.

42 Except as noted, this account is based on formerly top-secret records regarding the Red Orchestra held at the U.S. National Archives. RG 319, Boxes 59 and 60.

Chapter Four

STALIN MOVES

KILLING MACHINE

As 1941 began, the war was going much to Joseph Stalin's satisfaction. His most significant potential European enemy, Germany, was still bombing his other hated enemy, Great Britain. And although there was a rattling of sabers across the Atlantic, the Americans seemed inclined to do little.

Since the beginning of the war, Stalin appeared intent on taking advantage of the huge real estate fire sale that Hitler had offered him while also preparing to someday confront a depleted Germany. The offerings were many, and most came easily. Shortly after his understanding with Hitler, Stalin helped himself not only to half of Poland but to other territories mentioned in the secret protocols of the German-Soviet nonaggression pact. Those protocols gave Russia spheres of influence over Finland, Estonia, and Latvia and reached as far south as the northern border of Lithuania. Stalin soon read that to mean the southern border of Lithuania, and that country was also swept up into the Bear's embrace.

The carnage that was the Second World War followed Stalin into each country. The Poles lost at least 120,000 lives in combating their two invaders, but that was only the beginning of their travails.[1] Stalin deported 1.5 million Poles of the upper class. Only half of them survived the war. And he decapitated the cream right away. Fully 15,000 of the "officer class" were machine-gunned by his secret police in the Katyn Forest. Similar fates befell the ruling classes of the Baltic States.

Only in Finland—another nation deeded over by Hitler—were Stalin's ambitions blunted. The Finns didn't know about the secret protocols, but they did know that they had no wish to become a Soviet republic. Stalin started his war with Finland on November 30, 1939. It was expected to be a Soviet cakewalk, but advances of the 600,000-man Soviet army were sharply contested by a 150,000-man Finnish force with its back to the wall. The war did not last the twelve days that had been expected but dragged on for four months. Every inch of Finland was fiercely defended. By war's end, more than 27,000 Finns had been killed. Moscow admitted to 58,000 Red Army deaths.[2] The Russians did capture some land, but the Russo-Finnish war was finished without a loss of Finnish sovereignty. Stalin's Red Army had been humiliated by a much smaller force. All of Europe, and particularly Adolf Hitler, took note of that.

The sloppy Finnish campaign should have told Stalin that the Red Army had significant weaknesses in materiel and leadership. But on such matters, Stalin seemed to be a slow study. He screamed at Red Army marshal Klementi Voroshilov about the inept army command. Nikita Khrushchev, who would later rule the Soviet Union, said that the marshal shouted back: "You have yourself to blame for all this! You're the one who annihilated the Old Guard of the army; you had our best generals killed." Voroshilov then overturned a dinner table that featured a suckling pig.[3]

If this did occur, it was done by a man who had blood enough on his own hands from the army purges. It had been Voroshilov's letter to *Pravda* that sparked the purge against Marshal M. N. Tukhachevsky, a brilliant strategist who had gone a long way in revising Soviet military dogma. Tukhachevsky knew about the threat of armored spearheads and how a modern war based on the use of petroleum would take a far different course than any that Russia had seen in the past. But the one man most capable of blocking the coming German Blitzkrieg was reduced to the rank of enemy of the people. He was shot.

Voroshilov was certainly right about one thing: While a general war threatened to break over Europe in the 1930s, Stalin busied himself with destroying the two functioning arms of his government that he would need most to defend Russia in any war with Germany—the military and the intelligence services. The Finnish setback, as Voroshilov rightly shouted, had been no mistake.

Even by the later standards of the Second World War, Stalin's wanton killings were astonishing. Between 1934 and 1938, 75 out of 80 members of the Military Soviet were liquidated, as were all 11 deputy commissars. Thirteen out of 15 army commanders were killed, as were 57 out of 85 corps commanders. The divisional level was not left unscathed: 110 out of 195 were executed.[4]

On the intelligence side, things were just as grim. When Lavrenti Beria replaced Nikolai Yezhov as head of the NKVD in December 1938, he supposedly heralded the end of Stalin's great terror. But the terror did not end for many. The NKVD continued to purge itself and the GRU's Fourth Department with glee. By the end of 1938, 150 of Yezhov's top NKVD functionaries had been shot.[5] Scores more were added to the rolls in 1939 as Stalin dallied with Hitler. In total, the secret police killed 23,000 of it own.[6]

The killing machine was used against the residencies of the Fourth Department itself. By Stalin's standards, anyone who had contact with foreigners was suspect, especially those who had worked abroad.[7] Their controllers in Moscow were killed as well. They had, after all, been associates of enemies of the people.[8] This is the atmosphere to which Maria Poliakova had returned and somehow managed to survive.

The killing had been steady in the latter part of the decade. S. P. Uritsky, head of the Fourth Department, was arrested and shot in late 1937, just as Poliakova arrived. J. K. Berzin, who had held the post before Uritsky, had gone to Spain and there had virtually run the Republican Army. For these heroics, he was recalled to Moscow and shot in December 1938.[9]

Berzin's arrest had a strong effect on Leopold Trepper. After the war and his subsequent incarceration, Trepper lamented that good Communists such as himself had gone along with the terror "sick at heart, but passive, caught up in machinery we had set in motion with our own hands. Mere cogs in the apparatus, terrorized to the point of madness, we became the instruments of our own subjugation."[10]

It was so insane that most in the West at the time and even now have only a scant idea of how capricious and omnipresent the terror actually was. "I learned how the arrests and executions were conducted," Trepper wrote. "With rudimentary logic of mechanized inquisitors, veritable robots of injustice elevated to dogma, the NKVD decreed that all Jews born in Poland were salaried spies of the Polish government, and that those who came from Palestine were in the pay of the English."

This was enough for a death sentence that came often without appeal and "invariably ended in front of the firing squad."[11]

Berzin helped Trepper get an assignment to Europe, thereby circumventing Trepper's almost certain execution. In 1940, Berzin's Fourth Department replacement, Filipp Golikov, carried out another far-reaching purge of foreign residencies, explaining that "too many had been too long abroad, had too many foreign contacts, and were therefore security risks."[12] Foreign agents were being purged for doing their jobs—having contacts with foreign sources.[13]

Such madness knew few limits. Soviet census takers who reported a sharp drop in population were taught a lesson. Only enemies of the people would suggest that under Stalin's great leadership the Soviet population would shrink. So the members of the census board were shot. All of them.

It is unknown when, if ever, Stalin would have curbed his terror had not a former little corporal of the German Reich caught his attention. But as Hitler's rapid success against France and Great Britain contrasted poorly with Stalin's fumbling maneuvers against the Finns, the Soviet leader began to worry that Germany was winning too much at too little cost while his own troops were doing too little at too much cost.

Beria's appointment as head of the secret police might have marked a slowing of the terror based upon a practical view of a changing European power matrix. But it did not mean a slowing of Stalin's aggression. If the terror was tempered in 1940 and 1941, the tempering was evenly matched by an increase in

Stalin's plans against his new friend, Adolf Hitler. He began a mammoth buildup of forces in the West that oddly seemed positioned for an offensive.

But in Hitler, Stalin's treachery had met its match.

OVER HIS SHOULDER

It is true that Hitler was predisposed to view the Soviet Union as Germany's natural enemy and believe Britain to be her natural ally. But it is also true that Hitler knew that Germany would be taking a grievous risk if it attacked the Soviet Union while still engaged in a war with the British. Hitler's decision to take this step cannot be ascribed simply to his obsessions. Hitler had reason to believe that Stalin was as untrustworthy as he was himself.

Despite the decimation of Soviet generals and intelligence services, Stalin still looked like a huge potential threat to Hitler. As Stalin played for real estate in the Baltics, Finland, and Poland, Hitler suspected that the Russian dictator was really preparing to fight—on his terms. The Red Army, the largest in the world, became a nightmare that Hitler could not shake.

Stalin's moves did nothing to lessen the German dictator's anxieties. Shortly after Stalin's troops invaded Poland, the Soviet dictator began moving other forces, slowly at first, toward grounds on the Soviet Union's western frontiers, where they would become for the Germans uncomfortably close to the precious Romanian oil fields. Those were the fields upon which Hitler depended to fuel his mobile war. Without them, the Wehrmacht would simply come to a halt.

Throughout 1941, Hitler and his generals grew more and more concerned. Ribbentrop told his Nuremberg interrogators, "The overnight Russian invasion of Bessarabia and, even more so, the Bukovina, surprised the Führer and made him sense an expansive urge westward.

"The Führer believed that the Kremlin had concluded the 1939 treaty in order to dictate first economic, then political terms to Germany during a long war with the West. The Führer declared that he would not allow Soviet Russia to spring a surprise attack, which might crush him. He received reports of Anglo-Russian negotiations, and of a treaty with the Serbian Putsch Government. So the Führer ordered military countermeasures."[14] Granted, these are the words of a self-serving war criminal awaiting the gallows, but they seem to reflect what was actually taking place on the ground.

Halder confided his concerns to his diary, saying that he feared not a direct attack on the Reich but one on "Rumania which would threaten German oil supplies."[15] And Halder confirmed Ribbentrop's view of what bothered Hitler, writing that "Stalin is flirting with Britain to keep her in the war and tie us down, with a view to gain time and take what he wants . . ."[16]

Halder stood by this account after the war, telling American investigators that Hitler was alarmed by reports of an offensive buildup of Soviet forces.[17]

While the world's attention was focused on the air war over Britain, on August 30, 1940, Germany and Italy attempted to check Stalin by guaranteeing Romania's territorial integrity. This was an unmistakably aggressive step against Stalin, but it was hardly uncalled for.[18] If Stalin moved against Romania, he could strangle the Reich.

By November, relations between Russia and Germany had disintegrated to the point where both felt that a conference of German and Soviet foreign ministers—the last conference that the two would hold—was needed. Vyacheslav Molotov, the Soviet minister of foreign affairs, came to Germany acting much like a man who held the winning hand. By all accounts, he was hostile and uncompromising. He warned that Moscow might issue a "guarantee" to Bulgaria as the Germans had to Romania. He demanded a lease for a naval base close to the Bosphorus. He asked Germany to arrange concessions from Japan. To Hitler and his top German aides, Molotov was the perfect image of an implacable enemy.

German generals, who had thought that a Russian war might still be avoided, began swiftly changing their minds. Perhaps Hitler's intuition had again been right. Molotov and his master, Stalin, were the real threats to German interests.

On December 18, 1940, Hitler issued Directive 21, the plan

for Operation Barbarossa—the invasion of the Soviet Union. "There is no time to lose," Hitler declared. "War must come in my lifetime. My pact was meant only to stall for time, and, gentlemen, to Russia will happen just what I have practiced in Poland—we will crush the Soviet Union."[19]

Hitler confided that he "was haunted by the obsession that the Russians might take the offensive."[20] As Hitler contemplated his obsession, Stalin sped his military moves in ways suggesting that he was in fact preparing a first strike.[21]

Some tried to restrain Stalin from adopting a forces-forward strategy. Defensive troops, if that is what they were supposed to be, must be laid in depth, not bunched forward like a spring. Yet Red Army troops continued to bunch. Before Molotov's Berlin visit, fourteen Soviet divisions were in Poland, seven in Bessarabia, and twenty—including eight armored—farther south.[22] After the meeting, Stalin ordered even more troops forward.

By February, Stalin approved the latest version of mobilization orders.[23] That same month, Stalin was given precise information on the planned German invasion. He even knew that it was codenamed Operation Barbarossa.[24] It is perhaps true that Stalin ignored dozens of warnings about Hitler's designs, but that proposition cannot be proven by what he was doing on the ground. It is hard to understand how Stalin could have moved more aggressively without tipping his hand altogether. Trainload after trainload of Russian troops arrived in the Kiev district. Twenty-eight rifle divisions and four army commands moved to the frontier districts.[25] Fully 170 Soviet divisions were outside the prewar 1939 boundaries, or five-sevenths of Russia's strength.[26] All were pointed at the German Reich.

The numbers suggest that Stalin, far from reacting too slowly to the German buildups, reacted too much, too vigorously. More men and materiel had been shifted to the front than were needed there for the defense of the Soviet Union. Too little had been left in reserve. Hitler did not have time to wait and see exactly what Stalin had in mind. Besides, he always wanted to be the first to strike.

Zhukov accepted responsibility for the forward deployment of Soviet supplies, although without Stalin's forward deployment of troops, such supplies would have been unnecessary. Said Zhukov: "The Commissar for Defense and the General Staff, myself included, thought it necessary in view of the impending war to bring the materiel closer to the troops. What was seemingly correct, however, later turned out to be our common mistake."

And a grand mistake it was. When war finally came, the Germans "managed to seize in a short time the material resources of the districts, which affected the supply and the formation of reserves," Zhukov bitterly recounted.[27]

On May 5, 1941, General Golikov, the new head of Russian military intelligence, told Stalin that Germany had 103 to 107 divisions arrayed against her. That same day, Stalin showed his hand. He told a graduating class of Red Army officers what his intentions were. "The Red Army is a modern army, and the modern army is an offensive army. The war [will] be fought on the enemy's territory . . ."[28] War with Germany, Stalin said, "is inevitable."[29]

The Soviet leader continued pushing Soviet armies to the west. Zhukov reported that the 22d Army came from the Urals, the 21st Army from the Volga district, the 19th Army from the northern Caucasus, and the 16th Army from Transbaikal. Stalin called up 800,000 reservists.[30] By late May, there were more orders for movements to the west. By no later than mid-June, the armies aligned against Hitler would number some 2.9 million men, 1,500 modern aircraft, 35,000 guns and mortars, and 1,800 heavy and medium tanks.[31] Germany marshaled 3 million men and 3,350 tanks but only 7,146 guns.[32] The calculus of flesh and steel was close to balanced.

Stalin thought that the war was still eleven months off. Zhukov, though, thought that it could begin much sooner. He wrote to Stalin: "As Germany is now fully mobilized, and with her rear organized, she has the ability to surprise us with a sudden attack. To avert this, I think it essential that we deprive the German command of the initiative by forestalling their forces during deployment, by attacking them at the moment they are at the deployment stage and have not had time to organize a front or co-ordinate their forces."[33]

Stalin thought that he was moving as fast as he could. To do as Zhukov asked would take time.

And time was short. Hitler was almost ready.

HESS

Only one thing prevented a German first strike. Hitler had said that the main fault of the German leaders of the Great War was that they had allowed German forces to be divided on two fronts. He called those leaders "nitwits." As Hitler moved closer to at-tacking the Soviet Union, he also drew closer to repeating that vast strategic mistake. For years, Hitler had said that he would never do this. The resolution was repeated throughout *Mein Kampf* and repeated later again and again in Hitler's talks with his closest aides.

Though many thought that Hitler was willing to risk that in 1941, he wasn't. He needed some guarantee from the British that he could have a free hand in the east and not be subjected to a second front in the west. The Battle of Britain, which domi-nated the headlines at the time, was for Hitler a feint and a de-laying action more than a real military operation. Hitler sought to deceive Stalin about his real intentions by appearing to pound the British, whereas he intended to impress the British with a practical reason to compromise.[34]

To these ends, Hitler first told his airmen that "before every-thing the inflicting of great damages on the civil population must be avoided."[35] That resolution changed over time for many reasons, but the objective of the German air war did not. It was to prepare for Barbarossa, not Sea Lion—the name given to the theoretical invasion of the British Isles. Hitler warned his gener-als that the illusion must be kept up at all costs. "Cancellation of our plans [Sea Lion] would not remain a secret. It would ease the strain on the enemy's nerves, and consequently must not be ordered now."[36]

As Hitler drew closer to the Russian attack, he grew more ner-vous that he was following the path of the "nitwits." He needed reassurance from the British that somehow this wasn't so. As night bombings of Great Britain increased, so did secret liaisons between British and German agents.

Throughout the war, Hitler remained convinced that there was a strong "peace party" in Britain that could serve as a counterbalance to Winston Churchill. Before Churchill became prime minister—in fact, before the war even started—Hitler had sought out that peace party.

Then, persons of influence in Great Britain would dally with Hitler. The cream of the British Empire—including the Duke of Windsor and Lloyd George, the British prime minister during the First World War—had made pilgrimages to Hitler's doorstep. But after the empire's very existence was threatened at Dunkirk, Churchill took an iron grip on all peace overtures.

The first ones seemed to be sincere—almost desperate—attempts to find a formula to extract Great Britain from the war with a minimum cost to sovereignty. But after Churchill scented Hitler's turn to the east, the overtures were conducted to gain time, letting Hitler have rope enough to hang himself. Those contacts suggested to Hitler that there was progress in Britain at neutralizing the prime minister. Churchill's position was not firm. Cooler heads in Great Britain would prevail.

As the deadline for Barbarossa approached, Hitler grew more nervous. Was his intuition about the peace party correct?

On May 10, 1941, Hitler's strongest air raid of the war descended upon London. The center of the city was pummeled; Parliament was partially destroyed. Westminster Hall, Westminster Abbey, Gray's Court Hospital, and Queen's Hall were gravely damaged. Seven hundred acres of central London were incinerated. It was the harshest day of the Blitz, showing how England could be vulnerable to indiscriminate night bombing.

But a hundred miles to the north of the burning center of London, a single plane crossed the English Channel. Inside it was Rudolf Hess, Hitler's closest friend and the deputy Führer of the Third Reich.

The details of the Hess mission are too involved to go into here, but General Halder after the war gave a succinct summary:

"After the termination of the Polish campaign it was the general understanding in Berlin that the war would soon come to an end. Peace negotiations were conducted through a number of different channels. The most important one was the contact with the British Foreign Secretary established by the late Ambassador of Germany to the Holy See, von Hassell. [Halder] himself was associated with this move and was informed about all the details of the negotiations . . .

"Hitler's grand strategy though was to avoid a war against England. He made repeated attempts to gain England's cooperation in a war against Russia . . . Still believing, however, in some fundamental 'anti-Bolshevist' solidarity between Germany and England, Hitler dispatched Rudolf Hess to inform the British of his determination to wage war against Russia and to submit to them his 'last offer' to participate in this venture.

"The British 'double-crossed' Hitler, and informed Moscow of the nature of Hess's mission. At that point Hitler's hand was forced. He felt that Russia was alerted, and that further delays would be only to Russia's advantage."[37]

The whole matter was actually more involved than that. Hess flew to Scotland expecting to land safely. The British secret service had prepared a landing strip next to the Duke of Hamilton's estate. But for some reason, Hess did not find the strip and instead bailed out of his plane, only to be captured by the Home Guard. His presence made it into the press before a hapless group of intelligence officers could stop it.

The broad purpose of the Hess mission became clear eventually to the Americans and Russians. American military attaché Raymond Lee wrote to the chief of army intelligence that upon meeting British officials, Hess said that he had come "to tell them that Germany was about to fight Russia" and to seek ways to bring Great Britain on as "a silent partner in the crusade."[38]

Kim Philby, a Soviet agent in Great Britain's secret service, signaled Moscow that Hess had come to contact anti-Churchill peace elements with certain proposals, the specifics of which were not known. "Hess said in a conversation with [Ivone] Kirkpatrick that a war between the two northern peoples was a crime.

He thinks that there is a strong anti-Churchill party in Britain which stands for peace." Philby said, "It is not yet time for peace talks. As the war develops, however, Hess could become the center of intrigue for the conclusion of a compromise peace and could be useful to both the Peace Party in Britain and Hitler."[39]

Messages were sent from Hess to Germany through "devious" means.[40] These messages from the deputy Führer must have had a salving effect, for soon Hitler became convinced that he had a green light to attack in the east.[41]

On May 20, 1941, ten days after the Hess flight, Washington received word about the intentions of the Soviet side. A Yugoslavian military attaché had spoken with Zhukov, and the marshal had rewarded him with a rare look into Soviet secret planning. Zhukov told the attaché, "The Soviets will fight Germany later and are waiting for the United States to enter war, and that the Soviet Government distrusts England and suspects Hess flight as effort to turn war against USSR."[42]

In the end, it was a case of both dictators conspiring against each other, both seeking the right time for a surprise attack, both viewing the nonaggression pact as so much ink and paper and little else. While Germany amassed its forces in the east—explaining to Stalin that they were merely staying out of range of British bombers—Stalin pushed his troops west.

In early June, operating under the guise of mobile training camps, Stalin moved two additional all-arms armies into the Ukraine and Byelorussia. The operation was to be conducted under "extreme caution and operational secrecy."[43]

In the end, it was a matter of who would pull the trigger first. By June 22 Hitler was ready to. Stalin was not. The Soviet people would pay a heavy price for their leader's gamble.

BORMANN ADVANCED

Little known to most at the time was an aggressive move up the Nazi hierarchy by a man who would soon be second only to Hitler in Germany and who as such would play one of the most decisive roles in the Second World War. Martin Bormann, the deputy to Rudolf Hess, had a steady if fairly placid career as a Nazi. Not a politician or a public speaker, this son of a postal worker had won a brief period of fame in early 1923 for his role in the murder of Walter Kadow, an alleged Communist infiltrator in a freikorps movement in Bavaria. Actually, Bormann's role was smaller than he later let on, but it was clear that he had at least given orders that the suspect be roughed up. After that, things got out of hand. In his defense, Bormann pointed out that he was not at the scene. The judges listened carefully, and Bormann found himself out of jail in a year. Some others were not so lucky, though none of the conspirators served hard time. One of Bormann's confederates in the plot was Rudolf Höss, who later as commandant of Auschwitz would carry out Bormann's orders during the Holocaust.

Bormann himself joined the Nazi Party late, but he got along well handling the party's self-insurance program, a type of financial setup that could today be called a Ponzi scheme. Those being relieved of their money, however, were mostly the Brown Shirts, and they had ceased to be major players in Germany. Bormann got things done, and artists such as Hitler often thought that admirable. Other Nazis looked at Bormann with some scorn, if they looked at him at all. As Hess's deputy, he was the party's liaison to the Führer. That seemed to be about all.

But Joseph Goebbels took note of the short bulldog of a man and did not like what he saw. On December 4, 1940, the propaganda minister lamented in his diary: "Bormann intervened again on the Foreign Ministry's behalf in the broadcasting question. But for the moment, I remain immovable. I shall not allow myself to be [. . .] from that quarter."[44] Bormann continued to get under Goebbels's skin. By March 1941, Goebbels complained: "Bormann is making trouble about the Red Cross Appeal. Mere jealousy. In fact, he has been a general thorn in my side. He has also been criticising Ritter's film, *Over All in the World*. But I have managed to force through its release by an appeal to the Führer, who has now gone off to Munich. None of the members of that clique do any work; all they do is to intrigue.

But I shall not allow myself to be deflected from my goals."[45] Only days later, Goebbels lamented that Bormann "is crossing my path too often."[46]

Then disaster supposedly struck for Bormann. His boss, Hess, had flown off to England and, according to everything that Goebbels was putting out and what he also undoubtedly believed, had done so without Hitler's permission. Goebbels was beside himself with worry about Hess compromising the coming Barbarossa campaign against the Soviet Union. And he and others saw that no one as close to Hess as Bormann could long survive. Ten days after the Hess flight, Goebbels wrote: "Bormann has issued a circular to the Party, in which he introduces himself. His position is under the strongest possible attack from all sides. He is, I believe, neither honest nor clear-minded. He has intrigued rather than worked his way into this job. The Party leadership senses this instinctively and hence its rejection of him. He will have a lot of difficulty in getting his way.[47]

But Goebbels was being naive. The Hess flight had been the Führer's inspiration all along. As such, Hess's deputy would not be punished. Just the opposite. Two days after Hess's departure, Hitler named Bormann head of the party chancellery, investing him with powers that were second to few in Germany. From that position, Bormann would control the vast districts of the new Reich and the Gauleiters who controlled them. These were the lands onto which the blood of genocide would soon run.

The Führer tried to offer his propaganda minister some help in understanding the double game that he was playing with England and that England was playing with Germany. "The Führer," Goebbels reported in his diary, "has high hopes of the peace party in England. Otherwise, he claims, the Hess Affair would not have been so systematically killed by silence."[48]

War with Russia was only hours away.

DESPERATE MEASURES

Rachel Dübendorfer, code-named Sissy, sent her last courier to Henri Robinson in France in April 1941. Dübendorfer and Robinson, also a member of Maria Poliakova's cabal known as Gisela's family, had used courier contacts to exchange information for more than a year. Now couriers were too risky and too slow. A German-Russian war was looming. Time could not be wasted.

In May, Moscow Center ordered Dübendorfer to contact Rado, the man who would subsequently bolt from the spy plane in Cairo. Rado had been instructed to supply Sissy with necessary secret codes and wireless operators. The principal operator was Alexander Foote, the would-be Hitler assassin who was codenamed Jim.

By this time, Dübendorfer had already been awarded the Order of Lenin for her intelligence work.[49] But her best effort, through Lucy (Rudolf Rössler), was just beginning. Before long, Lucy would possess the most important links of all—those leading to Hitler's traitor, Werther.

Because many of Dübendorfer's secret messages went through the Rado radio net, some have mistakenly assumed that Dübendorfer worked for Rado. If she worked for anyone, it was certainly not Rado, whom she viewed at most as a cutout and more often as an inconvenient bore. She certainly worked for Poliakova, but at times even that was tenuous. Maria Poliakova was a spymaster at the center, and Sissy did not trust the center. It had once cut her off for months. During that period, she had heard not a word and had not received a Swiss franc to pay her agents. The Center's erratic nature was unsettling.

Throughout the war, Rachel's distrust would continue. She ignored the Center when she wanted to, hid her sources' identities, lavished them with whatever rewards she could gather, and in all remained her own commander. That she survived, becoming Stalin's most important spy, is a testament not to her demeanor but to her tradecraft.

Her dossier reported: "Professional jealousy appears to have affected negotiations between Dübendorfer and Rado from the first, but by June 1941, Rado realized the exceptional quality of the Lucy material and forwarded it to Moscow by W/T [wireless transmission.]"[50]

In handling this traffic between Dübendorfer and Lucy, Rachel used a cutout, Christian Schneider, a translator for the

International Labor Organization. His masters gave him the code name Taylor. It took the Russians many attempts to get straight exactly what role he played. Dübendorfer did not help, as she always tried to keep her operations as secret as possible. At times the Center identified Taylor as the source of the material; at other times the Center appeared not to know about him at all. Only in 1943 does it appear that the Center had a firm grasp about what was going on with Schneider.

Declassified American intelligence records known as the Red Orchestra files note that Dübendorfer was in contact with Lucy and her ring before Barbarossa and that Lucy gave Stalin the exact timing of the attack. Says the report: "The lack or poverty of communications never seems to have discouraged Dübendorfer as a collector of intelligence, and she was able to provide [Moscow] with her famous Lucy material from the very beginning of the Russo-German war."[51] If this account is accurate— and it does conform to one given by Foote after the war—this was one of more than eighty war warnings that Stalin received.[52] Rado also confirmed after the war that a warning message came through Taylor, Lucy's cutout, although Rado didn't know the source at the time.[53] That message, which came about two weeks before the attack, read: "About 100 infantry divisions are now positioned on the German-Soviet frontier. One third motorized. Of the remainder, at least ten divisions are armored. In Rumania, German troops are concentrated at Galatz. Elite divisions with a special mission have been mobilized. The 5th and 10th divisions stationed in the General Government are taking part."[54]

This report alarmed Moscow, not that the Germans were coming—because Moscow knew about Barbarossa—but because Moscow had misjudged its timing. Moscow felt that the Lucy report was too convenient and that agent provocateurs must be about. Years later, Foote said in a French publication: "The Center was very suspicious of Lucy. Her information was regarded as too detailed and exact, and Moscow thought that the German 'Abwehr' was to place a trap."[55]

Foote wrote that the Center ordered all contact with Lucy severed because she was assumed to be an enemy agent. Only days later, by most but not all accounts, a Lucy source later named Werther announced that a general German attack would be launched against Russia on June 22. Foote said that the source followed up this warning with a detailed report on the German Order of Battle.

This unnerved Rado. Should he follow orders and ignore Lucy and thus fail to send the war warning to the Center, or should he find a contrivance to disobey? "Rado," Foote said, "did not know what to do. If the information was correct, it was obviously of the greatest importance and should be transmitted without delay." But Rado was a bureaucrat not inclined toward daring action. He told Foote that, just like the Center, he believed Lucy's information to be an Abwehr trap. Yet Rado did not want to be the person who withheld from Moscow information that could stem defeat.

Rado's very existence as a Soviet agent in a foreign country produced enough anxiety; he did not need more. Finally, Rado found a way to rationalize his insubordination. He noted that the source's information gave details not only of the German battle plan but what the Germans knew of probable Russian countermeasures. Foote urged him on, saying that the Center was better able to decipher the source's truthfulness because it alone could assess what the Russian side had planned.

Foote argued that "it would be criminal on our part to suppress it [the Lucy information]."[56] Passing on this information to the Center was one of Rado's rare great acts of bravery.

Moscow distrusted the message and, by one account, lost interest in the source. But that would soon change. The Center started a special labeling system for messages from Switzerland, with those of most importance labeled "VYRDO." They went personally to Stalin. Almost all of the VYRDO messages came from Lucy.

American intelligence reports immediately after the war agreed with Foote's account of the timing of the first Werther message and its eventual effect. The Americans said that "by the autumn of 1941 . . . Moscow admitted that 'Lucy' warranted exploitation at all costs."[57] And those costs were heavy, not only in hours of human effort but in money. Funds earmarked for Dübendorfer and her Lucy net were specially handled, because they had to be foolproof and in the most important currency of the time—American dollars.

Hollywood played a significant part in funding the Lucy net. Money for Dübendorfer was first transferred to dummy corporations in the United States. In July 1941, only days after the Wehrmacht invaded the Soviet Union, an RKO Pictures representative in Switzerland began handing over the money to the Red Army spies.[58] It would prove to be a vital connection, one that kept Gisela's family functioning during the German onslaught.

As with most true spy stories, the exact timing of Lucy's appearance was made into a mystery by a 1979 report by the CIA. The agency said that Rachel probably began sending her Lucy reports in the summer of 1942 instead of the year before. Foote, whose other recollections were mostly correct, was somehow wrong here. The agency's analysis is flawed. It ignores not only Foote but also Rado and prior detailed intelligence findings obtained in the field. The CIA report was based on analyses of decrypted messages, which would have been definitive had they not been so sparse. The CIA decoded only 6 percent of the transmissions, most coming after 1942.[59] The message in question came in 1943[60] and referred to the "Taylor-Lucy"[61] group as having provided Moscow with information since the "summer of 1942."

Even the CIA conceded that the Center had a rough time understanding exactly what role Taylor played. Rado himself didn't understand who or what Taylor was until after the war. The author of the CIA report probably did not know in 1979 what we know today: Soviet intelligence was so confused at this time that it had even lost track of its star recruit, Kim Philby.

Most likely, Foote's, Rado's, and the early American assessment of the affair hold true: Lucy warned of the attack but was ignored by Moscow. Even after the attack, Moscow ignored Lucy, convinced that she was some sort of plant. But after a history of accurate accounts from Rachel's source, the Center changed its mind.

But the CIA was right about one thing: Rachel Dübendorfer's spies would play their major roles in the great battles of 1942 and 1943. In fact, the Center was soon to become obsessed by Rachel, Lucy, and Werther.

Notes

1 NAZ, p. 758.

2 Martin Gilbert, *The Second World War* (New York: Holt, 1989), p. 49.

3 Strobe Talbott, ed./trans., *Khrushchev Remembers: The Last Testament* (New York: Little, Brown and Company, 1974), p. 153.

4 Alan Clark, *Barbarossa, The Russian German Conflict 1941–1945* (New York: William Morrow, 1965), p. 34.

5 Robert Conquest, *The Great Terror* (New York: Oxford University Press, 1990), p. 432.

6 Dmitri Volkogonov, *Stalin: Triumph and Tragedy* (London: George Weidenfeld & Nicolson, 1996), p. xxiv.

7 Conquest, p. 209.

8 Voroshilov certainly knew that Stalin was willing to kill anyone. No exact total for the graves that Stalin ordered dug is possible, in part because he killed the census takers who reported a 1937 population below his expectations. Direct murders in state prisons and camps number 7 million at least. When the number of people who were starved as part of state policy is added in, Stalin may have killed 30 million to 40 million of his countrymen—far more deaths, in fact, than Hitler visited upon the Soviet people.

9 Conquest, p. 209; Trepper, p. 92.

10 Trepper, p. 55.

11 Ibid., pp. 63–64.

12 Christopher Andrew and Oleg Gordievsky, *KGB: The Inside Story* (New York: HarperCollins, 1990), pp. 257–58.

13 The Fourth Department of the GRU continued to run Foreign Intelligence, though with the ever-increasing intervention of the NKVD, or—as it was known after February 1941—the NKGB. In 1942 and 1943, though, Stalin had transferred most functions of the GRU to the NKGB. This, of course, disrupted intelligence gathering immeasurably. Even famed British spy Kim Philby fell into the abyss. A Soviet document from early 1940 describes a succession of Philby handlers and their fates. "Mar," who handled Philby from 1934 to 1936, is listed as "shot. German

and Polish spy." His successor, Theodor Maly, is also listed as "shot. German spy." Philby's next two handlers are likewise listed as being "shot," one as a Polish spy and the other as a German spy. Philby's last handler, Alexander Orlov, who actually did defect to the West but kept his secrets to himself, was listed as a "traitor." Naturally, when bright, new officers took the place of their purged predecessors, they did not know who Philby was. But the list of traitors who had handled Philby reveals that he entered not the shrine of Soviet intelligence that decades of spy lore granted him but relentless Soviet suspicion, from which he never fully recovered. New handlers did not know what he had done, to whom he had done it, and, most importantly, why he had done anything. And many of those "new" handlers were soon shot as spies themselves. No wonder that replacements viewed Philby as a new, unvetted source. Philby had been, and would later be again, one of the Soviet Union's most important sources, but for much of the war he was distrusted. This was astonishing, and it foreshadowed some of the confusion over Gisela's family in Switzerland. Past services meant nothing. In February 1940, Moscow ordered a cutoff of all contact with the mystery agent Philby, whom the Soviets had earlier entrusted with a mission to assassinate Franco. Contact was repaired in time for Philby to give his Russian masters key information about the 1941 flight of Rudolf Hess to Scotland.

14 RG 319, XE 000887, Box 8.

15 NAZ, p. 783.

16 Halder, p. 231.

17 Halder, U.S. Strategic Bombing Survey, APO 413, Interview 52, June 25, 1945, National Archives.

18 NAZ, p. 799.

19 Toland, p. 655.

20 Secret Interrogation of Joachim von Ribbentrop, RG 319, XE000887.

21 Fugate, p. 87.

22 Clark, p. 37.

23 Georgi Zhukov, *The Memoirs of Marshal Zhukov* (New York: Delacorte Press, 1971), p. 211.

24 Ibid., pp. 228–29.

25 Ibid., p. 218.

26 Clark, p. 40.

27 Zhukov, *Memoirs*, p. 215.

28 Volkogonov, p. 369.

29 Ibid., p. 393.

30 Ibid., p. 392.

31 Zhukov, *Memoirs*, p. 218.

32 NAZ, p. 817.

33 Volkogonov, p. 398.

34 For an in-depth examination of the Hess affair and the politics surrounding it, refer to Kilzer, *Churchill's Deception*.

35 Lukacs, p. 159.

36 Halder, p. 258.

37 U.S. Strategic Bombing Survey, APO 413, RG 226, 137995.

38 RG 319, Box 83.

39 Cable No. 338, KGB's Black Bertha file.

40 Secretly recorded conversations between Hermann Göring and Rudolf Hess, October 15, 1945; court reporter Frances Karr, National Archives.

41 Joseph Goebbels, *The Goebbels Diaries: 1939–1941*. Fred Taylor, ed./trans. (New York: Putnam, 1983), p. 424.

42 740.0011/11348 U.S. State Department Confidential File, National Archives.

43 Zhukov, *Memoirs*, p. 217.

44 Goebbels, p. 190.

45 Ibid., p. 277.

46 Ibid., p. 281.

47 Ibid., p. 374.

48 Ibid., p. 424.

49 Jozef Garlinski, *The Swiss Corridor* (London: J. M. Dent & Sons, Ltd., 1981), p. 58.

50 RG 319, Box 60.

51 Ibid.

52 Foote, p. 74.

53 Rado, p. 58.

54 A. Reed and D. Fisher, *Operation Lucy* (London: Hodder & Stoughton, 1980), p. 90.

55 RG 319, Box 59, Vol. 1.

56 Ibid.

57 RG 319, Box 60; see also Foote, p. 76.

58 RG 319, Box 60.

59 CIA, p. 185.

60 See CIA, *Rote Kapelle.*

61 "Taylor" was Christian Schneider, a man whom Dübendorfer used as a cutout between Rössler and herself.

Chapter Five

BARBAROSSA

HISTORIC TOUR

The battle that would end in Adolf Hitler's destruction was announced by the trembling thunder of artillery at 3:15 A.M. on June 22, 1941. It was Sunday, Hitler's favorite day of attack. The Russians had placed their army on full alert two hours earlier. But neither that nor anything else Stalin had done could prepare the Soviet Union for what would happen during the next few months. Germany was able to send into the breach 3 million men, 3,350 tanks, and nearly 2,000 planes. Russia was prepared to immediately counter with 2.8 million men, 1,800 tanks, and 1,540 modern aircraft. It had 5,000 obsolete aircraft that would soon become target practice for the Luftwaffe.[1]

The war began on a 930-mile front, toward the Baltic and the Black Sea. Three German army groups would delineate the fighting. Army Group North, under Field Marshal Wilhelm Ritter von Leeb, was to secure Baltic ports and eventually take Leningrad. Army Group Center, under Field Marshal Fedor von Bock, was to attack toward Moscow. Army Group South, under Field Marshal Gerd von Rundstedt, aimed toward Kiev, the Ukraine, and the Caucasus.

At 7 A.M., Hitler took to the airways to announce Barbarossa. "Weighed down by heavy cares, condemned to months of silence, I can at last speak freely—German people! At this moment a march is taking place that for its extent, compares with the greatest the world has ever seen. I have decided again today to place the fate and future of the Reich and our people in the hands of our soldiers. May God aid us especially in this fight."[2]

From Switzerland, Rado radioed the Center that Gisela's family was at work: "To the Director. In this historic hour we vow solemnly and with unshaken loyalty that we will fight with re-doubled energy at our forward outposts."[3]

Suddenly, Moscow was wide awake. No longer would there be orders for its secret agents to ignore Hitler and his Reich. The Center told Gisela's family in Switzerland: "Concentrate your whole attention on procuring information about the German army. Watch and report regularly on the regrouping of the German troops from France and other western zones towards the east."[4] By July 2, Lucy was able to report to Moscow Center: "The Germans currently have operational Plan No. 1 in force . . . the accent is on the central sector of the Front."[5] Foote later reported that "nearly every day new material from 'Werther' on the grouping of the German forces which were smashing their way towards Moscow came in and was sent off by me."[6]

At first, whatever the family might provide could affect the decision of the war only slightly. Lucy had not been fully vetted. In fact, she hadn't been vetted at all, and it would take months for the Center to rely blindly on her information or on her mystery agent Werther. Besides, there wasn't time.

Everywhere, the Russians were dropping back. Within four days of the attack, the Germans had streaked north 190 miles. By July 28 Minsk, some 200 miles into Byelorussia, had fallen. Soon, the cut-off pocket around Minsk collapsed, yielding 290,000 prisoners. Riga was captured on July 1. Two weeks later a huge pocket around Smolensk fell, and with it another 300,000 Red Army prisoners were taken.

It had the appearance of a rout. That was not the fault of the Russian fighting men, who often fought so doggedly that they were soon thought of as not really human by the German infantrymen. There was something crazy in the way they fought. Wave after wave of soldiers would throw themselves on a prepared German position and be mowed down again and again. It was not the spirit of these men that was lacking. It was leadership. Using diplomatic language after the war, Zhukov put the blame on Stalin's senseless purges. "When important, major organizational measures were carried out on the eve of the war there could be felt a shortage of skilled commanders, specialists, tankmen, artillery men and flying-technical personnel; the sub-stantial increase in the strength of our armed forces made the shortage still more perceptible."[7] Stalin saw things differently. He ordered Gen. D. C. Pavlov, head of the western front, and an unknown total of other commanders to Moscow. They were shot.

The German successes were so universal that the usually cau-tious General Halder declared on July 3: "It is thus probably no overstatement to say that the Russian Campaign has been won in the space of two weeks."[8] Two days later he declared, "The entire front is advancing in accordance with our intentions."[9] Thirty Russian divisions had been wiped out, and seventy others had lost half their numbers. Half of the Soviet fuel and ammunition dumps were destroyed within three weeks.[10]

The Führer was pleased. He would take victories on all three fronts if possible. On July 8 he told his generals that he intended "to level Moscow and Leningrad, and make them uninhabitable, so as to relieve [the German army] of the necessity of having to feed the populations through the winter."[11] He decided that ar-tillery and the Luftwaffe could take care of this, because tanks were unsuited for city warfare. With this accomplished, the So-viet Union would face "a national catastrophe which will deprive not only Bolshevism, but also Muscovite nationalism, of their centers."[12]

But shortly thereafter, the seemingly inexhaustible resources of the Soviet Union began to grind their way into the nerves of the German General Staff. The advance toward the south ap-peared to be going well, whereas resistance in the north and cen-ter hardened. Halder began talking of the "savage determina-tion" of the Russian fighter and soon wrote in his diary, "The whole situation makes it increasingly plain that we have under-estimated the Russian colossus who consistently prepared for war with that utterly ruthless determination so characteristic of totalitarian States."[13] By now, the Russian machine had mobilized an additional million men, who were asked to fight like the beasts the Germans thought they were. They were told, "If you are wounded, pretend to be dead; wait until the Germans come up; then select one of them and kill him . . . Tear his throat with your teeth. Do not die without leaving behind you a German corpse."[14]

Suddenly, choices had to be made. If the 1941 campaign was to be decisive, it was clear that the Germans had to concentrate their forces. Victory on all three fronts was not possible.

Hitler had for years made it clear that he had a bias toward the south. His concept of lebensraum, or living space, always pointed toward German expansion in the Ukraine, where, geopolitically, German expansion would least aggravate the British. With lebensraum, Germany would have enough food and raw materials to make itself immune to blockades and embargoes. This was the goal of the Thousand-Year Reich, during which Hitler believed that the British would first admit that the Germans were equals and eventually would be partners. But the goals of a thousand years were now being condensed into days.

Hitler saw little reason to go to Moscow instead of Kiev. His ideological bias toward the south met perfectly with present military reality. If Germany could now conquer the Ukraine, the region's resources would not only help the Reichswehr but would be denied to Stalin's forces. More immediately, Soviet military air bases that threatened the absolutely vital Romanian oil fields would be eliminated. Finally, success in Kiev could open a road toward the Soviet Union's own oil-producing areas of Baku and Grozny. If Hitler controlled these, he could feed the Reichswehr while starving the Red Army.

So one German spearhead would go to Kiev before Moscow. The other mass would, Hitler thought, go north, completing the OKW's goal of controlling the Baltic. Again, the goal was to gain a strategic advantage that would force Moscow to her knees without first having to go there. Control of the Baltic Sea would eliminate any hope by Russia or Britain of interfering with the transport to Germany of Swedish iron ore. That ore was second only to Romanian oil in importance to German arms.

On July 19 Hitler issued Directive 33, sending powerful panzer forces north to help attack Leningrad, whose surrender was vital to the campaign to control the Baltic Sea. Hitler also prepared to send other reinforcements south.[15] These decisions precipitated the most serious and injurious of Hitler's fights with his generals. Almost to the man, generals in the German army had developed Moscow as the aim and wouldn't see or embrace any broader concept of how the war could be won. Hitler was still not one to fight gratuitously with his generals, and most of them did not seem to realize that the Führer had made a decisive change in strategy.

BORMANN'S SPIES

At Hitler's headquarters, there were others taking note of Hitler's plans. These were not Russian or American spies. They were Germans, and they spied on Hitler for Bormann and the Nazi Party, whose Chancellery he controlled. Though not yet in the military planning room, they surrounded Hitler everywhere else. One spy was Werner Koeppen, who, at the request of Alfred Rosenberg, minister of the eastern territories under Martin Bormann, "had been circumspectly recording the Führer's table conversations . . . Koeppen assumed Hitler knew what he was doing and would furtively jot down notes on his paper napkin, then immediately after that meal write out only those parts of the conversation he could distinctly remember. An original and one copy of his records were forwarded to Berlin by courier . . ."[16]

Bormann personally recruited Heinrich Heim, his adjutant, into a scheme to secretly write down everything that Hitler said during his sometimes rambling but always revealing table talk. Heim was present when Bormann was not. But Bormann did not miss a thing. He told Heim that one thing was important above all others: secrecy. The Führer must never know that his words were being recorded.[17] For reasons that Heim could not understand, Bormann was careful never again to mention this operation. Heim later told historian John Toland: "So the matter went on, without Bormann giving me any instructions, expressing any wishes or anything else except to silently show his happiness that in this way much would be preserved and not forgotten."[18] Heim told Toland that for security reasons he omitted recording Hitler's specific military plans.

Nevertheless, Heim took notes under the table and Hitler never seemed to notice. Or if he did, he did not object.[19] Heim was certain that Hitler never knew what he was doing.

Although Heim tried to omit any discussions of direct military planning from his recordings, Koeppen did not.[20] If Bormann wanted to know, he could.

The intrigues began at the Wolfsschanze, or Wolf's Lair—Hitler's term for his spartan headquarters in an East Prussian pine forest. At the center of the headquarters was an unadorned concrete bunker, dank with mildew and surrounded by barbed wire, camouflage, and guards. There were wooden huts above the bunker where staff stayed and Hitler and his generals mapped out their war. It was swampy, and mosquitoes were everywhere. To Hitler, it was a far different environment than his spectacular residence in the Alps at Obersalzberg. Yet Hitler spent more of his days in this prison than anywhere else during Barbarossa.

At Wolf's Lair and at the front, Hitler's generals did what they had been accustomed to doing several times in the past: ignoring Hitler or, failing that, trying to subvert him at every chance. Said historian Brian Fugate: "Hitler had previously shown himself inclined to defer important decisions if they appeared likely to cause disagreement among his advisors, and it was this weakness in his character that Halder could use to his advantage."[21]

But by July 30, Hitler said that Army Group Center—the spearhead of the Wehrmacht—must pass to the defensive. This would leave the Center as a kind of strategic reserve for the main wings of the attack. Halder wrote in his diary that Hitler "reiterates the familiar points of view determining the pattern of the continuance of the campaign; as before, the emphasis is on Leningrad and control of the south (coal, iron, elimination of the enemy air base in the Crimea), with Moscow being brushed aside."[22]

Hitler was now turning away all arguments about taking Moscow. The generals saw that the man was serious. There were many options, obeying the Führer being one of them. But there were others as well.

SHOEMAKER'S APPRENTICE

Those who wanted to change course by arresting the Führer again came to the fore. The focus of the conspiracy against Hitler settled now in Bock's command at Army Group Center, the group having been denied the glory road to Moscow. The conspirators were so senior that it is unlikely that Bock himself was not involved.[23] Even his two top personal aides took part in the planning.

The conspirators approached generals throughout the army about possible participation in a coup, which produced a startling and improbable situation. Officers of an army that had been unbelievably successful at war and was ascendant throughout most of Europe were plotting to dispatch their head of state. Georg Thomas, one of the most persistent of the rebellious generals, was so openly plotting the fall of Hitler that finally an exasperated Walther von Brauchitsch, the army's commander in chief, scolded him: "If you persist in seeing me I shall have to place you under arrest."[24] But Thomas had no reason to fear for his freedom. As Brauchitsch had signaled before, he was willing to stand by and not interfere if others took action against Hitler. He said as much to Thomas,[25] who reported back that the chiefs of staff of Bock and Rundstedt were on board.[26] Hitler's head could roll.

It was a bizarre time, and even those Germans who hated Hitler had to wonder if their country's interests were being well served by the generals' treason.

Among those who now became active in the conspiracy was Field Marshal Günther von Kluge, one of Germany's best officers. Kluge sent an emissary, Fabian von Schlabrendorff, to Hassell asking "whether there was any guarantee that England would make peace soon after a change in regime was effected." Hassell marveled with "what naïveté the generals approached this problem." The problem, as always, was how to end Hitler without ending Germany. "I told him," Hassell wrote, "there were no such guarantees and that there could be none. Were it otherwise any shoemaker's apprentice could overthrow the regime."[27]

Without prior British approval, a "disillusioned people might declare that Hitler had been robbed of the victory within his grasp and the new rulers couldn't get peace either,"[28] said Hassell. He called it "the old dilemma."

Despite the old dilemma, some of Bock's officers were ready to eliminate Hitler, regardless of the British. They set their coup for August 3, when the Führer planned to leave the Wolf's Lair and travel to Army Group Center's headquarters on the eastern front.[29] Hitler was going there to try to calm his senior generals and get them to understand or at least accept his strategic decisions. He did not know or refused to acknowledge that his life was in danger.

Hitler frustrated the young officers who were to begin the coup by rescheduling his appearance several times. When he did arrive, he was accompanied by a heavy escort of SS that arrived in several staff cars instead of one. The conspirators did not know which car the Führer was in and never got close enough to him to shoot him with one of their guns much less arrest him.[30]

Hitler then set about assuaging his upset commanders. He interviewed each one individually: Bock, Guderian, Hermann Hoth, and Halder's representative, Adolf Heusinger. They were never allowed to form a united front; in fact, their discussions with Hitler showed divisions among themselves. Afterward, Hitler called them into a conference, where he stressed that his current goal was Leningrad and probably the Ukraine. The commanders left subdued but not beaten. Their more impulsive colleagues in the conspiracy left to fight another day.

Privately, Hitler told Guderian that he was impressed at the Russian resistance. "If I had known that the figures for the Russian tank strength which you gave in your book were the true ones, I would not—I believe—ever have started this war."[31]

Hitler's health added to his troubles. He became ill during this period, and his personal doctor took to attaching leeches to Hitler to stop the buzzing in the Führer's ears. Hitler was simply too ill to enforce his will. He would depend upon Prussian honor. He thought that once his generals agreed to an order while looking into the eyes of the state leader, they would carry through with resolve. Prussian honor, however, did not prevail.

Halder, like Guderian, did not change his strategic thinking, despite the Führer's determination. Halder wrote in his diary that OKH plans for Moscow were still the same and that, as such, "We could not expect to reach the Caucasus before the onset of this winter."[32] Halder complained of confusion at the top.

Perhaps the commanders were right, and taking Moscow would bring down the entire Red edifice. But taking Moscow before the flanks were secure was something that Napoleon had tried. The Wehrmacht's lines of communication were already stretched. Russian forces in pockets in the west outnumbered German troops that had crossed the Dnieper. And the Russians operating close to home were awaiting the Germans.

Halder's moods alternated. On August 8 he said that the Soviets were spent. "The number of divisions which have appeared to date is the maximum that can be got up . . ." Three days later, the general was far less assured. "The time factor favors them, as they are near their own resources, while we are moving farther and farther away from ours."[33] Guderian and Bock tried to keep the Moscow offensive alive by attacking at Roslavl and Yelnya as a prelude to attacking down the Moscow highway.[34]

Alan Clark noted that the days lost in the generals' subplots and subversion helped determine the course of the war that year. "We can now see that the Germans did the one thing which was fatal—namely nothing."[35]

ABSOLUTELY ESSENTIAL

On August 18, Brauchitsch submitted another OKH draft on the desirability of a march on Moscow. In it, Halder tried to talk Hitler out of the southern strategy, explaining that the "enemy therefore appear to regard an attack by Army Group Center in the direction of Moscow as the main threat. They are employing every means (troop concentrations, fortifications) in order to block this attack. It is unlikely that the enemy will significantly weaken their forces in front of Army Group Center in order to reinforce those in front of Army Groups South and North."[36]

If Halder had really thought that Hitler would not go to the Baltics or the Caucasus if he had told the Führer that the Russians would not strongly defend those two places, he seriously misunderstood Hitler. Hitler restated his goals: "Apart from the fact that it is important to capture or destroy Russia's iron, coal,

and oil resources, it is of decisive significance for Germany that
the Russian air bases on the Black Sea be eliminated . . .

"This measure can be said to be absolutely essential for Germany. Under present circumstances no one can guarantee that
our only important oil producing region is safe from air attack.
Such attacks could have incalculable results for the future conduct of the war."[37]

Again, Hitler reiterated his overall rationale: "The objective of
this campaign is finally to eliminate Russia as a Continental ally
of Great Britain and thereby to remove from Britain all hope of
changing the course of events . . . This is a strategic opportunity
such as fate only very rarely provides in war."[38]

Hitler had clearly had enough. On the same day, August 18,
he issued Directive 34, trying finally to put to rest his commanders' indecision and subversion. The main German effort
should shift to the south.

Still the German generals waited.[39] Bock decided that Guderian could do the job of changing the Führer's mind. On August
23, 1941, Guderian and Halder took off in a Ju 52 for one last
stab at Hitler. Brauchitsch, who had supported their efforts in
the past, was now nervous. Upon meeting Halder and Guderian,
he stated: "I forbid you to mention the question of Moscow to
the Führer. The operation to the south has been ordered."[40]

The order was ignored. Guderian gave a lengthy analysis as to
why Moscow mattered most. The Führer listened to him quietly,
offered his oft-repeated explanations, and remarked: "My generals know nothing about the economic aspects of War."[41] But
Hitler's mind was made up.

Then Guderian changed sides. He agreed to swing his panzers south, but he asked to bring his whole corps along, removing
any hope that Bock might have in a center thrust. Hitler agreed.
Some members of Bock's command never forgave Guderian for
the stab in the back.

HITLER WINS?

Before Barbarossa, Stalin suspected that Hitler would drive toward the flanks in order to force Russia to make a negotiated

peace. Wrote Zhukov: "Stalin was convinced that in the war against the Soviet Union the Nazis would first try to seize the Ukraine and the Donets Coal Basin in order to deprive the country of its most important economic regions and lay hands on the Ukrainian grain, Donets coal and, later, Caucasian oil. During the discussions of the operational plan in the spring of 1941, Stalin said: 'Nazi Germany will not be able to wage a major lengthy war without those vital resources.'"[42]

Now, in September 1941, Hitler appeared poised to do exactly what Stalin most feared and what the Führer most wanted. Hitler was shifting the juggernaut to the south. Stalin desperately asked Britain for a second front to divert thirty to forty German divisions away from the Soviet Union. He also asked for great direct material assistance through delivery of airplanes, tanks, and aluminum. With unvarnished candor, Stalin told Churchill, "Without these two forms of assistance the Soviet Union may be either defeated or weakened to such an extent that for a long period it may not be in a position to help its allies by active operations in the struggle against Hitlerism."[43]

But Britain and America could not deliver what Stalin needed. It quickly became clear that Guderian's and Rundstedt's attacks on the south would succeed. Red Army resistance around Kiev fell despite Stalin's order to hold the city at all costs. September 16 brought the capitulation of Kiev. More than 600,000 Red Army troops surrendered, their equipment forfeit. The surrender amounted to a third of the power of the Red Army as it existed at the beginning of Barbarossa.

On October 7, Stalin told Zhukov that Russia could not win the war. Secret negotiations between the two powers would begin on a compromise peace. Stalin was prepared from the start to cede the Baltic States, Byelorussia, Moldavia, and part of the Ukraine.[44] Stalin, Beria, and Molotov called in the Bulgarian ambassador to explain their offer and ask for Bulgaria to be the intermediary to the Führer. Only Molotov did any talking for the Soviet side.[45]

Hitler had won. He could have his lebensraum. He would have all the resources he needed to prosecute the war. He would control the Baltic. If he accepted what Stalin offered, Britain would surely not be able to continue the war.

Why did Hitler not take victory? The whole truth may never be known. Ribbentrop said that Hitler refused the offer, sent through King Boris of Bulgaria, "because he was convinced he could stand the immediate test and emerge victorious in the end."[46]

In general, it appears that Hitler became a victim of his success. On September 6, even before the German victory at Kiev was certain, Hitler issued an order providing for the *panzergruppen* to return to the Center for a possible push on Moscow.

The Führer began rethinking what his generals had told him. The way to the southeast was clear to his armies. The Wehrmacht could likely take Rostov, Voronezh, Stalingrad, and even Baku. It seemed at the time that this would be almost like punching into thin air.

Hitler decided to reverse course. He would take Moscow, just as his generals had always said. The rest he could mop up later.

Hitler told his soldiers: "After three and a half months' fighting, you have created the necessary conditions to strike the last vigorous blows which should break the enemy on the threshold of winter."[47]

At Vyazma, Hitler's decision seemed to be validated with the destruction of forty-five divisions and the seizing of 650,000 soldiers. By this point, October 16, 1941, Russian losses topped 3 million men, more than the Red Army's entire prewar strength. Yet Russian troops kept coming, seemingly inexhaustibly, and German soldiers soon developed a deep foreboding.

By November 12, German generals began to lose their nerve. A cruel cold had come over the eastern front. Mud and slush slowed down the Wehrmacht on the few roads that led to Moscow. And the Russians were more fanatical than ever, attacking at night, attacking sometimes with a single airplane, attacking with one hand grenade held over a single soldier's head.

Hitler did not see that this was the time to go over to the defensive; he thought that the Russians had no force behind their attack except desperation. That the Germans were desperate, too, is not in doubt, but a final push would do, or so Hitler had been told for five months.

MINCING MACHINE

But there was more than desperation that Stalin could call upon. The best fighting men that the Soviet Union possessed had not yet been pressed into battle. The Soviet army in Siberia, one that had decisively defeated a Japanese incursion in a prelude to the Second World War, was a final, strategic reserve of immense importance. Stalin had yet to call upon the Siberians for fear that he would so weaken Soviet power in the east that Japan would attack again. But he also knew that Japan was having a dispute with the Americans and faced a cutoff of her petroleum supplies. Japan had to develop a northern strategy or a southern strategy and had to do so quickly. And Stalin needed to know that decision.

In August 1941 Rado had sent the Center a crucially important message: "The Japanese ambassador in Berne has said that there can be no question of a Japanese attack on the Soviet Union as long as Germany has secured no decisive victory at the front."[48] Inside Germany, another of Stalin's spies, Harro Schultz-Boysen, told the Center on September 22 that the "OKW regards all intelligence about a special Russian winter army as false. OKW convinced that Russians have thrown everything into defeating present German offensive and have no further reserves left."[49]

The most important message came from a Soviet spy named Richard Sorge. Based in Japan, Sorge told Moscow on October 4: "The Soviet Far East may be considered guaranteed against Japanese attack."[50] The Japanese navy had won its argument with the army. Japan would secure her oil in Southeast Asia, a move that would bring her to war with America and Great Britain. She would not have the strength to attack Russia also.

Stalin now knew two things: He would not face an attack from Japan this winter, and the Germans were totally unprepared for the appearance of a strategic reserve.

It was as much information as Stalin would get, because suddenly lines to his spies went blank. Sorge's operation was exposed by the Japanese, and he was arrested on October 18. What happened to Rado and Dübendorfer the next day was altogether darker: At the moment of the most peril, with the German army pointed at the heart of the Soviet Union, the Center was killing its secret agents at a pace that would leave no one alive. The Center was consuming itself. It went off the air, and none of the spies in Germany, France, or Switzerland knew why.

They had no way of knowing that Stalin had ordered his entire intelligence operation moved nine hundred miles east to Kuybishev. The NKVD and the Fourth Department took the occasion to further their purges. Three hundred officers and agents were shot in the basement of the Lubyanka. More senior officers were evacuated and tortured at the same time. Said Beria: "Merciless beatings were administered. It was a real mincing machine."[51] In the chaos, spies in the field were neglected.

While Poliakova and the rest of the Center headed east, new Siberian troops came in wholesale to the west. Fifteen infantry and three cavalry divisions were dispatched west, together with four air divisions with 1,500 aircraft. Also arriving were eight tank brigades with 1,700 fresh tanks.[52] This force, equipped for winter fighting, would be commanded by a personality that even Stalin did not challenge, Georgi Zhukov.

Zhukov was a remorseless and fierce fighter, savage and determined, who would cut the throats of his enemies and any man in his command who wouldn't push forward. He was Stalin's kind of general. On November 30 Stalin gave the marshal permission for a winter offensive, a seemingly crazy idea, for at -44 degrees few machines of a modern army work well.

But Stalin's bet was that winter would work for the Soviets more than the Germans, and he was right. The German offensive was faltering and the Russian defense was strengthening; fresh Soviet troops could mean the difference. The Siberians made their first impression on the Germans on November 18, even before the general offensive was approved. The Germans were shaken. Some Wehrmacht soldiers abandoned positions. On December 5, when the real Soviet offensive began, it got worse.

The Russian offensive was overwhelming to German infantry-men. They had been told that the war was won. Now, immaculate Siberian troops, dressed in white fur and using guns that operated in the cold, were evidence that the war was just beginning.

Their presence caused panic in the high command as well. Retreat was the catchword. It reached -63 degrees, and Guderian recorded that under such conditions the mere attempt to defecate was potentially lethal. "Many men died while performing their natural functions, as a result of a congelation of the anus."[53]

Roles in the German High Command were again reversed. Hitler wanted to continue, or at least not retreat, whereas the generals, who were earlier so sure of the Moscow advance, now proposed a wild withdrawal. With engines that wouldn't run, guns that wouldn't fire, and a winter that wouldn't stop, the generals' suggestions looked reasonable. But Hitler wouldn't have it, sensing that a temporary reversal in momentum at the front could devolve into a rout. "Talk of Napoleon's retreat is threatening to become a reality. Thus, there must only be withdrawals where there is a prepared position in the rear," Hitler ordered.[54]

General Bock, who only weeks before fancied himself the conqueror of Moscow, was unnerved; he reported himself unfit for duty, suffering a stomach ailment.[55] He was replaced by Kluge. The army's commander in chief, Brauchitsch, recovering from a heart attack, tried to convince Hitler that he should call for a general withdrawal. Hitler sacked him on December 19. Instead of a replacement from the general staff, Hitler named himself the army's commander. He was done with generals who would not follow the orders of the head of state. He hoped that maybe they would follow the head of the army. "This little affair of operational command is something anybody can do," he declared.[56] During the crisis, Hitler cashiered thirty-five corps and divisional commanders.[57]

At the time, it was unclear what effect Hitler's stand-fast orders would have on the German army. Soon it became apparent. It is now largely accepted that December 1941 was Hitler's greatest moment as a military man, coming oddly not as a conqueror but as a defender. He held the army together, pulling back German troops in an orderly fashion and with a strong rear guard; in so doing, he left the Germans in control of the battlefield when the thaw came in 1942. Historian Alan Clark concluded: "As for Hitler, it was his finest hour. He had done more than save the German Army; he had achieved complete personal ascendancy over the ruling class."[58]

MID-SENTENCE

Stalin, who had never left Moscow, also scored a great personal success. His deployment of the Siberians had saved Moscow. The German army would never really threaten it again. Government offices, including the intelligence services, were ordered to return from Kuybyshev. Suddenly, communication with the Soviets' spy networks resumed. A message that had been cut off in mid-sentence six weeks earlier was resumed in December as if nothing had happened.[59]

Alexander Foote had little doubt about Lucy's role after contact was reestablished. "'Lucy' provided Moscow with an up-to-date and day-to-day order of battle of the German forces in the East . . . Russia, fighting with her back to the wall and scraping up her last resources, was obviously vitally interested in trustworthy information regarding the armed forces ranged against her, and this 'Lucy' supplied."[60]

The information, Foote was convinced, could have come only over the airways. Someone in Germany was daring enough or in a secure enough position to send intelligence from inside the heart of the Third Reich. "There was," he wrote, "no question of any courier or safe hand-route . . . [H]is sources, whoever they were, must have gone almost hot-foot from the Service teleprinters to their wireless transmitters in order to send the information off. It was this speed which was one of the factors that made the Center distrust this source, and only after bitter experience did they accept it at its face value."[61]

Unfortunately, most of the Lucy material from this period has never been found or decoded, so the exact extent of its influence on the winter campaign is hard to judge. That situation would change in the great battles of 1942 and 1943.

• • •

As Stalin's offensive ended, the Germans learned that they had an important counterintelligence problem. Mathematicians working for SS general Walter Schellenberg were able to decode two of Rado's messages. From that point on, Schellenberg knew that someone within Hitler's entourage and in the Wehrmacht command was betraying vital state secrets.[62]

There was a race to stop the leak.

THE OTHER MINCING MACHINE

As Hitler's armies headed into the belly of Russia, sinister forces traveled with them everywhere. Germany sent in four *einsatz-gruppen* units designed to murder tens of thousands of Jews, Communists, Gypsies, and other undesirables, often mowing them down over fresh trenches or attaching crude devices to small locked trucks in the first experiments on gas execution. These Germans were the pioneers of a type of ruthlessness that had not appeared much during the First World War or, in fact, during most wars among nations since Rome. The terror was made all the crazier because the responsibility was so opaque. Certainly, Hitler was the prime mover, but even his actions were muddied by the lack of clear-cut written orders for genocide. The man who sat on his right filled that void. As prosecutors at the Nuremberg war crimes trial would later say, Martin Bormann "was, in truth, an evil archangel to the Lucifer of Hitler."[63]

There is no rational basis to doubt Hitler's true intentions. From his writings, his table talk, and even his speeches, it is clear that he intended a bad end for the Jews of Europe. Before Barbarossa, Hitler intended to exile the Jews to Madagascar or other destinations. But after the push east, his intentions darkened. Before a month was over, Hitler spelled out the plan to Bormann, Lammers, Göring, Keitel, and Rosenberg. Of his plans in the east, Hitler said that it "was essential that we did not publicize our aims before the world, also there is no need for that; but the main thing was that we ourselves knew what we wanted. By no means should we render our task more difficult by making superfluous declarations. Such declarations were su-perfluous because we could do everything wherever we had the power, and what was beyond our power we would not be able to do anyway . . .

"What we told the world about the motives for our measures ought to be conditioned, therefore, by tactical reasons . . . [W]e shall emphasize again that we were forced to occupy, administer, and secure a certain area; it was in the interest of the inhabitants that we provided order, food, traffic and so forth, hence our measures. Nobody shall be able to recognize that it initiates a final settlement . . . But we do not want to make any people enemies prematurely and unnecessarily. Therefore we shall act as though we wanted to exercise a mandate only. At the same time we must know clearly that we shall never leave those countries."

The plan went on. The Germans would occupy the Crimea, evacuating all non-Germans. Other areas, too, were to be appropriated. Hitler's golden rule for taking land was, "First, to dominate it; second, to administer it; and third, to exploit it." Then, in a chilling foreshadowing of what was about to happen, Hitler mentioned: "The Russians have now ordered partisan warfare behind our front. This partisan war again has some advantage for us; it enables us to eradicate everyone who opposes us."[64] Bormann kept the notes as Hitler spoke.

But Bormann, for some reason, did not act as though he understood some of the subtlety in Hitler's Machiavellian scheme. Hitler had called for fooling the population into complacency before destroying or ejecting it, using eradication only when it was tactically beneficial. Bormann, however, began issuing orders that were not subtle in the least. He had earlier declared, "The lowest German peasant must still be 10 percent better than any Pole. All intelligent Poles were to be exterminated." For the Slavs he was just as harsh. "The Slavs," he said, "are to work for us. In so far as we do not need them, they may die. Therefore, compulsory vaccination and Germanic health services are superfluous. The fertility of the Slavs is undesirable."

At every juncture Bormann sought the severest measures in the east, and any Gauleiter who did not go along was removed or punished. German law, Bormann said in October, would never apply to the Eastern population. By December, Bormann issued an edict entitled Criminal Law Practices in Incorporated Eastern Territories.

Ever since Hess had flown to Scotland in May 1940, Bormann's role expanded geometrically. Nuremberg prosecutors would later call him "a prime mover in the program of starvation, degradation, spoliation and extermination of the Jews."[65]

Bormann's influence on Hitler had become pervasive. Speer complained that Bormann was "Hitler's permanent shadow" who followed Hitler's orders when they suited him and quietly subverted others.[66] Bormann's ambition, Speer thought, was to one day succeed Hitler. "I had the impression for a long time that Bormann consistently pursued this ultimate objective," Speer told his Nuremberg interrogators.[67]

But trying to impress Hitler by surpassing the Führer in cruelty did not help the German cause. Schellenberg recounted after the war that Bormann-inspired pogroms were beneficial to Stalin.

"The Russians," Schellenberg wrote, "used the harshness with which the Germans were conducting the war as the ideological basis for their partisan activities . . .

"My Russian advisers believed that in reality Stalin welcomed these German measures, and reports of whose validity I was practically certain supported this theory. One of them stated that the most important aim of the partisan warfare was ruthlessness in itself, that anything was justified which would make the population support the struggle. The brutalities committed must always be ascribed to the German invaders, so that a hesitant population would be forced, as it were, into active resistance."[68]

Perhaps Speer was not overstating when he told secret interrogators: "For Germany, Bormann's influence on Adolf Hitler was a national disaster."[69]

But there can be no denying that Hitler liked his Bormann and that their thoughts on cruelty in the east were synergistic.

On July 16, 1941, Hitler explained his vision to Göring, Keitel, Rosenberg, and Bormann. Bormann again took notes. "There can be no talk of the creation of a military power west of the Urals, even if we should have to fight 100 years to achieve this,"

Hitler said. "All the Baltic regions must become part of the Reich. The Crimea and adjoining regions north of the Crimea must likewise be incorporated into the Reich. The region of the Volga as well as the Baku district must likewise be incorporated into the Reich." Then, the Nuremberg prosecutors said, Bormann wrote that the plan involved the "enslavement and annihilation of the population of these territories." Göring and Keitel later said that they did not hear those specific words from Hitler.

Regardless, that became the plan, and Bormann became the point man for the Holocaust.

Notes

1 NAZ, p 817.

2 Robert Payne, *The Life and Death of Adolf Hitler* (New York: Popular Library, 1973).

3 Garlinski, p. 64.

4 Rado, p. 66.

5 Garlinski, p. 66.

6 Foote, p. 91.

7 Zhukov, *Memoirs,* p. 223.

8 Halder, p. 446.

9 Ibid., p. 450.

10 Volkogonov, p. 417.

11 Halder, p. 458.

12 Ibid.

13 NAZ, p. 820.

14 Clark, p. 43.

15 Ibid., p. 101.

16 Toland, p. 687.

17 Ibid., p. 682.

18 Ibid.

19 Ibid.

20 Ibid.

21 Fugate, p. 124.

22 Halder, p. 495.

23 Clark, p. 99.

24 Ibid.

25 Hassell, p. 222.

26 Ibid., p. 214.

27 Ibid., p. 219.

28 Ibid., p. 220.

29 Most of the following description is derived from Clark.

30 Clark, p. 101.

31 Ibid., p. 102.

32 Halder, p. 496.

33 Ibid., p. 506.

34 Clark, pp. 105–06.

35 Ibid., p. 104.

36 NAZ, p. 821.

37 Fugate, p. 234.

38 NAZ, p. 823.

39 Clark, p. 110.

40 Ibid.

41 Ibid., p. 111.

42 Zhukov, *Memoirs,* p. 211.

43 Churchill-Roosevelt correspondence, Warren Kimball, ed., p. 237.

44 Andrew and Gordievsky, p. 273.

45 Volkogonov, pp. 412–13. The account came from Beria during his interrogation after Stalin's death. Marshall K. S. Moskalenko, who investigated Beria, said that there was little reason to disbelieve the account, "especially as the former Bulgarian ambassador confirmed the facts in conversation with us."

46 Toland, p. 686.

47 Clark, p. 148.

48 Rado, p. 68.

49 V. E. Tarrant, *The Red Orchestra* (New York: John Wiley & Sons, Inc., 1995), p. 85.

50 Gordon Prange, *Target Tokyo* (New York: McGraw-Hill, 1985), p. 446.

51 Andrew and Gordievsky, p. 273.

52 Prange, p. 449.

53 Clark, p. 181.

54 NAZ, p. 828.

55 Toland, p. 696.

56 Ibid., p. 697.

57 Clark, p. 182.

58 Ibid., p. 183.

59 Foote, p. 98.

60 Ibid., pp. 74–75.

61 Ibid., p. 75.

62 Garlinski, p. 140.

63 IMT, Vol. 5, p. 334.

64 IMT, Vol. 4, p. 11.

65 IMT, Vol. 5, p. 319.

66 Intelligence Report No. EF/Min/1, U.S. Group Control Council.

67 Ibid.

68 Walter Schellenberg, *Hitler's Secret Service* (New York: Jove Publications, Inc., 1977), p. 266.

69 U.S. Group Control Council.

Chapter Six

PRESERVED

If Germany succeeds in taking Moscow, that is obviously a grave disappointment for us, but it by no means disrupts our grand strategy. The only thing that matters is oil.

—Soviet marshal Semën Timoshenko

TRAP

The Moscow battle proved one thing again to the German generals: Hitler still possessed warfare instinct. As spring broke, the German front was stabilized, her strength greater than the Russians'; the strategic initiative was again in her favor. Hitler's moment of megalomania, when he thought that he could defeat all of Russia and dictate a peace with Britain, was gone. He now reverted to his original plan, to capture those resources in the south still controlled by the Russians.

He told the Japanese ambassador to Berlin that Germany "was determined to take up once again the offensive in the direction of the Caucasus as soon as the weather was favorable. The thrust in this direction was the most important one: we must get to the oil and to Iran and Iraq."[1] To Mussolini, Hitler simply said: "When Russia's sources of oil are exhausted she will be brought to her knees."[2]

So far, the German war effort had come at great cost. By February 1942, there were nearly a million German casualties, including 199,448 dead.[3] But the foot soldiers and people at home still supported their Führer. Had a plebiscite been held—Albert Speer told his interrogators after the war—Hitler would have won by a substantial margin.[4] "If the workers regarded anybody as their protector, it was Hitler himself, whose way of life, views and post-war plans were well known to them."[5] The people were even ready to do more than Hitler was asking of them. Germany had yet to mobilize for total war, and unlike the other combatants, most German women were not in the workplace. Ordinary Germans would have gone further. "The people were in favor of total war at a much earlier date [than Hitler] and they were prepared to sacrifice everything in order to avoid a total defeat," Speer said.[6]

Though the Germans were ready for a new offensive, Russia was not. The Soviet Union had suffered 4 million casualties. Twenty thousand tanks—the number that Russia possessed at the beginning of Barbarossa—had been destroyed. Soviet factories were replacing them, but not as quickly as needed; the factories didn't have the necessities. Soviet coal production was down 57 percent, steel down 58 percent, aluminum down 60 percent.[7]

Yet Stalin was not willing to sit around waiting for Hitler to resume the attack. At a meeting in March, Marshal Boris Shaposhnikov tried to put before Stalin the idea of a strategic defense. The Russian dictator cut him off. "Are we supposed to sit in defense, idling away our time, and wait for the Germans to attack us first?" Stalin asked. "We must strike several preemptive blows over a wide front and probe the enemy's readiness."[8]

Stalin conceived of three attacks. The first was to hit Manstein's forces outside the Red Army's Sevastopol garrison. The Russians came as they had before, in wave after wave. And, as before, they were outmaneuvered, losing 100,000 men whom Russia could not afford to lose.[9] A similar fate awaited Siberian divisions striking German positions on the Volga River. The offensive was stopped, with heavy Russian losses.

But it was Stalin's main thrust—toward the vital rail junction of Kharkov—that caused a potentially decisive defeat, not because of the number of men lost but because it threatened the connection to Lucy. The drive was headed by one of the Red Army's best marshals, Semën Timoshenko, who later with Marshal Zhukov would defeat Hitler's best. But now was not that time.

Timoshenko's force would have made significant progress—maybe even produced a rare Soviet victory—had not Bock ordered a relatively small, tactical offensive, which collided accidentally with Timoshenko's.

The Russians had formed a bridgehead during the winter in the Izyum area, some fifty miles southeast of Kharkov. German generals were learning that Russian bridgeheads were consistently troublesome, and Bock decided that it was time to eliminate this one. He ordered forces in front of the salient to appear to loosen, encouraging Russian forces there to move forward. At the same time, Gen. Friedrich von Paulus's 6th Army was directed to descend from the north, on the Russians' right flank, while the powerful 1st Panzer Army of Gen. Ewald von Kleist came up from the south.

The problem for the Kremlin was that the Izyum bridgehead that Bock wanted to snip was exactly the spot through which Timoshenko, on May 12, 1942, was launching his armor for the march toward Kharkov. Had his forces and Bock's met each other head-on, they both would have been surprised. An uncertain battle, perhaps one even favoring Russia, could have ensued. But Timoshenko's forces were mostly through the pocket before the German pincers closed.

The Soviet marshal did not realize his peril until interrogations of German prisoners on May 17 revealed that some were from Kleist's panzer army, which definitely was supposed to be somewhere else. By then it was too late. The Germans found themselves the unexpected and largely undeserving recipients of a Russian prize. Kleist's and Paulus's forces closed around Timoshenko's, and only a quarter of the latter escaped the pocket. Another 200,000 Russians were in German hands.

Lucy became immediately suspect. The secret weapon that Joseph Stalin had increasingly begun to respect had not predicted the appearance of Kleist's panzers at the belly of Timoshenko's army. To the Russians, it appeared that the source might in fact represent a German double game.[10]

Hardly anyone on the Soviet side could conceive the truth: that Bock and Kleist had taken it in their own hands to clip the

Izyum bridgehead. Instead, the Center thought that such a move could have been made only after an order from the Führer. And because Werther had not given such a warning, something was wrong in the whole Lucy system.

Years later, the Soviet intelligence services were still trying to figure out exactly what went wrong at Izyum. It was this incident that caused the director and Poliakova to question Foote so heavily when he arrived in Moscow in January 1945.

But Stalin did not have years to make up his mind. He had only days.

NAME ON A MAP

In planning his great 1942 southern offensive, Hitler wanted to crush the Russian forces standing between the Wehrmacht and the Caucasus, and he was ready to do this in any way possible. "I am completely indifferent to what posterity may say about the methods I had to use," Hitler told Speer in May. "As far as I am concerned, there is only one issue which has to be resolved, namely, we must win the war or Germany will be destroyed."[11]

Hitler issued the high command's Directive 41 on April 5, ordering the southern front to "destroy the remaining military forces of the Soviets once and for all" while depriving the whole of Russia of "the most important economic resources necessary for the war effort"—namely oil.[12] Hitler planned to crush as many Soviet forces as possible at Voronezh, some 325 miles northwest of Stalingrad. The retreating Russian units would fall back into the bend of the River Don, an area approximately 200 miles wide and 200 miles deep. The OKW thought that Timoshenko's remaining forces, unable to retreat quickly over the river, would be decimated. "It was hoped," said German panzer general F. W. von Mellenthin, "that many Russian divisions would be trapped in the great bend of the river between Rostov and Voronezh."[13]

The tip of the Don Bend was a mere forty miles from Stalingrad, a city twenty miles long and three miles wide that wormed along the west bank of the Volga. Thinking that the Russians would perish on the banks of the Don, no one much considered that this city would become synonymous with one of the war's great battles. Said Kleist, who was to spearhead the drive into the Caucasus: "Stalingrad was, at the start, no more than a name on the map to my Panzer army."[14]

What the Germans missed, and what would soon become obvious, was Stalingrad's strategic importance if the Red Army did not oblige the Germans and surrender or die in the Don Bend. If enough Red Army troops and materiel made it to Stalingrad, they could threaten the left flank of German operations in the south while keeping open the Volga for oil and raw materials heading north.

For now, the Germans did not consider this nightmare. Their focus was the Don. Command for the German attack down the bend fell to Gen. Friedrich von Paulus's 6th Army and Gen. Hermann Hoth's 4th Panzer Army. On paper, at least, Paulus and Hitler had every reason to be optimistic. The Red Army had fought stupidly in the past, throwing away its chances through simple boneheadedness. The Germans believed, and they were right at the time, that the Russians had only a handful of divisions to contest Paulus, and almost no reserves. To counter these thin forces, Paulus had an army that was quite real. In all, Hitler assigned some sixty-eight German, twenty-seven Romanian, and thirteen Bulgarian divisions to crush whatever hopes the Soviet dictator might have for a fair issue from the war. D day was June 28, 1942.[15]

SECRETARY

One person who should have known the broad scope of the plan was Martin Bormann, a man hardly known to the outside world or, in fact, to the vast majority of citizens of the Reich. But even now, Bormann's personal access to the Führer was unparalleled. Except for the highest military officers, Bormann determined whom Hitler saw and did not see. Bormann was the only one ever entrusted by the Führer to issue orders in his name, as though Hitler himself had signed them. At Nuremberg, prosecutors accused Bormann of orchestrating the Holocaust on Hitler's behalf.

From this position alone, Bormann likely knew of Hitler's plans for the southern campaign. But if he needed more insight, he could always have availed himself of the work of the two spies he had inserted into the Führer's headquarters: Koeppen and Heim.

Koeppen, sitting at the same table as Heim but not knowing that his colleague was a fellow spy, surreptitiously recorded Hitler's views, including precise military matters. Those notes were sent to Nazi headquarters in Berlin.[16] It is not known whether Bormann studied Koeppen's notes, though it is almost impossible to think that he did not. Bormann ran the Nazi Party as though it was his personal valet. Regardless, it is clear that Bormann saw Heim's notes, and these alone were enough to reveal the Führer's general intentions. Heim, for instance, recorded this Hitler declaration: "We must at all costs advance into the plains of Mesopotamia and take the Mosul oil fields from the British. If we succeed here, the whole war will come to an end, for the British have now only Haifa as their sole loading port for oil."[17]

Anyone hearing this would know that to get to the plains of Mesopotamia, the German army would need to attack Russia's own oil fields beyond the Caucasian Mountains. And anyone with any military insight could look at the map and tell where Hitler would eventually have to secure his left flank—those forty miles between the Don and the Volga.

Just as Bormann was receiving this insight, so too was Lucy, who in turn relayed the German plans to the Soviets.[18] But Lucy was not yet rehabilitated, the sharp smart from the Timoshenko affair still on the Center's mind. So the first weeks of the German offensive toward the south saw Stalin remaining loyal to his misconceptions. He thought that the German move might be a trap, so he carefully husbanded seventy Red Army divisions—the bulk of the Soviet forces—behind the Moscow front, where they were not needed. He had only two hundred tanks and a few divisions in the south, where Hitler threatened.

But after Paulus's panzers reached the strategic objective of Voronezh only seven days into the German offensive, Lucy's messages suddenly took on new meaning.[19] Even if this was a German feint, it could not be ignored. If the oil was lost, it didn't matter if Hitler's phantom forces conquered Moscow. The war would be lost anyway.

Two million executions argued that Joseph Stalin preferred suspicion over trust, that he could never believe Werther or Lucy after Izyum. And in the years following the war, no one has been able to explain why he did what he did. But during these darkest days of the war, when he had every reason to jettison the suspect spy, Joseph Stalin made up his mind that he would trust Lucy, an unknown spy who existed only in the ether of code tapped on a wireless.

His decision came on July 12, 1942. If Hitler saw the Don-Volga isthmus as the key to the war, Stalin resolved to check him there. And there was no better way to do that than to lure Hitler into the city that bore the Russian dictator's name. Stalin established the Stalingrad front, and for the next twenty-one days the Russian reserves that had been preparing to save Moscow headed south instead.

Stalin ordered Marshal Georgi Zhukov, who had defeated the Japanese in a major clash before this war and had stopped the unstoppable Wehrmacht before Moscow, to perform his magic again.* "The Supreme Command was sending to Stalingrad all that it was possible to send . . . ," wrote Zhukov.[20] When the mass move was completed, 60 percent of Russian armor was placed on a front around Stalingrad and was backed by seven of the nine Russian reserve armies. More than a million men were ready to contest the Führer's armies.[21]

Stalin summed up the stakes clearly. If the city fell, "we should lose our main waterway and soon our oil, too!"[22]

---

*Zhukov replaced Timoshenko on the southern front. Previously in Stalin's Russia, a general replaced was a general liquidated. But Stalin now knew that he could not insanely throw away the few brains that remained in the Red Army. Timoshenko, therefore, landed the important task of fending off the German siege of Leningrad.

ERROR

Had Hitler known that Stalin was committing the majority of his forces to the south, he would not have plunged ahead. More certainly, he would not have divided his forces, which he was about to do. But from what Hitler could tell, he was facing only paper-thin Russian strength as his soldiers rushed down the Don Bend.

What Hitler didn't know was the reason for the lack of resistance. He believed that it signified a final Russian collapse, but it didn't. For one of the few times in the war to date, Russian generals as a whole began acting as if they belonged to a nation of chess players. Instead of opposing Hitler from exposed positions where they could not hope to prevail, the Russian forces had been ordered to retreat en masse. They were headed for Stalingrad. Hitler was falling into a trap that his heretofore near perfect instincts did not scent. In mid-July he told Halder: "The Russian is finished."[23]

This error was fatally magnified on July 23 when the Wehrmacht conquered Rostov, a city second only to Stalingrad in strategic importance for the German operations in the south. It was a defeat that produced Russian prisoners in numbers that had been seen far too often. In all, 240,000 Russian soldiers surrendered and were sent to a most uncertain future in the West. Rostov, some three hundred miles southwest of Stalingrad, was to be the right flank of Kleist's Caucasian Army Group. With the city secured and the Red Army eliminated there, Hitler thought it safe to try to capture the prized oil immediately. The Russians had done little to convince him that they posed any real danger in the Don Bend or Stalingrad. "There followed," wrote German general F. W. von Mellenthin, "one of the greatest misfortunes in German military history—the splitting of our effort between Stalingrad and the Caucasus."[24]

Only eleven days after Stalin decided to move Red Army firepower to the south, Hitler revised Directive 41. He ordered Hoth's 4th Panzer Army to break away to the south toward Kleist's forces, "with the aim of taking possession of the Caucasus with its oil resources." That left Paulus and the 6th Army alone to "attack Stalingrad, smash the enemy concentration there, take the town and cut off the isthmus between the Don and the Volga."[25]

Hitler's plan was wrong. If he continued to force the 6th Army into Stalingrad, he could lose it, not because of anything clearly seen on the board but because of what was not seen. Hitler did not know that the Russian army was streaming in from the north. In fact, Hitler did not realize that the Russians had any real armies in the north that could be sent anywhere.

Compounding this massive intelligence failure was Hitler's own indifference to betrayal inside his own headquarters. He told General Halder on July 3: "The enemy knows our operational plans. Clear [from the time of] our approval."[26] Yet Hitler, though he sensed the massive betrayal that was taking place, chose to shrug it off. There is no record that Hitler did much at this crucial time to determine who the traitor or traitors were. From a German perspective, it was criminal conceit. Hitler seemed at this point unconcerned about what the Russians knew or did not know. He was certain that the Red Army was defenseless against the Wehrmacht no matter what.

Others held darker, more anxious suspicions. The Red Army collapse in the Don Bend seemed eerie and foreboding to some. The great German army seemed to be charging into a fog. A Berlin correspondent noted: "The Russians, who up to this time had fought stubbornly over each kilometer, withdrew without firing a shot. Our advance was only delayed by destroyed bridges and by aircraft. When the Soviet rearguards were too hard-pressed they chose a position that enabled them to hold out until night . . . It was quite disquieting to plunge into this vast area without finding a trace of the enemy."[27]

STALINGRAD: THE BEGINNING

It was Stalin, not Hitler, who decided that the battle would be joined at Stalingrad. Besides its clear strategic position in the Don-Volga isthmus, it was a perfect place for the Red Army to take on the Germans. In fact, if Stalin had sought to deliberately build a fortress to defeat the Wehrmacht, he could hardly have improved upon Stalingrad. Here were thirty-three square miles of man-made obstacles: masonry buildings and factories that could and would provide cover and camouflage. As important, those same structures limited greatly the Wehrmacht's advantage in maneuver. Tanks, almost everyone understood, did not do well in cities. Vision from them was reduced to nil by buildings and narrow streets, and antitank guns and even Molotov cocktails could come fatally close. So what at first appeared to the Germans a mere point on the map was to Stalin the ideal place to trap General Paulus. If the Red Army at Stalingrad could last until Stalin's huge movement of northern troops and armor reached the Volga, he would finally be in a position to win a major battle, if not the war.

The key here was that Stalingrad must last long enough for Stalin's forces to make a difference. As it was, the retreat of Soviet forces in the Don Bend came so rapidly that the Germans threatened to reach Stalingrad before the Russian reinforcements could do much to stop them. If the Germans succeeded, the Stalingrad front would prove meaningless. So in July, Stalin ordered that the headlong retreat be stopped. The Soviets were to fight again, delaying the German drive.

Paulus noticed the change. The Russians suddenly began fighting as they had in the past, contesting every inch. Paulus's men fought well for an army at the end of a 1,500-mile supply line, but they were exhausted. Worse, it was clear that the mass of the Red Army had already escaped from the Don Bend and was re-forming at Stalingrad. Paulus decided that Hoth's panzer army would likely be needed now to capture the city and command the territory between the Don and the Volga.

Still, there was little alarm. German armies had faced adversity before and had carried through. The taking of Stalingrad would not be as easy as first thought, but it would not be that much trouble either. The Russians were fighting again, but that was all. They had no depth, no reserves.

Hitler agreed with Paulus that Hoth's panzers might be needed, and he issued orders that the two forces be joined again. Already within sight of Russian oil derricks at Baku, Hoth reluctantly turned his forces north. Hitler also dispatched Richthofen's 8th Air Corps to join the battle. The airmen would eventually get to Stalingrad, but Hoth's panzers never would.

The front that Paulus faced had a seventy-mile base and a fifty-mile bulge stretching from Stalingrad to Kalach. Inside that bulge Russia had eleven infantry divisions—on paper no match for the Wehrmacht. At the front, the Germans had nine infantry, two mobile, and three panzer divisions, not to mention the forces that Hoth was trying to bring up.

On August 19, Paulus began the assault on Stalingrad in earnest, attacking along the broad front. The attack went well. By August 22, the German 14th Panzer Division had breached Russian defenses and reached the Volga. Göring let loose the Luftwaffe on August 23 in the largest single raid since Barbarossa began, and on a much smaller, more concentrated front. Soon Stalingrad was ablaze. German sentries said that at night they could read their newspapers a mile away by the light of the conflagration.

Fortunately for the Russians, Paulus forgot a lesson that he should have learned by then. Behind the German army—on the west bank of the Don—was a small, quiescent Red Army pocket. Paulus was more concerned with the offensive than with a mopping-up, rearguard operation, which he thought was all the clearing of the pocket at Kletskaya demanded. So Paulus gave the task of dispatching that bridgehead to the Romanian 3d Army. The Romanians, however, did not believe in picking unnecessary fights. Because the Russians in the pocket did not seem to be misbehaving, the Romanians decided to leave them alone. It would be three months before the Russians taught the Romanians their error.

Provoked by the increasing Russian stubbornness on the Stalingrad front, Hitler, on August 23, 1942, finally ordered the Wehrmacht to capture the entire city. He later tried to explain his reasoning to old First World War comrades. "Stalin," Hitler said, "expected us to attack in the center—I had no intention of attacking in the center. Not only because Mr. Stalin may have believed that I wanted to, but because I was not interested. I wanted to get to the Volga and Stalingrad."

"I did so because it is a very important place. Thirty million tons of transport can be cut off there, including nearly nine million tons of oil."[28]

STENOGRAPHERS

Certain that one more push could win the city, Hitler ordered Paulus to his Ukrainian headquarters so that the general could hear and understand the plan. When Paulus arrived on September 12, 1942, he found some unfamiliar faces at the table.

Martin Bormann no longer was satisfied with his secret spies at Hitler's dining table. He told Hitler that professional stenographers should attend all his military conferences to ensure that, after the Führer was dead, historians would have an accurate record of his glory. Otherwise, unscrupulous generals would try to take credit that was due to the Führer.[29]

From the conference with Paulus on, the stenographers performed admirably, producing an average of five hundred typewritten pages a day that delineated every thought of the high command—a blueprint of Wehrmacht plans down to tactical details. Obviously, this was a dangerous operation. A new bureaucracy would be involved in recording, transcribing, and transporting these military secrets. If a Soviet agent somehow burrowed into the system, all of Hitler's secrets would be compromised.

But that was unthinkable. Hitler's own most trusted servant had devised the system. And it was that servant, Martin Bormann, who controlled the transcripts.

Simultaneously with the arrival of the stenographers, the level of detail available to Gisela's family soared. Moscow Center suddenly thought that it could demand specific answers to military questions that could be posed only to someone with the highest access inside Germany. "Was Guderian really on the eastern front?" Moscow asked. "Were the 2nd and 3rd Armies under his control? Was the 4th Panzer Army attached to [Field Marshal Wilhelm] List's army group, or had another panzer army been posted to him?"

The questions continued: "Who was commanding the 18th Army—Lindermann or Schmidt? Had the 9th Army Corps been posted to Army Group North, and what were the divisions that constituted it? How was [Gen. Walther] Model's group made up? Who was attached to it? Which sector of the front was he responsible for, and where was his headquarters situated? How was Kluge's group organized? What had been allotted to it? Was the headquarters of the 3rd Panzer Army at Vyazma? Who was attached to this army, and who was in command?"

There were also questions that could decide the war pertaining specifically to the defenses at the points where the Red Army planned its secret counterattack. Rachel Dübendorfer asked Rudolf Rössler—Lucy: "Where were the German defenses to the southeast of Stalingrad, and along the Don? Where had lines of defense been established on the line from Stalingrad to Kletskaya and exactly where were the 11th and 18th Armored Divisions and the 15th Motorized Division which were previously engaged on the Briansk-Volkhov front?"[30]

The defenses south and east of Stalingrad and at Kletskaya were the staging grounds for the planned Red Army offensive. Information about the German defenses there—or, as it turned out, the lack of German defenses—would be crucial to the offensive's success or failure.

On November 10, the director asked Rado to contact the Lucy group immediately and answer the following questions: "1) What is the current position of the 11th and 18th armoured divisions and the 25th mobile division that were previously engaged in the Bryansk-Bolkhov sector? 2) Is Weichs's army group already in existence? Composition and staffs? 3) Is there yet a Guderian army group? Which armies belong to it? Where are their staffs?"[31]

When the main battle came, Moscow would be informed.

Inside Stalingrad there developed surreal fighting unparalleled in this war. Every pile of rock and every toppled rooftop seemed to hide a Red Army sniper. Whole battalions fought over single scarred and blackened structures that often passed hands several times before one side could claim victory. The Russians fought with a tenacity that the Germans could not believe. More than a few soldiers wrote home complaining of the "subhumans" who fought crazily, ignoring danger and disdaining all forms of civilized warfare.

But slowly a pattern developed. The Germans, haltingly but more or less steadily, contracted the Russians into an ever-smaller pocket. Hitler, it seemed, was winning.

To improve this illusion while at the same time ensuring that Hitler did not, in fact, win, Marshal Zhukov had to get enough troops into the Stalingrad pocket each day to stop the Germans. He had to do this in such a way that he did not seriously deplete the Red Army forces gathering in the wings for the main offensive. His choices were limited. The only way to reinforce the Soviet's Stalingrad fortress was by boat across the Volga. And the only time that this had any chance of succeeding was at night, when German gunners would be hampered by the darkness. So Zhukov organized a ragtag flotilla of boats and near boats to make the daring sprint across the Volga.

For the often-raw recruits who had to cross the Volga, the only thing worse than arriving at Stalingrad was running the gauntlet to get there. German gunners made great sport of sinking the Russian craft, darkness or not. Thousands of raw Red Army troops bloodied the river. Zhukov knew that some men would decide that the risk was not worth it and would jump off the rafts and boats and try to make it back to the safety of the east bank. To discourage this, NKVD machine gunners shot those in the water who tried to return.

Through such desperate measures, Zhukov managed to ferry five Red Army divisions across the Volga and into the inferno. These men neither increased nor decreased the Red Army forces. They merely replaced "wastage."[32]

Once in the city itself, the Russian troops had only a marginally better chance of surviving. But now any possibility of retreat was gone. With their backs against the Volga, these men faced the guns of the Wehrmacht only a few hundred yards away. They could not go forward or backward; they were trapped in a crushing vice. Fearful men could die as heroes or cowards. Because dying seemed inevitable either way, most chose to be heroes. These soldiers brought a new type of fighting to a new type of war. These were the "subhumans" whose fight was not only hard and strong but was conducted with that certain arrogance of men who knew that they had already cheated death. These men became the legends and heroes of Stalingrad.

KLETSKAYA

Though most of the soldiers who got across the Volga were killed, wounded, or captured, their sacrifice served the Red Army well. Paulus became preoccupied with this steady and irritating stream of men, and as he heaped more lead on them he ignored what was happening on his flanks.

There, the Red Army was assembling. Stalin's massive gambit was about to unfold.

Zhukov knew that his sheer numbers of men would not be enough to beat the 6th Army. Russians had often had superior numbers, but so far only Hitler had clear victories. The Wehrmacht was nimble and could improvise successful escapes. Besides, the 6th Army was only part of the mass of Germans in the south that could be counted on to try to reverse any short-term Russian advantage. Two things were needed besides overwhelming superiority in men and machines: The Russians needed surprise so that Paulus could not maneuver to meet the enemy or escape, and they needed speed. To win, Zhukov would have to surround Paulus quickly, leaving him with nowhere to go. The plan was for the Russians to adopt German methods of lightning warfare, tactics that the Red Army had paid a price in blood to learn. Still, no one knew for sure if the Russians could successfully conduct a blitzkrieg.

Zhukov planned to launch the northern pincer from the bridgehead across the Don at Kletskaya, which was being defended by the 3d Romanian Army. Mellenthin later complained bitterly about the Romanians and about German leadership that did not make sure there was no bridgehead across the Don. "Nobody could understand why Rumanian formations had given up part of the huge Don Bend," he complained, "allegedly to save troops for other purposes, but actually yielding an area which it would have been easy to defend, and thus handing over a most valuable bridgehead to the Russians."[33]

Zhukov said that Romanian troops in contrast to the Germans were "not so well-armed nor battle-wise or efficient . . . Their soldiers and even many officers did not want to die for interests foreign to them . . ."[34] Therefore they would prove the ideal formations to attack.

A military pincer movement demands two pincers. The Kletskaya bridgehead in the north would have to be aimed at another coming up from the south. The Soviets wanted to know from where exactly the southern pincer should emerge and had asked Gisela's family in Switzerland to tell them. Lucy, with her impressive sources inside the Third Reich, provided the answer. She told the Center: "The German army high command sees no possibility of the Soviets assembling troops in the uninhabited semi-desert known as the 'Black Fields' south-east of Stalingrad. The flank of the German army is consequently unprotected here."[35]

The Center's demands on Gisela's family now increased steadily. At the end of October, the Center radioed Rado: "The work of your organization is at present more important than ever. You must do everything to continue the work."[36]

THIS DAY WAS DIFFERENT

The great Russian offensive against the flanks of the Axis forces began at 5 A.M. on November 19. From the fog-enshrouded area around Kletskaya came first the hiss of the feared Russian Katyusha rockets, followed by the roar of 2,000 heavy guns and 1,500 mortars. In Stalingrad it had been an unusually quiet night, but by dawn the foot soldiers who heard the distant concussion knew that the war had suddenly changed. "Although the Russian artillery had always been quite good," observed one German soldier, "they would not keep up their fire for long periods at a time. But this day was different . . . continuous drum-fire since dawn with the scream of a Katyusha discharge every minute or so."[37]

Zhukov had achieved the first part of his master plan. The Germans were caught completely by surprise. Not only did Hitler have no sources in Stalin's High Command, he even lacked routine tactical intelligence that should have detected the vast Red Army force that had been collecting at Kletskaya.

It had been a grievous error. But even now, as the most concentrated artillery bombardment in the war was well under way, the German leaders could not actually convince themselves of what was apparent. They had been fools.

At 8:48 A.M. the great barrage ended. Two minutes later, Russian tanks and infantry poured into Romanian lines. Within a mere six hours, the Romanian 3d Army was in total rout and the Russians raced toward Kalach, a vital junction west of Stalingrad. If the Germans were to stand any chance of escape, they had to act decisively and immediately. They did not; instead they believed that what was happening could not be happening. The 48th Panzer Corps, stationed behind Kalach, had been held in strategic reserve. Hitler and his generals believed that this force could deal with what they still convinced themselves to be a local anomaly northwest of Stalingrad. Besides, the Germans believed, Paulus's right flank was intact. If an escape was needed, the 6th Army could always escape to the south.

This illusion evaporated the next morning as the second Russian pincer exploded from the southeast, cutting through the Romanian 4th Army and heading to join the northern arm near Kalach. Finally, the Germans were alarmed. If the Russians succeeded in this offensive, the 6th Army would be surrounded.

Still, neither Paulus nor Hitler grasped the true peril. What needed to be done—punching through the closing vice—no one yet proposed. To be fair, even if they knew exactly the Russian positions, it is not clear whether Hitler or Paulus could have done much about it. The Germans had not had enough power to conquer Zhukov's more limited forces at their thin bridgehead in Stalingrad. How could the 6th Army be expected to turn around and beat Zhukov's much superior force in the rear? By the evening of November 21, Hitler at least knew that the focus of the 6th Army would have to change to give it a chance to survive. Instead of pointing east toward Stalingrad, it would have to hold the perimeter in the west and southwest "under all circumstances."[38] This meant defending the army's communications through Kalach. But it was already a mere two days into the battle, too late to do even this. On November 22, the great Red Army pincers closed around the 6th Army's neck twelve miles southeast of Kalach.

The next day the Germans were on the verge of doing something that could have actually been useful. On November 23, German engineers were ordered to demolish the great bridge at Kalach. Though it was over this bridge on the Don that vital German supplies had for months passed through to Stalingrad, the Germans now realized that the bridge was more important to the Russians than the Germans. The 6th Army was already cut off. But as the German engineers strapped the explosive charges to the bridge's columns, they saw three armored personnel carriers from the 22d Panzer rushing from the west—reinforcements, they assumed, against the Russians. A German lieutenant ordered troops to raise the bridge barrier to let the reinforcements through.

It was not a good decision. The carriers stopped dead on the bridge and disgorged sixty Russians with Tommy guns. The engineers were killed or captured. The Russians secured the bridge, and soon twenty-five Russian tanks streamed over it toward Stalingrad.[39]

Paulus was now alarmed. But his telegram to Hitler showed that he still did not fully understand the situation. He told the Führer, "[The] enemy have not yet succeeded in closing the gap to west and south-west," when in fact that gap was closed. Paulus, however, did tell Hitler that it was time to break out. "[I]t is essential to withdraw all our divisions from Stalingrad and northern front. Inevitable consequences will be that army must be able to drive through in south-west, neither north nor east fronts being tenable after this withdrawal."[40]

The next day Hitler told Paulus that the 6th Army was surrounded and could not immediately escape. "The Army must be persuaded that I shall do all in my power to supply it adequately and to disengage it when the time is convenient," Hitler reassured Paulus.[41]

The OKW war diary betrays a certain cynicism in the Führer's reassurances. It reads: "25 November, 1942. The 6th Army which is now surrounded has held its fronts, though its supply situation is critical and, in view of the unfavorable winter weather and the enemy superiority in fighters, it is very doubtful whether the 700 tons of food, ammunition, fuel, etc. per day, which the Army has requested, can be transported to the pocket by air. Air Fleet 4 has only 298 transport planes, whereas 500 are required."[42]

Even 500 planes would not have been enough. It soon became clear that if the 6th Army were to be relieved, it would have to be by land. The only force that had a chance of doing that was Hoth's.

CAPTURED

As Hitler dispatched the fateful news to Paulus,[43] the German secret police began to close in on the Red Army spy network in Belgium and France. Conducted by the Sonderkommando, a special unit of the Abwehr, and parts of the Reich Main Security Office (RSHA), this effort would eventually have a major impact on Gisela's family and the conduct of the war.

The Sonderkommando had two main targets: the head of the Red underground, labeled by the Germans as the "grand chef" (great chief), and his lieutenant, called the "petit chef" (little chief). The great chief was Trepper, whom the Germans considered one of the most important men in Europe at the time. The little chief was known to the Germans as Victor Sukulov (sometimes known as "Sukolov"), or simply "Kent," who had helped establish a Red Army intelligence network inside Germany itself. The two originally operated in Belgium under the cover of the Foreign Excellent Trenchcoats Company. After the invasion of the Low Countries, Trepper left for Paris, where he established a new firm called Simex. Sukulov remained behind as managing partner of a sister company called Simexco. It was excellent cover. Trepper did business with the Todt Organization, one of Nazi Germany's major contractors. As such, he received a special passport allowing him to travel freely around Nazi-occupied Europe as he collected intelligence from dozens of sources.

But Trepper's most important contact was with Sukulov in Brussels. Sukulov controlled the best and at times the only wireless link to Moscow that served not only Trepper's interests but those of a Red underground organization in Germany itself. Collectively, the Germans called the organization the Red Orchestra.[44]

It would have been better for the orchestra had the German wing been able to secure wireless contact on its own, but it was never able to do so. As such, the two key German spy rings—one headed by Harro Schulze-Boysen, a liaison officer for the Luftwaffe's chiefs of staff, and another by Oberregierungsrat Arvid Harnack, a top civil servant in the German Reich Ministry of Economics—depended on Sukulov's network.[45]

That was a fatal flaw. To handle intelligence from Germany, France, and his own group in Belgium, Sukulov's key transmitter was obliged to operate for five hours a day, from midnight to 5 A.M.[46] The Germans intercepted the signals, but not even the best German mathematician was able to decode them. The Abwehr was tasked to locate the transmitter. At first it could tell only that the broadcasting station was in Brussels. German agents lost precious time trying to infiltrate the Belgium Communist Party, an organization that knew nothing of Sukulov's operation. But owing to the five-hour nightly broadcasts, German radiomen were able to pinpoint Kent's radio operators. On December 13, 1941, German soldiers, wearing socks on their boots to reduce noise, raided the station. The Germans almost won the grand prize as Trepper managed to arrive just as the Germans were conducting their search. He passed himself off as a rabbit salesman and escaped to bedevil the Germans for another year. Warned by Trepper, Kent was also able to escape, slipping away to Marseilles.[47]

But the bleeding that was to kill the Red Orchestra had begun. With the help of some of those arrested and an abundance of seized coding material, the Germans by July 16, 1942 had realized that the agent they knew of only as "Choro" was Schulze-Boysen, and the agent known as "Wolf" was Dr. Harnack.[48]

The Gestapo did not immediately arrest the principals but tried to determine how extensive their network was. It was almost embarrassing for the Gestapo to learn that this important web of spies had seen little need to disguise their operations. The Red agents used uncoded and easily tapped telephones to arrange their meetings and even sent one another their plans through the public mail service, again with nothing in code.[49]

The Gestapo arrested Schulze-Boysen on August 30. Within four weeks, sixty others were arrested and shipped off for interrogation at Gestapo headquarters on Prinz-Albrechtstrasse. Subjected to "intensified interrogation," the Red Orchestra sang out the names of fifty-seven others who had helped.[50]

While the Gestapo executed Schulze-Boysen and his wife, Libertas, as well as Harnack and scores of others, the Germans closed in on Sukulov. The task of tracking down the "chefs" fell to Karl Giering and his Sonderkommando. Giering arrested Sukulov on November 12, 1942.[51] The Germans soon learned of the connection of the grand chef to Simex, and the company was raided. The arrest of Trepper, known to unwitting Simex employees as Jean Gilbert, was almost sure to follow.*

As with so much of the history of the Red underground, there are at least three differing but sympathizing versions of exactly what happened next. Intelligence historian David Dallin wrote that the Germans recovered a notebook from "Gilbert's" office at Simex that listed the date of a dental appointment.[52] The CIA instead found that the director of Simex, Alfred Corbin, told the Germans of the dental appointment.[53] Trepper himself said that it was Corbin's wife—warned that her husband's life depended on her answer—who gave up the information.[54]

For whatever reason, Giering's forces surrounded the offices of one Dr. Maleplate on November 16 (Dallin's version) or November 24 (Trepper's version) or December 5 (the CIA's version). But in all versions the consequence was the same. As Trep-

---

*One report by Dallin, p. 165, has Trepper being arrested first. This appears to be in error.

per was about to sit down for the dental examination, the Germans burst in.

"Hände hoch," shouted a burly man with a revolver aimed at Trepper's head. Trepper slowly raised his hands and said that he was not armed.

As with the precise date of his arrest, what happened in the hours and days following the arrest also depends upon who is telling the story. The Germans say one thing, the Americans another, and Trepper still a third. What is clear is that Trepper's arrest ushered in a new and dangerous time for the Soviet spy networks and the conduct of the war.

German reports claim that Trepper almost immediately offered to turn against Moscow and help the Sonderkommando roll up the Red Army underground in Europe. In exchange for his cooperation, Trepper asked only that the Germans conceal his predicament by allowing him to continue to communicate with the Center. Of course, he said, all such messages would be written by the Kommando itself. Trepper explained the reasoning behind this audacious plan: He was worried that his family in Moscow would be liquidated if the Center knew of his arrest. The Germans were skeptical and demanded that Trepper provide proof of his new allegiances. He did so by arranging for the arrest of his personal assistant, Hillel Katz.[55]

The Germans were amazed. The person whom they thought was their most dangerous secret enemy had turned on a dime.

Within three weeks, they began a "playback,"or *funkspiel,* game with the Center. The Germans explained that they were determined to keep Trepper's transmitters working in order to ferret out Red Army operations in Europe. To the Germans, the game succeeded, and they learned much from Trepper and the director in Moscow.

One German commander of the operations said that Trepper told "much more than we ever hoped and much more than was necessary under the circumstances."[56]

Trepper's version is quite different.

After his arrest, Trepper said that Giering told him in a fit of excitement: "I'm delighted. It's been two years since we started

looking for you in all the countries Germany occupies."[57] Giering
then telephoned Hitler and Himmler with the news.[58] Noting
the slippery ways of the "grand chief," Himmler joked, "The best
course could be to tie his hands and feet and bury him alive."[59]

Instead, Giering treated his new ward with respect and civility,
albeit interrupted briefly by a dark threat. After offering Trepper
a cup of coffee, Giering sat back and commented: "You have lost,
and I imagine that you know what fate awaits you. But let me re-
mind you that it is possible to die twice. The first time you will be
shot as an enemy of the Third Reich. But in addition, we can also
have you shot in Moscow as a traitor."[60]

This double entendre Trepper did not immediately understand. How could he be shot in Moscow? Giering did not explain. The next day, in Trepper's account, Giering corrected
this. And there was an important new player in the great game.
Heinrich Müller, head of the Gestapo, watched quietly as Giering no longer threatened death but instead offered Trepper not
only the chance to save his own life but to serve the Soviet Union
in the process.

Giering, Trepper says, began with an astonishing statement:
"The sole objective of the Third Reich is to arrive at peace with
the Soviet Union. The bloodbath that is spreading between the
Wehrmacht and the Red Army can please no one but the capitalist plutocrats. The Führer himself has called Churchill an al-
coholic and Roosevelt a miserable paralytic. But although it is
easy to establish contacts with representatives of the Western
powers in the neutral countries, it is almost impossible to meet
with emissaries of the Soviet government. This problem was in-
soluble for us—until the day we hit upon the idea of utilizing the
Red Orchestra. The broadcasting stations of the network, once
they are working for us, will be the instruments of this advance
toward peace."[61]

Giering went on: "For several months we shall continue to
make these little sacrifices for the greater cause. But when the
time comes that we are convinced that not a shred of suspicion
remains on the Russian side regarding the networks in the west,
then the second phase will begin. On that day your Director will

begin receiving reports of capital importance originating in the highest circles in Berlin, all confirming the fact that we are seeking a separate peace with the Soviet Union.[62] I have revealed our program to you because you are no longer an obstacle to its realization," Giering supposedly said. "You have your choice: either you will collaborate with us, or you will disappear."[63]

Trepper said he assumed at the time that the Germans were "lying brazenly" and the real idea was to set up a channel of disinformation to the Center. However, Trepper said that he thought there could be an advantage to the Center if the game was played well. For a while, the Germans would have to surrender accurate information to the Center in order to gain its confidence. In the meantime, Trepper planned to tip off the Center to the game so that the director could play it on his terms.

Trepper said he betrayed no one, and he denounced those in the network who broke under Gestapo torture.[64]

Trepper's assessment of the potential for the *funkspiel* proved so remarkably true that even he began to have dark questions. The Germans relentlessly surrendered military secrets to the Center. Only days after Trepper's arrest, his group was "obligated to send valuable material in order to reassure Moscow that no transmitter had fallen into the hands of the enemy."[65]

As the battle continued, Moscow demanded that Trepper send more and more detailed information about the exact disposition and intentions of German troops. The Germans obliged.

Soon, Trepper came to an astonishing conclusion. "Careful examination of the questions revealed that Moscow was trying not so much to obtain information as to verify information already in their possession."[66]

Though Trepper did not know it, it was clear where that other information was coming from.

Moscow's only other source of such specific military information was Maria Poliakova's Lucy spy ring. And it was at precisely this time, after Paulus's army was surrounded at Stalingrad, that Werther stepped up the volume and detail of his military intelligence.

Yet there is still a third assessment of Trepper's actions—by the Americans. In a formerly top-secret report on the Red Orchestra and in a later analysis released by the CIA, the Americans agree with the Germans that Trepper betrayed a large part of the Red Orchestra. The report says that Trepper "hastened to give proof of his desire to collaborate by ringing up Hillel Katz, his right-hand man, in the presence of the Germans. This was accepted as a sign of good faith, and in the following weeks Trepper amply fortified their confidence. Directly or indirectly he put his finger on an impressive collection of agents, including his great partner, [Henri] Robinson, in Paris . . . Whatever may have been the truth about the extent of Trepper's authority in the creation and manipulation of R.U. [Russian] networks in the Low Countries and France, there can be no doubt of his importance in their death and destruction."[67]

But the Americans concluded that Trepper was involved in a deeper game than any of his immediate German wardens realized.

Both the top-secret report and the subsequent CIA analysis said that this betrayal was part of a cynical and deadly plan designed by the Center itself. Said the CIA: "As a result of the arrests in the Low Countries [that is, the previous shutting down of Sukulov's network in Belgium] Trepper undoubtedly had seen the writing on the wall and had realized the probability of his own capture. He had ample time before his arrest to discuss this likelihood with Moscow, and it is probable that he and his superiors drew up a 'triple-cross plan' against such an eventuality."[68]

"Within a fortnight," said the American top-secret report, "Trepper seems to have lulled all the suspicions of his enemies and on Christmas Day they began a playback to Moscow on a wireless station which Trepper was supposed to have set up in Paris."[69]

In this case, Trepper was not alone in this treachery. Said the American report: "If it is accepted that Trepper from the first intended and practiced a triple-cross then it seems likely that Sukulov entered his German captivity with a similar plan."[70] The flow from the great game could continue from two sources, both in Russia's service and also—at first unknown to Trepper or Sukulov—perhaps in the service of someone else in the German High Command.[71]

The CIA did not say who this "someone else" might have been, but it clearly referenced his existence. In a 1979 report on the Rote Kapelle, the agency noted: "It is said" that a number of top RSHA officials believed "in the necessity for a compromise agreement with Russia."[72] The agency did not identify the Reich officials who sought "a channel of communication between Russia and the Nazi authorities."[73] But for whatever reasons, the CIA concluded that the *funkspiel* turned sharply against the Germans. The agency said that a review of the intelligence exchange between Trepper and the director revealed "that Moscow profited much more than did Berlin."[74]

The Russians seemed to think so. While Trepper adjusted to his new role, the Center sent his wife, who had been evacuated to central Siberia, a message: "Your husband is a hero. He is working for the victory of our country."

The message was signed by Major Leontiev, Colonel Epstein, and Major (Maria) Poliakova.[75]

Notes

1 NAZ, p. 836.

2 Ibid., p. 838.

3 Goralski, p. 204.

4 RG 226, XL 17234.

5 Ibid.

6 Ibid.

7 Clark, p. 195.

8 Zhukov, *Memoirs,* p. 366.

9 The following descriptions of the three battles, except where noted, came from Alan Clark's *Barbarossa,* pp. 187–219.

10 See Foote's account in *A Handbook for Spies.*

11 NAZ, p. 829.

12 Ibid., p. 839.

13 F. W. von Mellenthin, *Panzer Battles* (New York, N.Y.: Ballantine Books, 1984), p. 189.

14 Clark, p. 192.

15 Ibid., p. 206.

16 Toland, p. 682.

17 Bormann, p. 499.

18 Paul Carell, *Scorched Earth: The Russian German War 1943–1944* (Boston: Little, Brown and Company, 1970), p. 111.

19 Mellenthin, p. 192.

20 Zhukov, *Memoirs,* p. 377.

21 NAZ, p. 843.

22 Volkogonov, p. 461.

23 Clark, p. 209.

24 Mellenthin, p. 193.

25 NAZ, p. 841.

26 Halder, p. 632.

27 Clark, p. 208.

28 NAZ, p. 842.

29 David Irving, *Hitler's War* (New York: Avon Books, 1990), p. 484.

30 Reed and Fisher, p. 141.

31 Rado, p. 153.

32 Clark, p. 232.

33 Mellenthin, p. 199.

34 Zhukov, *Memoirs,* p. 383.

35 Rado, p. 151.

36 Reed and Fisher, p. 143.

37 Clark, p. 246.

38 NAZ, p. 844.

39 Edwin Hoyt, *The Battle for Stalingrad* (New York: Tom Doherty Associates, 1993), pp. 210–11.

40 John Erickson, *The Road to Stalingrad* (New York: Harper & Row, 1975), 11/23/42.

41 Ibid., 11/24/42.

42 NAZ, p. 844.

43 RG 319, Box 60.

44 Ibid.

45 Ibid.

46 David Dallin, *Soviet Espionage* (New Haven: Yale University Press, 1955), p. 152.

47 Ibid., p. 153.

48 Tarrant, pp. 58–59.

49 Ibid., p. 59.

50 Ibid., p. 89.

51 RG 319, Box 60.

52 Dallin, p. 163.

53 CIA, p. 105.

54 Trepper, p. 170.

55 The German version is given in various postwar accounts, including Perrault's *The Red Orchestra* and the CIA's *Rote Kapelle.*

56 CIA, p. 110.

57 Trepper, p. 171.

58 Ibid., p. 172.

59 Ibid.

60 Ibid., p. 174.

61 Ibid., p. 186.

62 Ibid., p. 187.

63 Ibid.

64 Ibid., pp. 186–92.

65 Ibid., p. 191.
66 Ibid., p. 250.
67 RG 319, Box 60.
68 CIA, p. 107.
69 RG 319, Box 60.
70 Ibid.
71 Ibid.
72 CIA, p. 121.
73 Ibid.
74 Ibid., p. 114.
75 Trepper, p. 229.

Chapter Seven

STALEMATE

If we do not capture the oil supplies of the Caucasus by the autumn then I shall have to face the fact that we cannot win this war.[1]

—Adolf Hitler, January 1943

MANSTEIN

After the Russian counterattack at Stalingrad, there were two wars being fought by Germany—one to rescue the 6th Army, the other to save the German armies farther south. At the time, the world knew only of Stalingrad, where the questions seemed simple: Could the 6th Army be saved? Was the Red Army poised finally to win? Could Germany be facing its first major, and perhaps decisive, defeat?

But while the world invested heavily in the symbol of Stalingrad, the German army was vulnerable to a far greater calamity elsewhere. With the 6th Army surrounded and immobile, Stalin was positioned to charge west, into the left flank of the whole of Army Group Don, and from there he could turn south to Rostov. That move would cut off the Caucasus, decapitate Army Group A, and destroy all remaining hopes for the Third Reich. Rostov, not Stalingrad, was the strategic prize of ultimate importance. As bad as the loss of the 6th Army would be, it could not bring an end to the war. The fall of Rostov could. "The issue," wrote Field Marshal Erich von Manstein, "was no longer the fate of a single army but of the entire southern wing of the front and ultimately of all the German armies in the east."[2]

If Stalin had known this, he could have won the war that year. But he became as mesmerized by Stalingrad as the rest of the world was. Though he sent armies to the west to test the Germans, he never broke their back. The chance for victory was missed.

Hitler had his own obsessions. The Führer was not blind to the threat in the south, but he was reluctant to accept the cost of preventing a tragedy there. He had fought this war as much on economic terms as on military ones, believing that possession of the oil at Maikop and the coal of the Donetz Basin were critical for the Reich. Now he might have to choose one or the other or even abandon both. This was a reality that the dictator shunned.

In the first days after the Russian counterattack at Stalingrad, Hitler equivocated. Neither he nor the rest of his general staff realized that his hand would soon be forced. Hitler's first instinct, as it had been the year before at Moscow, was to hold out. He forbade Paulus and his 6th Army from breaking out of Stalingrad— not in a single order, and not absolutely, but evidenced over time by a steady resolve. The Stalingrad wasteland, Hitler decided, should be held. The Führer told Paulus to adopt a "hedge-hog defense" and wait for reinforcements.

At first Hitler acted as though he had faith that through this action the city could actually be held. Göring had promised 550 tons of supplies a day from the air, and General Hoth said that it was possible to bring his imposing 4th Panzer Army, now lodged to the south of the battle, north to punch a hole into the belly of the Russian forces. Hitler grasped both chances. He told Göring to start his air armada immediately and ordered Hoth to "bring the enemy attacks to a standstill and recapture the positions previously occupied by us."[3]

Hitler was hoping for a miracle, but he was not blind to a broader view. He cast a wary eye at Rostov, the German Achilles' heel. But he did not know what to do to stave off defeats at Stalingrad and Rostov, nor did his generals. For the first time, the general staff sensed that the Führer was adrift. The German War Diary reported: "As before, no decisions were taken: it looks as if the Führer is no longer capable of making them."[4]

It was a harsh and temporary judgment by a group of men who had never been sympathetic toward Hitler. However, Hitler was in a box. All the complaining in the world could not show him or anyone else an easy way out. Worse, Hitler was by habit almost functionally incapable of handling the situation. He had proven himself a great offensive strategist who now confronted the type of war he did not understand. In the past he had gambled everything for the sake of victory. Now he needed to wage the same stakes on the mere chance of a stalemate. Hitler brooded, casting about for some simple answer. A tremor started in his left arm. He lost sleep. The Wolfsschanze became as cold and dank as Hitler's heart.

Yet Hitler did one thing that proved critical. When he was least able to act on his own, he knew enough to appoint someone in authority. He called upon Manstein, a general who rivaled Hitler in strategic vision but also knew about defense and strategic reserves. There are few times in history when two leaders have had more synergy than what grew between Hitler and Manstein. To this day no one knows who should be given the most credit for their combined plan to invade France. There they sought success. Now they needed to avoid defeat.

Hitler continued to incline toward standing pat, fighting to the last. Manstein, the Blitzkrieg general, favored maneuver and strategic depth. Neither appeared willing to compromise. The tension between these points of view saved the Third Reich for a year.

As Manstein headed south to take up his new command as leader of the newly created Army Group Don, which included the 6th Army, he met von Kluge, commander of Army Group Center. Kluge offered Manstein only pessimism, warning, "You will find it impossible to move any formation larger than a battalion without first referring back to the Führer."[5]

Even without such interference, Manstein felt that he faced overwhelming odds. The 6th Army and its twenty divisions were encased by sixty Russian divisions.[6] Hoth's 4th Panzer Army farther south had little space to move, and the 48th Panzer Corps, which had been defending the rear of the 6th Army, was being savaged by Russian armor. Added to this dismal picture was a sudden appearance in quantity of the new Russian tank, the T-34. Nothing in the armies or the rest of the world, including the Wehrmacht, had an answer for the T-34. The Germans could not disable it at a distance and faced suicide trying to get in close. The Russians were also machining artillery as only the Russians could: huge, simple, and deadly.

Facing a paucity of materiel and reserves, Manstein sought aid from von Kleist's Army Group A in the south. But neither Kleist nor Hitler was immediately moved. Kleist wanted to keep his force intact, whereas Hitler still held to the dream that he could retain the Caucasus.

More immediate to Manstein than any problems to the south was the plight of the 6th Army. Saving this force was Manstein's first responsibility. On the evening of November 24, Manstein thought that it was "still possible" for at least the armor of Paulus's forces to break out of the Stalingrad pocket. But Manstein knew that such a move, if possible at all, would come at an enormous, perhaps unbearable, moral price. For although there just might be enough petroleum to power the heavy armor away from the Stalingrad pocket, there would be nothing left for the infantry. The foot soldier would have to be sacrificed.[7] Added to this burden, Manstein faced the clear inclination of Hitler, who had seldom been wrong in the past. "We can never replace what we have there," said Hitler. "If we give it up, we in fact give up the whole object of this campaign."[8]

Manstein hesitated. Göring was promising relief, and Hoth was preparing to drive his panzers north. Manstein said that the 6th Army should stay put until the Red Army checked these moves. Hitler himself set forth the calculation: If Hoth got within twenty miles of Stalingrad, Manstein could try his breakout. If not, there were other things to worry about.[9] Simple logistics argued against the quick breakout, which some postwar historians seem to think was possible. Manstein knew that even if an immediate decision was made, the army could not simply decide to break out and be done with it. It would take a "ram" formation to attempt a breakout, and at least four full days would be needed to put the ram together. As such, the earliest that the Germans could attempt the breakout was November 28.[10]

Even then, all depended on Hoth's panzers. If they could not make it to within the Führer's dictated twenty-mile minimum,

Paulus could ram the Russians all he wanted. He would not break out.

Hoth could not begin his main thrust to relieve Stalingrad until December 10. The plan—code-named "Winter Tempest"—aimed to reach Beketonskaya, where German forces would be close enough to the 6th Army that Paulus could try the gamble with his armor. If getting to Beketonskaya proved too difficult, Hoth was to link up with the 48th Panzer Corps farther west, where they could combine to punch through Red Army lines. Hitler told Paulus that he could move if Hoth's forces achieved either goal. Paradoxically, Hitler also ordered that in such a case, the 6th Army must maintain its perimeter.[11] Obviously, an army could not retreat and maintain its perimeter at the same time, so Manstein ignored this stricture. If the situation of a breakout presented itself, the perimeter could be damned.

By December 17, the leading tanks of the 4th Panzer Army were at Aksia, only thirty-five miles from the Russian siege guns at Stalingrad.[12] For a shimmering moment, it seemed that the impossible plan was possible after all.

Then hope died.

ZHUKOV ACTS

German plans had called for Marshal Zhukov to behave like a Russian, a slave to inflexible doctrine, committed to mass attack and mass defense. According to this, the Germans thought that Zhukov would send the bulk of his armor south to meet their advance. If there was one thing that the Germans had demonstrated so far, it was their superiority at maneuver. This was the one real chance that Germany still had for Stalingrad. But for reasons not understood at the time, Zhukov did not oblige. Some armor went to meet Hoth, but Zhukov had different plans for his striking force.

The Germans did not know that the German traitor Werther was already sending Stalin the German rescue plans. Nor did they know that somehow this spy had direct access to the deliberations of the high command. But several generals were becoming increasingly annoyed about the stenographers who were always at the staff conferences. Göring complained, "The working methods of the headquarters [are] quite wrong, especially the fact that stenographers are always present during the staff conferences and take down every word."[13] Bormann's stenographers were relentless.

Even with the leaks from the high command, there was so far in this war scant evidence that even the best-informed Russian general could counter the battlefield wits of the Germans. Marshal Zhukov, if he mishandled the precious intelligence, could go down like the others, a Red Army gnat.

But Zhukov was not like his predecessors. Though as ruthless as any man in this war, as merciless as Stalin himself, Zhukov knew how to win. And he alone in this conflict had the will to stand up to the Soviet dictator, to force upon the *Stavka* his own vision of how the battle could be resolved. Zhukov, as well as Manstein and Hitler, could read a map. If Hoth's forces were invested in the south, then the west, according to Werther, was largely open. If that was where the Germans were not, Zhukov reasoned that it was there that the Russians should be. It is not known whether Zhukov saw all the way to the prize of Rostov, but it is clear that he was looking in that direction.

By December 7, two Red Army tank brigades crossed the principal German defensive line along the River Chir, west of Stalingrad. It was a preliminary action, but for the Germans it was the first of many shocks. By nightfall, the Russians had penetrated twenty miles into the German lines, settling in at State Farm 79. A German division had been trying for a counterattack and asked desperately for help. It was now that one of Germany's best panzer generals came to the fore. General Hermann Balck, commander of the 11th Panzer Division, was ordered to relieve the 336th Infantry. But as German generals would do during the next five months, he decided to interpret his orders liberally. Instead of rushing headlong into the enemy's strongpoint, Balck daringly drove his troops and tanks at nighttime in a wide arc around the state farm. At dawn on December 8, just as the Soviets were preparing to mop up the 336th Division, Balck attacked from the rear and pulverized the enemy.[14] He continued to have success for several days. Soon it was apparent that if Zhukov was to win in the west, he would have to obtain it with more force. The German generals were still masters of open warfare.

It was not a great loss for Zhukov. In fact, it showed him the way. As for Hoth's mighty panzer army coming up from the south of free Stalingrad, Zhukov seemed to shrug. Even if they reached Paulus, they would merely become enveloped in a larger pocket. Army Group Don would still be isolated and destructible. Instead, Zhukov would gamble. He would attack to the west in as much force as Stalin would allow.

Stalin did not fully understand the concept; but like his German counterpart, he had begun to loosen his iron grip on his most gifted general. If Zhukov wanted to attack to the west, Stalin would let him do it—but within what Stalin considered reasonable bounds.

On December 16, Zhukov began his move. This was not a probing attack, nor was it an all-out offensive. But it was far more than the Germans expected. They were suddenly outnumbered and surprised. Worse, the Soviets had again chosen to attack the weak link in the Axis line, the area mostly defended by the Italians. Germany's hapless cousins were quickly overrun, and a sixty-mile-wide breach opened in the front. Suddenly, little stood in the way of the Red Army and the road to Rostov on Don. The Red Army was only 185 miles from the prize.[15]

Manstein, Hoth, and Hitler knew that they now faced a critical juncture. If Zhukov pressed, von Kleist and the entire southern front would be cut off.

Manstein's hand was forced. He could not afford to keep Hoth's panzers together as a single attacking *schwerpunkt* (spearhead). Hoth had to relinquish one of the three panzer divisions under his command—the 6th Panzer—to meet Zhukov's threat. Stripped of its most powerful unit, Hoth's army lost any realistic chance of reaching Stalingrad.

"At this juncture," summarized German general F. W. von Mellenthin, "the Russian Command showed strategic insight of a high order—Marshal Zhukov was commanding their armies on the Volga-Don front, with Marshal Vasilievski as his chief of staff. Instead of concentrating their reserves to meet Hoth's thrust, they unleashed a new offensive on a massive scale against the unfortunate Italian Eighth Army on the middle of the Don . . . The crisis on our own front and the collapse of the Italians not only forced the cancellation of the 11th Panzer's attack across the Don, but compelled Manstein to draw heavily on Hoth's Fourth Army in order to build up a new front to cover Rostov. This decided the fate of the Sixth Army at Stalingrad."[16]

As clear as this was after the war, it had not yet fully crystallized for the generals fighting the battle. Hoth was fifteen miles from Hitler's goal, and Manstein was not ready to admit that the job he had been asked to do could not be done. Manstein made one last and futile effort to convince Hitler to let Paulus try to ram through to Hoth's army. That would be suicide without benefit, Hitler said. Even Paulus agreed, saying that he had insufficient fuel for such an operation.[17]

The decision was a relief to the commander of Army Group Don. Released from a moral obligation to Paulus and his men, Manstein could concentrate his considerable powers on the task of repairing a front that was at risk of being shredded. If there was guilt to be carried, it would be Hitler's, Manstein reasoned.

Hitler did not flinch. The 6th Army still had a purpose, still could contribute greatly to the Reich. Wrote Manstein: "After the start of the Soviet offensive, it was clear that the [6th] army was to be lost for good and that the best it could do within the framework of the operation as a whole was to tie down the largest possible body of forces for the longest possible period."[18] But to tie down the Red Army meant that the 6th Army could not surrender. So that was what Hitler now ordered. The army was to fight to the last bullet.

Many historians after the war ascribed this decision to the Führer's legendary callousness and indifference to life. The decision, though, was far more practical. Hitler wanted to use the 6th Army for the same goal that Manstein later wrote about—as a lure to distract Stalin from the greater prize farther south.

The lure was attractive. Paulus still had under his command 230,000 men, 100 tanks, and 1,800 big guns. That this force had already been defeated might have been clear to Zhukov and a few others, but it was not clear to Stalin. The Soviet dictator restrained the marshal from charging full force into his new western offensive while the task behind was not complete. Stalingrad, he said, must be reduced before fully undertaking the new ambitious adventure.

The consequences of Stalin's obsession are clear. More than half the Red Army forces in the south were devoted to the singular task of crushing Paulus. As long as the 6th Army stayed where it was, the Red Army would also be immobile. Hitler's tactic worked. If it was morally bankrupt, Hitler did not care. "Whatever succeeds is right," he told his generals.[19]

Was Hitler solely responsible? Long after the war, historian Alan Clark noted: "The whole question of Stalingrad and the fate of the 6th Army is so clouded with guilt in the German mind that in holding an inquiry twenty years after, it is almost impossible to find any 'witness' who had told the whole truth."[20] Clark noted, however, that it was "conventional fiction" to believe that a breakout by the 6th Army was prevented by Hitler. The taking of the Kalach bridge prevented an easy breakout, and it was Hitler who had ordered that defending the Kalach area was the 6th Army's primary goal. Once that operation failed, little could have been done that was not done.

Hitler's responsibility for the debacle came before the Russian counterattack, not afterward. Hitler ignored all evidence that there was a spy working beside him, and he did little to ensure that the Germans had quality intelligence of their own. That Russians were able to concentrate more than half of all their forces in a small front along the Volga and the Don without the Germans knowing their peril will be remembered as one of the world's greatest intelligence failures. Hitler had lost track of the Red Army, had too long ignored the bridgehead at Kletskaya, and had completely overlooked the bunching of Soviet forces in the southeast. Those failures, and not Hitler's subsequent orders, lost Stalingrad.

MOBILE DEFENSE

Away from the tragic pocket, Manstein grasped for a much more mobile defense than the one Hitler had used in front of Moscow the year before. There, Hitler had said to hold to the last, and that formula had worked. Manstein knew that such tactics could not succeed again, because there were simply too many vital targets where the Germans were vulnerable. Worse, the Russians now were fighting with a certain smartness, aided by their Swiss friends to be sure, and were not going to miss for long the main chance. Besides, whereas it had been so cold in front of Moscow that both sides froze to a stop, the weather was more moderate in the south. Both sides now could move. Manstein intended to use that to his advantage.

He planned a leapfrog defense, with the first aim of protecting the rear of the Southern Army Group long enough for it to extricate itself from most of the Caucasus. That accomplished, he would shore up communications to make it possible for that army to survive. Only then would he counterattack.[21] The plan involved great risk and would take great luck to succeed, but Manstein thought that it was the only way. To win, he said, "The German command had to improvise again and again, and the fighting troops [had to] perform unparalleled feats."[22] His visions of a mobile defense were in keeping with the ones that Lee had perfected in Virginia. Of course, Lee finally lost that argument to Grant, but not before he proved that vulnerable forces could survive if they refused to join battles where they did not hold an advantage. Manstein had no intention of losing this one to Zhukov.

Through brilliant counterstrokes and some miscalculation by the Russians, by late December Manstein had stemmed the Soviet threat to Rostov, at least for a moment. On the twenty-ninth came Hitler's reluctant approval of the plan to withdraw the eastern wing of Army Group A. This went a long way—but not all the way—in erasing forever Hitler's goal of controlling the Caucasus.

While Manstein tried to salvage the future of the southern wing, the Russians prepared for the final implosion of Stalingrad. That battle for the remaining pocket at Stalingrad, one of the great mismatches in military history, would begin in early January. There was now no question of Paulus breaking out and no delusions that the 6th Army could do anything worthwhile for the German war effort except to function—as Hitler had planned—as a lure. The 6th Army could exist for only a few more days. Paulus pleaded with Hitler to allow the Germans to surrender when it was no longer possible to "avoid complete annihilation." Hitler refused. As Paulus should have known, the Führer wanted the army to "fight to the last man."[23] Hitler was merely playing out his hand. The men who would perish in the effort, he thought, should be quiet and die well.

Hitler took it for granted that Paulus would see this, fight until there was nothing left, then put his final bullet in his brain. Paulus fulfilled much of the bargain, and the results were as Hitler wanted. As January advanced, Zhukov kept the bulk of the Soviet southern forces encamped around Stalingrad, where they outmanned the Germans more than two to one.

On January 8, Zhukov had seen enough. The fighting, he thought, was doing neither side any good. He sent Paulus an offer for an "honourable surrender . . . sufficient rations . . . care for the wounded . . . officers to keep their weapons . . . repatriation after the war to Germany or any other country."[24] Though spiritually beaten down, Paulus did not yet surrender. So on January 10 the Russians began their final offensive against the German pocket. Now it seemed only a matter of days, or even hours, before the Germans would be crushed. In fact, it took three more horrible weeks of dying. In part, the Germans were roused by a rumor that spread after Paulus had rejected the Russian ultimatum. Zhukov, the rumor said, had issued orders that no German soldier would be taken alive.

On January 23, the last German airstrip was captured. With that, no more supplies could reach the Germans. Seven days later, Stalingrad's southern pocket collapsed and Paulus was captured. He had not put a bullet in his brain. Two days later, all resistance ended. To the world, the Russians had gained a decisive victory.

Hitler was beside himself, not in rage but in disbelief. He had known for weeks that the battle was lost, but he could not figure out Paulus. Hitler had named him a field marshal knowing that no other German field marshal had ever allowed himself to be captured. Paulus had acted selfishly. "There will be no more field marshals in this war," Hitler declared. "We'll only promote them after the end of the war. I won't go on counting my chickens before they're hatched."[25]

Hitler asked his courtiers, "What is life? Life is the nation. The individual must die anyway. But how anyone can be afraid of this moment of death, with which he can free himself from his misery, if his duty doesn't chain him to that Vale of Terror? Na!"[26] Hitler predicted that in a few weeks Paulus and the other surrendering general officers, after the Russians forced them to make anti-Nazi speeches, would find themselves "in the Lubyanka, and there the rats will eat them. How can one be so cowardly? I don't understand it."[27]

Paulus might well have improved his standing in German history if he had done what Hitler suggested—fight to the last. When he finally surrendered, 90,000 Germans were still alive. Although most never made it to the Lubyanka, they died terrible deaths nonetheless. Only 6,000 were to survive the war.[28] Some 84,000 would have been just as dead had they fought a few days longer.

HITLER'S MATCH

Away from Stalingrad, where critical battles were shaping up, Manstein had done wonders. He had kept open escape routes for Army Group A in the Caucasus while closing and concentrating his forces. With the defeat of Stalingrad on his mind, Hitler seemed less able than ever to take over the map room and run the war in detail. He had found his general in Manstein and, for now, he was going to stick with him. He was also begrudgingly coming to believe that Manstein might be right: The way to defeat the Russians was to turn their advantage back upon themselves. "Space is one of the most important military factors," Hitler told Jodl. "You can conduct military operations only if you have space . . ."[29] Where the Russians had blunted the best Hitler could offer the year before by disappearing into the vast steppe, the Germans could now do the same.

But Hitler was nothing if not a man of habit, and retreating was not one of his. So although he understood the military concept of depth espoused by Manstein, Hitler hardly liked to see all those swastikas being moved back on the situation room map. During the next few days, wherever Hitler looked, he found that Manstein was taking too much advantage of this new approach. A red tide seemed to be sweeping west. The general had abandoned Millerovo, Russochska, and Kantemirovka, and he was insisting on a withdrawal for the Mius. What was being gained, the Führer wondered, from such headlong losses? Hitler had allowed Manstein freedom of movement, but he had balanced that with orders to defend wherever possible. But for the general, the possible never seemed to exist. Manstein later recalled: "If Hitler thought he could order us, in the face of that preponderance of forces and with such an expanse of territory to cover, to make the army hold some 'line' or other, or else to obtain his approval before undertaking any withdrawal, he was seriously mistaken."[30]

Hitler continued to indulge Manstein's plans, even allowing a tactical withdrawal from the Caucasus of the 1st Panzer Army on January 24. But when Manstein showed that he was clearly ready to surrender parts of the Donetz Basin, albeit for only a short time, Hitler had had enough.

On February 6, Hitler ordered Manstein to attend a conference at the Wolf's Lair. Everyone expected it to be a stormy affair. Manstein was the commander who had been sent to rescue the 6th Army, and now the 6th Army did not exist. He had been entrusted to stop the Red Army before it could threaten the Caucasus, and now the Caucasus was being evacuated. The Donetz Basin and all its coal reserves seemed next on Manstein's list of tactical withdrawals. No one expected Hitler to stand for any more of Manstein's gambles. The general would be lucky to leave the conference with his head intact.

But instead of seeing bombast, Manstein saw the side of Hitler unknown to most of the world, the side that Guderian had seen.

"Hitler," Guderian told interrogators, "was able to convince every-body that his decisions were right through his personal charm, throughout the war."[31] This was one of those occasions. Instead of accusing Manstein of losing Stalingrad, as many expected, Hitler took all the responsibility on himself. He did not berate Manstein. The fault, Hitler said, was none of Manstein's, nor was it any other general's. Hitler said that he alone caused the defeat. "I had the impression," Manstein later wrote, "that he was deeply affected by this tragedy, not just because it amounted to a blatant failure of his own leadership, but also because he was deeply de-pressed in a purely personal sense by the fate of the soldiers who, out of faith in him, had fought to the last with such courage and devotion to duty."[32] The hard general even admitted to being a bit taken by Hitler's demeanor. "Whether deliberately or uncon-sciously, he had thus shown considerable psychological skill in the way he opened our discussion. He always did have a masterly knack of adapting his manner to his interlocutor."[33]

If Hitler was softening up his prey, it was not yet clear what his endgame was. The two talked about the Donetz Basin, with Hitler wanting to keep it and Manstein wanting to use it for the third phase of his plan—the trap. Hitler, he said, listened to this theory "with the utmost composure." But it was clear that the Führer did not agree. For four hours the men went at it, debat-ing as gentlemen, almost as equals. Finally, in Manstein's version, he (Manstein) refused to consider any more of Hitler's talk about halting the withdrawal of Manstein's army group. Hitler's will, Manstein believed, was finally broken on the back of hard reality. The Führer agreed to the withdrawal of Manstein's army from the Mius.

Hitler saw things differently. He thought that he had carried the day, having persuaded Manstein to slow his withdrawals and, wherever possible, strike back. Hitler had taken special ac-tion to ensure that the vital junction of Kharkov was not surren-dered to the Russians, and he was sending orders to Stalingrad to the SS crack units there—the Leibstandarte, Das Reich, and Totenkopf—to make sure that it wasn't. The Mius operation, in Hitler's mind, was a consolation prize for his general.

Manstein did not realize what the Führer had intended, or he ignored it to spite him. "The circumstances at Kharkov," Manstein later wrote, "proved stronger than Hitler's will."[34] When those forces were in danger of being surrounded, Manstein countermanded the Führer's orders and instructed the SS to leave the city. They did so on February 15.

Again, there was a hush in Hitler's map room. On paper, the withdrawals looked like a rout. The Führer was peeved. On February 17 he headed to the front for another showdown with Manstein. This time Manstein would surely meet the Führer of legend. But again something happened to Hitler in front of his general. Hitler did not become Hitlerian. There were no dismissals, no shouting, none of the tantrums that he was so adept at putting on for foreign emissaries. Hitler treated his recalcitrant general with calm respect when everyone had expected fire and bombast. All the same, Hitler tried to hold firm. The retreat must stop immediately and Kharkov must be retaken.

But Manstein did not relent. The retreat, he explained, was necessary not only to prevent the capture of the German forces but also because the Russians had charged through the Kharkov gap and were now headed into the expanse of the Ukraine lacking the logistics to sustain a force there. Manstein argued that if Hilter gave him a chance, he would pick off the Red Army "like a ripe apple."

By the third day of the conference, Hitler had again softened. He agreed at last to one major Manstein proposal—to transfer all forces possible from Army Group A to the Southern Army Group.

When Hitler left the room, he again thought that he had won major parts of the arguments and that most of the withdrawals would stop. He soon learned that Manstein had ignored him again. But before Hitler could act—and this time he may well have dispatched his obdurate general—Manstein handed him a series of quick and decisive victories. The Russians were pushed back pell-mell. The Germans retook Kharkov and Belgorod. By March 1, the Germans were again ascendant on the battlefield. The Red Army's great offensive had, as Manstein had predicted, turned into a vast trap. Manstein and Hitler shared the glory of the moment. Historian Clark noted: "Few periods in World War II show a more complete and dramatic reversal of fortune than the last fortnight in February and the first in March 1943. The German Army had done more, it seemed, than demonstrate once again its renowned powers of recovery; it had demonstrated an unassailable superiority, at a tactical level, to its most formidable enemy. It had repaired its front, shattered the hopes of the Allies, and nipped the Russian spearhead. Above all, it had recovered its moral ascendancy."[35]

Though the world still talked on and on about Stalingrad, there was now a stalemate on the eastern front. Neither side had a winning advantage. If there was an upper hand, it was again on Hitler's side, not Stalin's. The world war had not yet been decided.

The main credit goes to Manstein, whose dramatic gambits had turned back the Red Army. But some credit must be shared with Hitler himself. Who knew what would have happened had not some brakes been applied to Manstein's ambitious plans? Besides, Hitler had allowed blatant insubordination on a level seldom seen in this war, either because he believed that Manstein might just be right or because, for a time, he had lost his own self-confidence. Wherever the cause, it worked. Hitler had chosen the right man and had tolerated him. Germany was better served than it had any right to be.

Conspiracy Returns

But such was the case with the conspiracy against Hitler that, following this great victory, the participants finally decided to assassinate the Führer. Former chief of staff Ludwig Beck was the motivating force. He had earlier declined assassination on moral principles but now had resolved this internal conflict. Carl Goerdeler, former Leipzig mayor and a major leader of the civilian resistance, made the same moral choice.[36] But it would be men and armies in the field that would have to carry out the coup. The ever-traitorous Hans Oster, number-two man in the Abwehr, prevailed upon Field Marshal Günther von Kluge to provide the services of assassination host. Goerdeler had also worked Kluge, commander of Army Group Center, in December, and Kluge's continued acquiescence in the operation seemed assured.

As originally planned, the assassination was to take place on March 13 after Hitler flew into the army group on Kluge's invitation. Lieutenant Colonel Freiherr von Boeselager and other officers in the 23d Cavalry Regiment were to shoot Hitler.[37] Oster and Olbricht (chief of the Heeresamt) were to orchestrate simultaneous takeovers in Berlin, Munich, and Vienna.

But once Hitler and his SS entourage were on the ground, Kluge got cold feet. Because of Manstein, Hitler once again was seen as a victor. Kluge thought that the German people would not accept the coup, stressing that "we ought to wait until unfavorable military developments made the elimination of Hitler an evident necessity."[38]

The conspirators were not deterred. Perhaps they couldn't shoot down Hitler while Kluge was nearby, but they could certainly bomb him into oblivion when he left on his plane. General Erwin Lahousen agreed to supply the means: small blocks of nitrotetramethanium. General Henning von Treschkow would deliver the device in the form of two bottles of brandy.

When Hitler's departure approached, Treschkow walked over to a colonel standing beside Hitler's plane and asked if he would be so kind as to take the brandy back to a friend at Rastenburg. The colonel said "of course," and the two bombs, each separately fused, were loaded on board.[39]

As usual, Hitler's would-be assassins came up short. The fuses failed, and Hitler arrived back home knowing nothing of the mortal danger that had traveled with him. To the relief of the conspirators, no one discovered the bottles, which were delivered to their stated designee, who was part of the plot.

Although the conspiracy would not fully come to ground until July 20, 1944, one of its major advocates was now in harm's way, not from the failed bomb but from a general sense that something was going wrong from within the Reich. Even before the death of Reinhard Heydrich, the ever-dangerous head of the RSHA, in June 1942, German secret agents knew that the Abwehr's Hans Oster and maybe even the Abwehr's chief admiral Canaris had been involved in secret peace feelers to the west being sponsored by the Vatican. Heydrich had given the group a code name: Schwarze Kapelle, or Black Orchestra.[40] The surprise Allied landing in North Africa in late 1942 had been another grave intelligence failure, and suspicions fell squarely on the Abwehr. Walter Schellenberg, the intelligence chief of the SD (the security and intelligence arm of the SS), later told the Allies, "Hitler's confidence in Canaris was completely destroyed."[41]

It was worse for Oster. Suspected of treason since May 1940, the Abwehr's number-two man was now under scrutiny by the Gestapo and the SD. His phones were tapped, his letters opened, and his movements followed constantly.[42] Schellenberg later recalled that Hitler and Himmler suspected Oster of being involved in "one of the most important cases of treason in the whole history of Germany."[43]

Himmler hesitated to actually arrest a man as powerful as Oster, but he began zeroing in on subordinates.[44] The end came in April. On the fifth, senior judge advocate Dr. Manfred Roeder showed up at Oster's office with the Gestapo and demanded that Oster be present for the arrest of Dr. Hans von Dohnanyi, the Abwehr's legal expert and a committed member of the conspiracy against Hitler. Though Canaris had warned Dohnanyi of the imminence of his arrest, the former *Reichsgerichtsrat* (supreme court justice) seemed surprised when the men arrived. Certain inculpatory papers were left in the open, a situation that Dohnanyi tried to correct by whispering excitedly to Oster: "Those papers, those papers."[45] Conspirator Hans Bernd Gisevius later wrote that Oster was placed in a terrible position: He could either ignore Dohnanyi and let the Gestapo find the papers, or he could try to somehow spirit the papers to safety. Feeling that Dohnanyi would not have conducted himself so brazenly unless the papers were of supreme importance, Oster resolved upon the second approach. The Gestapo man, however, noticed the move and within hours Oster—whom Gisevius called the Third Reich's "most dangerous adversary"—was removed from his position; he was soon arrested.[46] The papers that

Dohnanyi had tried to protect proved to be damning evidence of the Black Orchestra and also detailed some of the planning behind the recently failed bomb plot against Hitler. Wholesale arrests began, with Gisevius "by a very devious route" managing to escape to Switzerland.[47] Within weeks, the Abwehr itself was broken up and in large part consumed into the Gestapo. The part of the conspiracy against Hitler that had long sought an understanding with the west—the part that until then had been dominate—was crippled, leaving the field open for those looking toward Stalin.

WERTHER ENTERS

In Switzerland, Rachel Dübendorfer went about her job much as she had before. Obsessively independent and suspicious, she did all she could to stay personally and professionally away from Rado, the titular Soviet chief of station in Switzerland. Rachel's finest gem was still Rössler—Lucy—the man who controlled the mysterious Werther. In Moscow Center, Maria Poliakova, still in control of the operation, was from the beginning of December 1942 under intense pressure by her own masters to find out exactly who Lucy was and what his sources of information were. Failing that, she was to have a special agent sent to Switzerland to take over control of Lucy from Dübendorfer.

Rachel was simply behaving too strangely and too possessively. In short, she was driving the Center mad.

But Dübendorfer wouldn't or couldn't get Rössler to reveal his sources. And she refused point-blank to turn over her cherished Rössler to anyone else. All she would tell Moscow was that Werther operated from inside the OKW, the Wehrmacht's supreme command where Hitler held sway. Other sources included Teddy in the OKH, the Army High Command, and "Stephan" and "Ferdinand" in the Luftwaffe.[48]

It did not satisfy the Center, but it would have to do. The Soviet dependence on the source, evident before the Red Army pincers closed around Stalingrad in November 1942, now became absolute. As Manstein, acting much on his own, was trying to stave off a total defeat, the Center told Rado on December 2 that the "top priority task in the near future is the most accurate determination of all German reserves in the rear of the Eastern Front."[49] As the German demise at Stalingrad became more certain, the Russians realized that German intentions away from Stalingrad were pivotal. If the Russians could prevent Manstein from saving the German armies to the south, they could win the Second World War outright.

On Christmas Day 1942, Poliakova told Rachel, in one of the messages sent directly to Rachel in her own code: "'Werther' is to state clearly how many replacement divisions in all are being formed from recruits by 1st January. Reply urgent."[50] This was a fateful message that would have repercussions throughout the Reich and the history of the war. The Germans were able to decode this snippet. It was the first they had heard of Werther and the clearest evidence that there had long been a traitor, not in the Abwehr or the field or the Luftwaffe but at Hitler's side.[51] However, that realization would not come for two years. By then the Reich could not recover.

The pressure built for the Swiss ring to produce more and more as the Stavka seemed desperate to press the advantage for fear that Manstein might somehow slip away or, worse, regain the upper hand. On January 16, 1943, the Center told Rado: "Lucy's and Werther's information about Caucasian front and all top priority information about Eastern Front, as well as on dispatch of new divisions to Eastern Front, to be sent to us without delay with precedence over all other information. Last information from Werther was most valuable. Director."[52] The next day, the Center ordered Rado to get from Lucy "information on the Caucasian front and the most important news on the eastern front as well as the dispatch of new divisions to the eastern front without delay and with priority over all other information."[53]

Werther acted immediately. Within twenty-four hours of receiving this request, the Center sent the Swiss net the following message: "Our thanks to Werther for the information on the Caucasus front."[54]

In February Rado was told to "convey to Lucy our thanks for her excellent work. The last report from her group concerning the middle sector of the front is extremely important."[55]

So important were the messages sent over Jim's transmitter that Moscow was willing to broker any and all risks. Foote stayed on the air for hours at a time, sending and receiving, a breach in tradecraft that could have cost him his life. Moscow seemed to reason that Foote could be replaced but Werther's stunning reports could not.

On January 18, a day after the previous message, Moscow sent Rado one marked "very important": "Find out from 'Lucy' which divisions and how many of them have been moved from the west to the eastern front, how many are supposed to be moved, and how many are already under way."[56]

The demands kept coming. On January 20, the Center asked the Swiss ring to "find out what plans and concrete intentions the Wehrmacht High Command has to counter Red Army's offensive and above all how they mean to ward off or neutralize the Red Army's assaults. What differences of opinion are there in the Wehrmacht High Command as regards the measures to be taken and the plans that have been adopted? Pass this order on to all members of the Lucy group . . ."[57]

By January 30, when Paulus was captured, the whole force of the Russian war was set to make a quick and decisive end to the Wehrmacht. Rado was ordered to "give urgent commission to 'Lucy' to find out whether Infantry Divisions No. 326, 334, 343, 347, 365 exist in the army, whether they were newly organized, where and when; where they are located now; also if Divisions 196 and 199 remain in Norway."[58]

In early February, on the same day that Manstein first sat down with Hitler to discuss the German withdrawals, Poliakova told Rado to order "'Lucy' to find out as soon as possible how OKW plans to occupy the new defense line, whether it is to be done with retreating troops, or with new troops coming up from the rear. Tell 'Lucy' that we are not only interested in decisions made by the OKW on this matter, but also in all the discussions of the General Staff and OKH."[59] Obviously, the Center now knew that Hitler—head of OKW—was not the only one devising war plans for the Wehrmacht. Manstein was a semi-independent force. Therefore, it was necessary to discern what the Army High Command as well as the Supreme Command was thinking. The message also revealed that the Center by now knew that Werther had tentacles throughout the German armed forces.

As the southern battle unfolded, the Center's urgency increased. On February 16, Poliakova ordered Rado to "find out at once from Werther through Lucy whether Vyazma and Rzhev are being evacuated."[60] Six days later this message arrived: "Immediately get from Werther OKW plans about objectives of Kluge's Army Group."[61]

On the same day, Lucy was asked "with urgency" these questions: "A: What new types of tank T-3 or T-4 are being built at present in Germany . . . B: The monthly production figures for these tanks. C: Have T-3 and T-4 tanks been modified and of what do these modifications consist. D: Are there any plans for the summer of 1943 to re-equip armored divisions with new tanks and new artillery or with old, modified tanks with thick armor and possibly new armament."[62]

And as if this wasn't enough for one day, the Center sent another message: "We have to know the Wehrmacht High Command's plans as regards the Kluge army group in the middle sector. Everything you can tell us about the middle sector or the front is of the first importance."[63] Moscow's growing concerns were well founded. Manstein was about to begin his counteroffensive, which would devastate the Stavka's planning.

As spring came to the eastern front, Hitler began considering one last major offensive, one that could finally smash the Red Army. The general staff was divided, and Hitler himself vacillated. If he took the next step, Germany would either win or lose the war. The stalemate would disappear.

As Hitler contemplated his move, Poliakova and the rest of her family redoubled their efforts. If Hitler made up his mind, the Red Army would know every detail of the plan.

The point on the map that Hitler was focused on was a town called Kursk.

SECOND FRONT

What Hitler did not know was how strained the relations were now among the Allies. Whether he could have exploited these divisions will never be known. But certainly had he known about them he would have tried. Hitler knew that he was out of easy victories.

The central issue dividing the Allies concerned a second front in Europe. Since the beginning of Barbarossa, Stalin had asked Britain and later America to form such a front so that Hitler would be forced to retract thirty to forty German divisions from the heart of Russia. Only two months after Barbarossa began, Stalin told the Allied leaders the stark truth: If the Soviet Union did not get major help from a second front soon, it could be too late. Hitler might be able to dictate peace terms with Russia, thereby leaving the Western Allies to face the Wehrmacht alone.

And Stalin was telling the truth. It was during this period that the Soviet leader sent peace feelers to Hitler through Bulgaria.

Had Germany and the Soviet Union settled their differences then, the world today would surely be far different. But in the greatest miscalculation of his life, Hitler rebuffed Stalin. It was that decision alone that kept the war going.

Churchill and Roosevelt talked about keeping Stalin in the war, but for varying reasons Stalin did not find that the Allied leaders did much to help. Mostly, they encouraged him to hang on, promising more assistance than they had the will or the capability of delivering. There was constant talk of a second front, but that would remain just talk until June 1944.

What Stalin did not know was that President Roosevelt actually wanted to launch a second front, whereas Churchill only dissembled. Roosevelt aide Harry Hopkins was so alarmed by Stalin's warning about bowing out of the war that he instructed military leaders to consider aid to Russia as the top American priority.[64] Churchill did everything he could to resist that. He promised a second front—in 1941 and 1942 and even in 1943—but he told insiders that it was not to be.

Churchill was disingenuous in his plans. While telling Stalin that massive German forces were in France, perhaps preparing for a cross-Channel invasion of their own, he told Roosevelt in March 1943: "The fact is that as a result of the Russian offensive a redistribution of divisions in France has been taking place since the end of November. Divisions have been taken from France to Russia. These have been partially replaced by training divisions and by a few battered divisions from Russia. The net result in the South of France has been a considerable reduction in strength and in quality since the end of November."[65]

Roosevelt thought that this would bode well for an invasion of France in 1943, but Churchill would have none of that. He would promise and then renege until the American military, if not Roosevelt, felt conned. The British Mediterranean strategy advocated by the British looked more and more like one designed to prevent, not encourage, an invasion of France. The Americans began to suspect that the British were prosecuting the war not to defeat Hitler but to preserve the British Empire.[66] George C. Marshall was constantly threatening that America should change from a Europe-first strategy to a Pacific-first strategy if the British did not stop dragging their feet.

In the Kremlin, Stalin felt that the Allies were letting the Red Army bleed to death while the West waited to pick up spoils.

That Churchill was kneading scheme into scheme became clear when the Duke of Alba, the Spanish ambassador to Great Britain, reported to his Japanese counterpart a conversation that he'd had with Churchill. According to the duke, Churchill said: "The war is 50% over . . . the British and Americans are again rulers of the waves. America's entry into the war, accompanied by the assurance that we would get plenty of arms, makes our victory absolutely beyond doubt." With that said, Churchill continued: "The United States is certainly anxious to whip Japan. She is going to fight her to the bitter end . . . But you know in Government circles here in London there are plenty of people who remember the Tokyo-London alliance and who say it was a mistake to have forsworn it for the sake of America. These Japanese have a lot of stamina. I fought in the Boer War and other wars too and have known well warriors of various climes, and judging from what I have seen of Japanese prisoners, I can only express admiration for the fine military spirit of the Japanese race."[67]

The Japanese ambassador encoded these remarks in the so-called Magic cipher and sent them on to Tokyo. British agents decoded the message, and Churchill, who knew that the Americans had the same ability, quickly told the president that he was merely playing a little game.[68] The simple conclusion that Churchill was hinting at a willingness to discuss a redefinition of relations among the world's three major sea powers was, Churchill indicated, not so.

Of course, the whole enterprise could have meant that Churchill was, in a backhanded and dangerous way, letting Americans know of the possible consequences of any change in the Europe-first alignment.

Whatever, Roosevelt, implicitly trusting Churchill, did not change American policy.

Stalin, when shown similar evidence of double dealing, was not as trusting.

In October 1942, just before the Stalingrad offensive, a Soviet resident agent in London sent Beria a message that he immediately relayed to Stalin. It concerned information gained by Colonel Moravec, chief of Czech military intelligence in exile. It read: "The widely spread opinion that Hess flew to Britain unexpectedly is untrue. Long before that flight Hess corresponded on this question with Lord Hamilton discussing all the details of his forthcoming flight. Hamilton did not personally participate in the correspondence, however. All the letters addressed to Hamilton failed to reach him. They were received by the intelligence service. Hamilton's alleged answers were also written by the intelligence service. This is how the British managed to trick Hess into flying to Britain.

"Col. Moravec also said that he saw the Hess-Hamilton correspondence with his own eyes. According to Moravec, in his letters Hess sufficiently clearly laid down the plans of the German government connected with the attack on the Soviet Union.

"The letters also contained well argued proposals on the need to discontinue the war between Britain and Germany."[69]

This document, the substance of which is confirmed in American intelligence reports,[70] told Stalin that powerful forces in

Britain had been in contact with the Nazis about the planning of Barbarossa. Stalin publicly declared that he had acquired new evidence that Hess had flown to Great Britain "in order to persuade the British politicians to join in the general campaign against the U.S.S.R."[71] He demanded not only that Hess be tried immediately for this act against the USSR but that a second front be established to prove that there was no strategic collusion against him. On November 28, Stalin told Churchill that he hoped the prime minister had not changed his mind "with regard to your promise given in Moscow to establish a second front in Western Europe in the spring of 1943."[72]

Annoyed by the lack of response, Stalin said on December 7 that he was too busy to attend a joint-power conference at Casablanca. In that message, Stalin pointedly issued the refrain: "I am waiting your reply to the paragraph of my preceding letter dealing with the establishment of the second front in Western Europe in the Spring of 1943."[73] Roosevelt, alarmed by the message, asked Churchill to pay special attention to Stalin's request.

As for the Hess affair and any relation it had to Stalin's demands, Churchill kept Roosevelt in the dark. Churchill wrote to the president: "All this chatter about Hess [by Stalin] may be another symptom. I am frankly perplexed and would be grateful for your thoughts at the earliest moment because time is passing."[74] As far as Roosevelt knew, a British commitment for a second front in France was still solid.

But there was to be no second front in the spring of 1943. Historians will debate for decades how the world may have differed had the Western Allies attacked Germany's weakly defended rear. Instead, as the American chiefs of staff feared, the North African offensive took so much time, materiel, and vital shipping that, far from hastening Hitler's fall, it actually prolonged his reign.

By the spring of 1943, Stalin and Hitler knew that the Reich would not have to pull its panzer armies west to defeat an Allied invasion. If the war was to be won or lost this year, it would be in the east. And the more the generals and leaders looked at the map, the more they saw a bulge 120 miles wide and sixty miles deep into German lines roughly surrounding Kursk.

That is where the battle would be fought. And the man who would most determine that battle was still known only by a code name.

Werther would decide the war.

Notes

1 Clark, p. 280.

2 Manstein, p. 367.

3 Clark, p. 251.

4 Warlimont, p. 278.

5 Clark, p. 257.

6 Mellenthin, p. 207.

7 Clark, p. 254.

8 Manstein, p. 285.

9 Mellenthin, p. 231.

10 Manstein, p. 302.

11 Clark, p. 265.

12 Ibid., p. 267.

13 Warlimont, p. 279.

14 Mellenthin, pp. 214–15.

15 Manstein, p. 369.

16 Mellenthin, pp. 216–17.

17 Clark, p. 271.

18 Manstein, p. 372.

19 Warlimont, p. 289.

20 Clark, p. 255.

21 Manstein, p. 375.

22 Ibid., p. 367.

23 Toland, p. 729.

24 Clark, p. 283.

25 Warlimont, p. 302.

26 Clark, p. 290.

27 Ibid.

28 NAZ, p. 843.

29 Clark, p. 291.

30 Manstein, p. 386.

31 RG 165, Entry 179, Box 721A.

32 Manstein, p. 406.

33 Ibid., p. 407.

34 Ibid., p. 422.

35 Clark, p. 306.

36 Gisevius, p. 468.

37 Clark, p. 308.

38 Ibid.

39 Ibid., p. 309.

40 Schellenberg, *Hitler's Secret Service,* p. 342.

41 Report on the Schellenberg case, p. 42.

42 Toland, p. 790.

43 Schellenberg, *Hitler's Secret Service,* p. 343.

44 Gisevius, p. 477.

45 Ibid.

46 Ibid.

47 Ibid., p. 478.

48 Garlinski, p. 75.

49 Carell, p. 100.

50 Ibid.

51 Reed and Fisher, p. 145.

52 Carell, p. 100.

53 RG 319, Box 59.

54 Rado, p. 153.

55 Ibid., p. 154.

56 RG 319, Box 59.

57 Garlinski, p. 138.

58 RG 319, Box 59.

59 Ibid.

60 Carell, p. 101.

61 Ibid.

62 RG 319, Box 59.

63 Garlinski, p. 138.

64 Kimball, Vol. 1, p. 238.

65 Message C-273 from Churchill to Roosevelt, per Kimball, Vol. 2.

66 Kimball, Vol. 2, p. 121.

67 Message C-249/2 from Churchill to Roosevelt, per Kimball, Vol. 2.

68 Kimball, Vol. 2, p. 102.

69 Cable No. 450, KGB, Black Bertha file.

70 November 5, 1941, letter from Raymond Lee to General

Sherman Miles, RG 319, Box 83.

71 *Facts on File: 1942, Persons Index* (New York: Facts on File, 1943), 428-j.

72 Kimball, Vol. 2, p. 51.

73 Ibid., p. 70.

74 Message C-172 from Churchill to Roosevelt, per Kimball, Vol. 2.

Göring and Bormann at Göring's Karinhall estate. Albert Speer warned Göring that he must act against Bormann or else Hitler would be isolated from all other advice. Göring hesitated, and soon lost his battle with the Führer's secretary.

Deputy Führer Hess and Hitler at a Nazi rally. Behind them stares Bormann, a short, stocky man who was Hess's secretary. Hess promoted Bormann to be his eyes and ears at the Führer's headquarters. Eventually, Bormann used that position to supplant Hess.

GILBERT

A rare picture of the master Red Army spy Leopold Trepper code-named "Gilbert," Trepper was a figure straight out of an Ian Fleming novel. After he was captured by the Gestapo, Gilbert agreed to play back messages to Moscow Center authored by Bormann. In the end, he came to believe that the separate peace Bormann wrote about might well have been real.

Victor Sukulov, code-named "Kent," was Trepper's number two. He participated in the Gestapo's "*funkspiel*" even after Hitler's death. Bormann and Gestapo Müller wrote the most important *funkspiel* messages. Were they real, or a deception?

KENT

In a rare smile, Martin Bormann exchanges pleasantries with German officers.

Deputy Führer Rudolf Hess helped Hitler write *Mein Kampf* while the two languished in Landsberg prison. He came to believe in Hitler's obsession about a German-Anglo pact. When the time came, he sacrificed himself for Hitler's dream.

Nazi propaganda chief Joseph Goebbels first plotted to limit Bormann's power. Later, he tried to accommodate the Führer's secretary. Neither strategy worked well.

Martin Bormann looks out at the Alps from the Führer's Berghof estate at the Obersalzberg. Bormann was responsible for much of the building at the estate, a feat that endeared him to the Führer.

Bormann preferred to stay in the shadows, only rarely allowing his picture to be taken. However, on occasion he was forced onto center stage, as he was here at an official state function.

A United States intelligence officer prints an arrow to identify Martin Bormann in a photo of the two at the Wolf's Lair that was captured after the war.

Goebbels faces his chief rival for the Führer's affection, Martin Bormann. Goebbels was always considered a genius, but could never outmaneuver the man he considered boorish.

Chief of the general staff General Ludwig Beck refused to overthrow Hitler in 1938 when he had a chance. Later, he regretted his decision and became the lighting rod for the generals' conspiracy against the Führer.

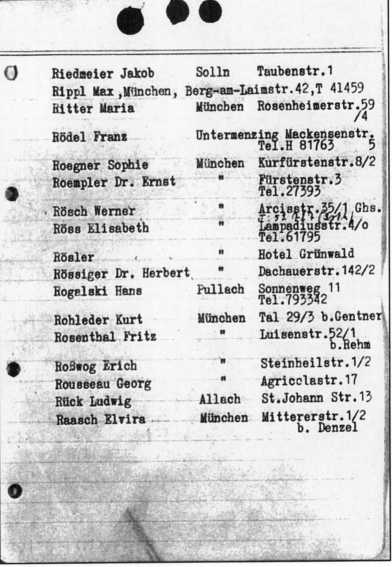

```
Riedmeier Jakob        Solln      Taubenstr.1
Rippl Max ,München, Berg-am-Laimstr.42,T 41459
Ritter Maria           München    Rosenheimerstr.59
                                               /4
Rödel Franz            Untermenzing Mackensenstr.
                          Tel.H 81763           5
Roegner Sophie         München    Kurfürstenstr.8/2
Roempler Dr. Ernst       "        Fürstenstr.3
                                  Tel.27393
Rösch Werner             "        Arcisstr.35/1 Ghs.
Röss Elisabeth           "        Lampadiusstr.4/o
                                  Tel.61795
Rösler                   "        Hotel Grünwald
Rössiger Dr. Herbert     "        Dachauerstr.142/2
Rogelski Hans          Pullach    Sonnenweg 11
                                  Tel.793342
Rohleder Kurt          München    Tal 29/3 b.Gentner
Rosenthal Fritz          "        Luisenstr.52/1
                                              b.Rehm
Roßwog Erich             "        Steinheilstr.1/2
Rousseau Georg           "        Agricolastr.17
Rück Ludwig            Allach     St.Johann Str.13
Raasch Elvira          München    Mittererstr.1/2
                                      b. Denzel
```

A page from Martin Bormann's addresses book. The entry for "Rösler" and the Hotel Grunwald may be meaningless, but it is the only entry in the book without a first name. Could this be Rössler also known as the Red Army spy "Lucy?"

After Hess flew Hitler's mission to Scotland, the three reigning powers were Hitler, Göring, and Bormann. Though in 1939 Hitler proclaimed Göring as first in the line of succession, by 1942 Bormann was Hitler's de facto number two.

Brauchitsch and Halder discussing the German invasion of the Soviet Union—Operation Barbarossa. Halder, the chief of staff, had wanted to overthrow Hitler but was afraid that this would not be enough to satisfy Western powers. Brauchitsch, the army commander, knew of the conspiracies around Hitler, but never told the Führer.

SS General Reinhard Heydrich was perhaps the most ruthless Nazi after Hitler. As head of the Reich Main Security Office (RSHA) Heydrich oversaw the organs of the police state, including the Gestapo. Heydrich chaired the Wannsee conference where the "Final Solution" of the Jewish question was resolved.

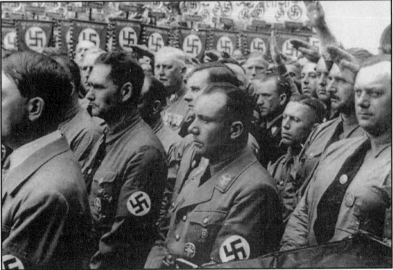

Hitler, Hess, Bormann, and Ernst Rohm at a party rally. Hitler would later liquidate Rohm and bring Rohm's Brown Shirts to heel.

Many people do not realize that the dictator Hitler largely ruled with not only the consent but often the adoration of the governed. Here he meets with enthusiastic German women and soldiers.

As the war progressed, fewer and fewer German civilian officials, including Himmler, could see Hitler without Bormann's OK. Hitler said he liked Bormann because he got things done where other couldn't.

From late 1942 on Bormann insisted on sending more and more of the Wehrmacht's secrets to the Russians through the *funkspiel*. Was this to help the Führer, or to destroy him?

Hitler ponders alone at his East Prussian headquarters called the Wolf's Lair. The dank surroundings were said the be harmful to Hitler's health. Yet the Wolf's Lair was the nerve center for much of the eastern campaign against Russia.

WANTED   GESUCHT

$1000⁰⁰ REWARD
FOR INFORMATION LEADING
TO THE APPREHENSION OF
MARTIN BORMANN

NOTIFY NEAREST
COUNTER INTELLIGENCE
CORPS DETACHMENT

BELOHNUNG $1000⁼
(ODER GEGENWERT
IN AMERIKANISCHEN
LEBENSMITTELN)
FÜR ANGABEN, DIE ZUR
FESTNAHME VON
MARTIN BORMANN
FÜHREN

It was only after the war that the Americans began to realize the significance of Martin Bormann in the Nazi universe. Here, an early wanted poster offered $1,000 for his capture.

Chapter Eight
INDECISION

For Adolf Hitler, 1943 began as a puzzle. In March, his troops recaptured Kharkov, winning 615 tanks and 1,000 guns.[1] Manstein had regained control and the question was which side, if either, would take the offensive in 1943. Stalin was anxious to do something. Hitler was not. Stalingrad and Manstein's high-wire act had given the Führer a terrible scare. Most of the German generals were also cautious, but one limited objective caught their eye. Between Manstein's army in the south and Kluge's in the north, the Russians had a massive bridgehead bulging from the general vicinity of Kursk. Manstein wanted to snip the Kursk salient with still another pincer attack.

Hitler could not decide. Manstein's plan seemed too ambitious. Perhaps, Hitler thought, he could wait for the indefatigable Speer to build up the German economy into one for total war, something that Hitler had so far avoided. Better still, Speer was promising wholesale production of the new Tiger and Panther tanks. Hitler had great faith in these, though there were too few presently available to make any difference. So while his generals asked him for a decision, Hitler stalled.

General Heinz Guderian, whom Hitler had just named inspector general of the armored troops, thought that the idea of doing anything in 1943 was foolhardy. The front was stabilized, the Red Army had not shown that it could sustain a deep offensive, and the Germans were exhausted. They needed time to rebuild. Guderian told Hitler: "The task for 1943 is to provide a certain number of panzer divisions with complete combat efficiency capable of making limited objective attacks. For 1944 we must prepare to launch large-scale attacks."[2]

But Hitler couldn't bring himself to take this approach either. Doing nothing was not one of Hitler's distinguishing characteristics. Yet he couldn't figure out what he wanted, much less how to get it. Never had Hitler been so paralyzed. His wrenching indecision was apparent to all at a March 9, 1943, meeting at his Werewolf headquarters in Vinnitsa. There, Guderian outlined his ideas for 1943. Nearly universal dissension arose among the generals, who let the Führer know that they liked little of Guderian's plans. The meeting reached its nadir after Guderian suggested that the assault artillery be placed under his command. Hitler was powerless to defend his newly named commander. He simply turned toward Guderian and said plaintively: "You see, they're all against you. So I can't approve either."[3] And that was about all the Führer would say today. Wrote historian Alan Clark: "For the first time in twenty years Hitler was silent. He had no ideas."[4] Guderian was so exhausted by the conference that when it ended, one of Germany's fiercest panzer commanders fell to the floor in a faint.[5]

Manstein did not yet agree with Guderian. To Manstein's mind, doing nothing invited defeat. "Obviously," Manstein later wrote, "after so many major formations had been lost, there would no longer be forces available to mount another crucial offensive on the scale of 1941 and 1942.

"What did still seem possible . . . was that the Soviet Union could be worn down to such an extent that it would tire of its already excessive sacrifices and be ready to accept a stalemate. At the time in question this was far from being wishful thinking. On the other hand, such an aim could not be realized by going over to purely defensive, static warfare."[6]

Instead, Manstein advocated a "strategic defense," in which short-term military moves, such as the one he favored toward Kursk, would knock the Red Army off balance and reduce the chance of a successful Soviet offensive in 1943. Such a strategy was named the "forehand." As an alternative, Manstein suggested a "backhand" plan, in which Germany would try to lure the Red Army into a logistical trap. In essence, it would repeat Manstein's tactics that had succeeded in stemming the Red Army after Stalingrad.

The general saw no way that Joseph Stalin would be content to sit on his hands while Hitler struggled with his doubts. After the 6th Army surrendered at Stalingrad, the Soviet dictator would surely want a follow-up show of Red Army prowess, lest the world catch on that Stalingrad was not the great strategic victory that the Soviet propaganda machine had made it out to be. Manstein feared that the Russians would resume their offensive against the southern German armies with the same goal that they had failed to accomplish before—to separate German forces and wedge open a door into the Balkans.[7]

What was clear in early March was that a decision had to be made. Was Hitler up to the task, or was he now so gripped by uncertainty that German policy and German fate would simply be left to drift? On March 13, the Führer issued Order Number 5 for the action against the Kursk salient.[8] But no one, including Hitler, knew if the order would stick.

In addition to German generals who watched Hitler's every inflection to detect his intentions, the director in Moscow was watching too, though at a safer distance.

BACK CHANNELS

On the same day that Hitler was meeting with his generals at Vinnitsa, Moscow Center sent a message to Leopold Trepper's phony transmitter requesting detailed information about German reserve forces in Western Europe. According to Trepper, the Sonderkommando was thrown into confusion. How could they respond without giving away valuable military secrets? Worse, the message asked Trepper to confirm information about specific locations of divisions; in other words, the Center already had the information from another source. There was a leak at the highest level of the high command. How could this be? And how could Germany confirm the traitor's information?

But orders came down from Berlin: If the game was to work, there was no recourse but to reply accurately to Moscow Center.

"Almost every day, very precise dispatches arrived from the Center, to which the Sonderkommando would reply in just as much detail," Trepper later wrote. "Such was the price that the architects of the 'separate peace' had to pay."[9]

Trepper also noted what he called "an interesting question." Who, he asked, had the power to approve giving correct answers back to Moscow, answers corroborating what the Center already knew from some other secret source? Was it Heinrich Müller alone? Or did something on such a grand level demand an even higher authority?

While Trepper looked for answers, the rupture in Hitler's secret wall widened. On March 13, as German conspirators were planting a bomb on Hitler's plane while he visited with Kluge, Rachel Dübendorfer reported to the Center that her Lucy ring had a source willing to sell German plans for the German "East-Wall" defensive structure to the highest bidder. The Center radioed Rado: "Agreed! Buy 'Ostwall' plan for 3,000 Swiss francs. What does 'Lucie' [sic] know of the genuineness and authenticity of these documents? It is most necessary to find out what other documents 'Lucie' can deliver."[10] Five days later, Moscow sent Rachel another urgent request "to determine: numbers of the Army Corps in the Donetz and Kharkov areas with regard to the Ostwall . . .1. How far back do the fortifications go? 2. What financial and material means have been set aside by OKW for the construction of the Ostwall? 3. How is the construction board organized?"[11]

The Center got its answers. After the war Marshal Zhukov acknowledged that "by early April we had obtained rather full information on enemy forces near Orel, Sumy, Belgorod and Kharkov"—forces that would constitute those available to attack the Kursk salient.

CONSERVATIVES

As Werther sent the Third Reich's secrets to Stalin, others in Germany were anxious to sell out Hitler's regime to the West. Walter Schellenberg, head of foreign intelligence for the Reich Main Security Office, told interrogators after the war that during March 1943 he committed two direct acts of treason against the Reich. He first met with the wife of Putzi Hanfstaengl, an American once in Hitler's inner circle, to discuss plans for kidnapping

Hitler. Mrs. Hanfstaengl asked Schellenberg to prevail upon his ever-duplicitous boss, Heinrich Himmler, to spirit the Führer to his Obersalzberg estate, where he would be held under house arrest. A so-called Council of Twelve, headed by Himmler, would then rule Germany while Hanfstaengl would surreptitiously contact Randolph Churchill, Winston Churchill's son, about a separate peace.

Far from laughing off such a scheme, Schellenberg said that he advanced Hanfstaengl 500,000 marks to help carry it out.[12] Schellenberg later told interrogators "that under other circumstances he would probably not have employed this woman for she had a somewhat hysterical temperament, but since her employment was virtually at Himmler's instigation the chance was too good to be missed."[13]

It was not Schellenberg's only betrayal this month. The other came in Switzerland. In part, it stemmed from Germany's displeasure that a Red Army cell was working within Switzerland with little local interference. Gisela's family had the attention of the Sonderkommando. If the Swiss could not cut off this source and prove their true neutrality, the Reich had drawn up preliminary plans for an invasion. Schellenberg managed to hand those plans to Roger Masson, his counterpart in Swiss intelligence.[14] To help ward off an invasion, the Swiss then gave Schellenberg a signed declaration that it would retain its neutrality throughout the war. Gisela's family, however, still operated.

The whole matter put Germany in the odd situation of planning to invade Switzerland partly because a spy ring there was passing to Moscow information almost identical to what Müller and Bormann were sending through another channel.

Also in March, treason was afoot in still another unlikely corner of the German High Command. Carl Friedrich Goerdeler, the former mayor of Leipzig, was the heart and soul of the conservative conspiracy against Hitler. Heinz Guderian was the newly appointed inspector general of armored troops, whose task it was to try to find victory in the east. Even though their goals appeared to be far different, the two met to discuss removing the Führer from power.

Exactly what happened during several meetings cannot be known, but even Guderian's exculpatory explanation is stunning. He wrote after the war that Dr. Goerdeler met him at his (Guderian's) office and "explained to me that since Hitler was incapable of performing his duties as Chancellor of the Reich and Supreme Commander of the Armed Forces, it was desirable that his activities as such be curtailed."[15] Goerdeler's proposal was almost identical to the Hanfstaengl plan and therefore may have had a common heritage. The Führer, Goerdeler said, was to be interned in the Obersalzberg while emissaries were sent to contact the West. Guderian then asked the question that had in the past prevented the conspiracy against Hitler from succeeding: Would the West agree to any German government? "Dr. Goerdeler," Guderian said, "could not guarantee foreign support in the event of his plans succeeding."[16]

That was not the answer that Guderian needed if he were to assist in the plot. "It was apparent that during his long-drawn-out attempts to establish contacts abroad he had been given a somewhat cold shoulder. Our enemies had refused to abandon the 'unconditional surrender' slogan, even in the event of Dr. Goerdeler being successful."[17] Goerdeler still insisted that Guderian not turn away from the plot, because the man behind the efforts—former chief of the Army General Staff Ludwig Beck—commanded respect in many circles.

Did the inspector general of the armored troops throw the conspirator and his accomplices into jail for plotting to overthrow the commander in chief? Of course not. This was the Third Reich.

Instead—and this is Guderian's own admission—the new inspector general queried frontline commanders about whether they would participate in the plot. Guderian later told Goerdeler that he could find no generals who were ready to overthrow the Führer, which meant that Guderian was lying or had not made much of a search. Anyway, Guderian said that he came to believe "that Dr. Goerdeler's plan would be harmful to our general interest."[18] This did not prevent Guderian from meeting with Goerdeler several more times.

While Goerdeler approached Guderian, General Beck himself wrote to Manstein begging for a *putsch*. The conspirator's main line was simple: The war was lost. Germany had to now get the best deal possible. Manstein disagreed, replying: "After all, a war is not lost until one gives it up for lost."[19] Kluge, meanwhile, was plotting against Hitler. Thomas was too. Assassinations were being attempted. And Hitler appeared to have suspected none of it. Whereas the man in the Kremlin suspected everybody of treason where none existed, Hitler suspected few while traitors were everywhere.

ZHUKOV IN COMMAND

In the Kremlin, things were much as Manstein had predicted. Stalin wanted to act, to take up the offensive again. The Soviet leader spoke of a "preemptive offensive" somewhat along the lines of Manstein's "strategic defense." He thought that the Red Army should move before the Wehrmacht could repeat its devastating performance of 1940, 1941, and 1942. But there was someone around Stalin with real backbone, and that person did not like the boss's ideas at all. Marshal Zhukov thought that a blind offensive would be the surest way to lose. Hadn't Stalin's ideas of mass attack been proven faulty in nearly everyplace save one? It would be better to take on a chess player's attitude. Because the Russians knew where Hitler was likely to hit—the Kursk salient being the only area now debated in Germany—it made sense to build up forces there that could deliver a crushing blow to the Wehrmacht and hand the strategic initiative back to the Red Army. It was Zhukov's version of deep defense envisioned by the Russian chess grand master Nimzovitch.

On April 8, Zhukov told Stalin his unvarnished opinion. He said that it would be "unwise to launch a preventive attack in the next few days. It would be better if we first wore the enemy down with our defenses and destroyed his tanks, and only then, after having moved up fresh reserves, went over to a general offensive and finally destroyed his main force."[20] Few generals during the war felt that they could simply contradict Stalin. Most were sure what he would do in return: He would have them shot. But Zhukov did not appear to be cowed, and Stalin decided to listen to his plans.

Stalin had another reason to wait to hear in detail about Zhukov's plans. The same day that Zhukov sent his message, the Red Army's Swiss network of spies notified the Center that any decision to attack Kursk had been delayed from the beginning of May.[21] Stalin, in other words, had time.

The Soviet dictator called for a conference on April 12 to discuss Zhukov's ideas. After hearing out the arguments that were supported by all but one top commander, Stalin reluctantly agreed. There would be no wild offensive. Instead, Stalin ordered Zhukov to build up unbreakable defenses in the Kursk salient.

LEAKS

Hitler was also nearing a decision. He had received from his army officers a detailed memorandum on the planned pincer movement at Kursk. The Führer called for a meeting on April 15 to discuss the issue.[22] Under the strictest secrecy, Hitler gave preliminary approval for the attack: "I have decided to launch the 'Citadel' attack as the first of this year's offensive blows as soon as weather conditions permit."[23] The attack must be "quick and conclusive . . ."

He continued: "All the preparation must be carried out with great care and energy. The best units, the best weapons, the best officers, large quantities of munitions must be deployed at the centers of gravity of the attack. Every officer, every soldier must be convinced of the decisive importance of this attack. The victory of Kursk must shine like a beacon to the world."[24]

Secrecy was primary. The enemy, Hitler said, must be "left uncertain about the timing of the attack" because the Wehrmacht must "carry out the attack so swiftly that the enemy can neither evade encirclement nor bring up strong reserves from other fronts . . ."[25]

Only thirteen copies of the plans were made, for Hitler and the twelve commanders. No one else was supposed to know anything further until Hitler gave a green light. "It is vital to ensure the element of surprise," Hitler insisted.

Someone did not obey the Führer. Bormann's stenographers had been in the room with Hitler and the twelve commanders. Two days after the conference, Gisela's family sent Moscow detailed information about German mobilization.[26] On April 20, Hitler's birthday, Werther told the center the preliminary date for the attack: June 12.[27]

Werther began delivering incredibly detailed information, not only about military plans but about troop dispositions and even the personalities and allegiances in the high command. In April, Werther sent the following:

"Composition of the 4th tank army, under command of General Hoth: 3rd, 25th, 27th armoured divisions, the SS division 'Viking,' the 12th, 26th, and 103rd mobile and light divisions. Temporarily attached as reinforcement are the 9th and 11th armoured divisions; the 6th and 7th armoured divisions have been detached for the summer operations cannot be complete before some time in May . . .

"The conference opened under Göring's chairmanship without Hitler, then Hitler arrived and also took part. The conference revealed the existence of fundamental differences of opinion between Göring on one hand and Halder on the other [Halder had been invited to attend in an advisory capacity] . . .

"Göring was supported by Donitz, Keitel, Manstein, List, Zeitzler, Fromm, Milch, and Jeschonnek, all of whom were present at the conference. Kluge, Küchler and Rundstedt . . . were not invited to take part."[28]

The Center, now betting everything on the information from Werther, revived its back-channel communications directly with Dübendorfer. The Center was desperate to find out who the players were in this most important game. Even with confirmation from the Trepper playback and the steady stream of accurate information given so far by Dübendorfer, Lucy, and

Werther, the Soviets felt a twinge of doubt. Could this all have been a plot to lead the Red Army to one devastating defeat? A message sent directly to Dübendorfer on April 23 read:[29]

> To Sissy:
>
> Dear friends, since the summer of 1942 you have worked with the Taylor-Lucy group. Which has provided us with a great deal of varied material, some of it valuable. But despite the long cooperation this group remains wholly unclarified for us . . .
>
> Determine and inform us by radio exact reports on Taylor, Lucy, Werther, Anna, Olga. Especially important is a personality sketch of Lucy. Who is he, what is his name, what were his circumstances earlier and what are they now, for what motives does he work for others and for us?
>
> Answer this telegram in your own code. You do not need to inform Albert [one of Rado's code names (the other is Dora)] of our telegram or of your answer . . .
>
> To Sissy [Rachel] only: We send you the title of a new book for your code; but, we shall give you instructions about how to work according to the book. Albert is not to know about the new book. It is called *Tempete sur al Maison* . . .
>
> How are you? What is Mara doing? Greetings to her and both of you from Gisela.

NOT AT HIS BEST

Though on April 15 Hitler appeared to have approved the Kursk offensive, his doubts about the operation would not go away. On May 3 in Munich he held a stormy meeting with his generals to review the whole operation. By now, lines were clearly drawn. Guderian was definitely against the Kursk operation; Zeitzler, the army chief of staff, was totally for it. Kluge, who would command one of the two pincers, was squarely behind the plan. In general, army commanders backed their boss whereas leaders of the OKW, which was assuming more of an advisory role than that of the central command, leaned toward Guderian. General

Walther Model broke from the pattern. According to Guderian: "Model had produced information, based on air photography, which showed that the Russians were preparing deep and very strong defensive positions in exactly those areas where the attack by the two army groups was to go in."[30] This should have told Hitler that there had somehow been a serious breach of his demand for secrecy. But this revelation did not stop Hitler from going ahead. It only caused him to hesitate.

Manstein, who Guderian knew had changed his mind about the Kursk attack, apparently did not state this clearly enough at the crucial May 3 meeting. "Manstein," said Guderian, "as often when face to face with Hitler, was not at his best. His opinion was that the attack would have had a good chance of succeeding if it had been launched in April; now success was doubtful and he would need a further two full-strength infantry divisions in order to be in a position to carry it out."[31] Hitler said that there would not be two more divisions and demanded Manstein's opinion. Guderian said that Hitler "received no very clear answer" from Manstein.

Guderian had once lamented that Hitler and Manstein had not been able to work more closely together. "Their characters were too opposed," he concluded. "On the one hand Hitler, with his great will-power and fertile imagination: on the other Manstein, a man of most distinguished military talents, a product of the German General Staff Corps, with a sensible, cool understanding, who was our finest operational brain."[32] But at this meeting, in Guderian's view, Manstein's brilliant mind failed to make its way inside the conference room.

Although Hitler kept the final decision to himself, a planning date of June 13 was affirmed for the operation. By then, Speer said, 250 of the new Panther tanks would be available.

Though preparations were now in high gear, Hitler could not control his doubts. On May 10, he asked Guderian to come to the Reichschancellery to discuss Panther production. Speer, a genius when it came to industry, said that by May 31 there would actually be 324, not 250, of the new Panthers available for Operation Citadel. Though impressed, Guderian did not surrender his previous position. After the conference, he pulled Hitler aside and asked what was to be gained by attacking "in the East at all this year?" Keitel, standing nearby, said that the attack must go on for "political reasons." Guderian was incensed. "How many people do you think even know where Kursk is?" he asked. "It's a matter of profound indifference to the world whether we hold Kursk or not. I repeat my question: Why do we want to attack in the East at all this year?"

Hitler was at least momentarily impressed. "You're quite right," he said. "Whenever I think of this attack my stomach turns over."[33]

Stalin's stomach was little better off. There had been too many deadlines and too many delays. General Vatutin, in charge of the forces in the southern part of the Kursk salient, and Nikita Khrushchev, the principal Communist leader there, suggested a preemptive strike. Stalin liked the idea, but Zhukov disagreed.[34] We must not escape from the trap, Zhukov said. We must set it.

Certainly, the spies were saying little to discourage Zhukov. On May 6, Werther reported to the Center that any attack would be delayed at least four weeks. The next day, the Center told Rado to "discover from Werther through Lucy all details about the plans and intentions of OKW and report to us urgently."[35] Rado did, the next day.

Werther warned Moscow on May 13 that "German reconnaissance has identified Soviet concentrations near Kursk, Vyazma, Velikiye and Luki."[36] That was the exact information that Model had told Hitler at the May 3 conference. No German secret, it seemed, was safe. On May 23, Werther reported that "all preparations of von Manstein's and Kluge's army groups were completed; all motorized and armored units stationed on the second line are in a state of alert, ready to leave for the front."[37] On May 30, Werther received an "urgent" message. He was asked to immediately answer three questions. "1) At precisely what point of the southern sector of the Eastern Front is the German offensive to open? 2) With what forces and in which direction is the thrust to be made? 3) Apart from the southern sector, where and when is a German offensive planned on the Eastern Front?"[38] Zhukov later wrote that by the end of May to early June, the Soviet leadership knew "virtually all the details of the enemy's plan."[39]

On June 4, 1943, the Center ordered Rado to concentrate all his resources on the Kursk sector.[40] This was exactly when Hitler's mind became settled. Kursk would indeed be Germany's 1943 strategic objective.[41] And it would be the only one. Hitler would not look back.

The Russians were growing increasingly concerned about two things in particular. Could their forces stop the new German Panther tank? And did Hitler plan to use poison gas? On June 12, the director asked the Lucy network to describe the construction technology of the tank, the strength of its armor, and whether it was equipped with flamethrowers. The Russians also wanted to know the number of Panthers they would face.[42] Though no reply has yet surfaced, the west to this date had released decryptions of less than 10 percent of the Gisela traffic. Judging from Werther's past performance, Moscow learned what it needed to about the Panther.

BORMANN WRITES

At the same time that Werther was being asked about the Panthers, the Center sent to the Trepper organization questions about its other major concern. Trepper was asked to "contact the manufacturer and find out whether the army of occupation is preparing to make use of gas. Is this type of material being transported at the present time? Are gas bombs being stored on the airfields? Where and in what quantity? What is the caliber of these bombs? What is the gas to be used? What is the degree of toxicity? Are tests being made with it? Have you heard the name of 'Gay-Hellé?'"[43]

The German commander in the field said it was "completely impossible to answer these questions."[44] Rundstedt seconded the remark. "I do not see the necessity for continuing the game," he said.

The Abwehr told Berlin: "The High Command of the Army is of the opinion that for some time the Director in Moscow has been asking questions that are too specific . . . The military High Command can no longer give accurate answers when, for example, Moscow asks the number of divisions or regiments, the names of the commanders, etc.

"The High Command of the Army feels that they can no longer furnish this type of information without posing formidable security problems."[45]

But the high command was overruled. The CIA said that this order came from the "Special Command" of the Reich Main Security Office. Trepper agreed that Gestapo chief Heinrich Müller, head of the Gestapo division of the RSHA, had a major role in the playback. But Müller did not have enough power to overrule the generals. Only two people in Germany had such power: Hitler himself and Martin Bormann, the Führer's shadow. Trepper said that it was Bormann who took over the playback.

After the war, Trepper wrote this of Bormann: "After Bormann took matters into his own hands, however, the situation changed. He possessed the necessary authority to silence the reservations of Ribbentrop and Marshal von Rundstedt combined. From this point on, the Great Game was referred to as 'Operation Bear.'"[46]

Trepper went on: "Not only did he [Bormann] appoint a group of experts to prepare the material that would be used for the Great Game, but he wrote the dispatches with his own hand . . ."[47]

Although the CIA's report differs from Trepper's on many accounts, on this one they agree: On June 5, von Rundstedt did object to any more cooperation with the "Great Game," stating flatly: "Moscow station had for some time been putting questions of a military type in such a precise form" that continuation was no longer possible.[48] The "RSHA Special Command" overruled his objection, and on June 17 von Rundstedt again was forced to provide information for the playback.[49]

Trepper's account—that it was Martin Bormann himself who took control of the operation and wrote some of the dispatches to Moscow—was confirmed by David Dallin.[50] Dallin, however, as-

sumed that Hitler's deputy had been "assigned to do an important job of misinforming" Moscow.[51] In this, Dallin brushed over
a key fact: No one in the Third Reich but Hitler could "assign"
Bormann to any task—not Göring, Keitel, or even Himmler.

If Bormann was involved in the *funkspiel*, it could be only
through his own volition or by order of the Führer. And Hitler
was not in the habit of divulging secrets to Joseph Stalin.

Russia did not always possess the best tanks or planes or generals. But it always had the best intelligence. And that factor
would now be decisive. Nothing Hitler could do, save call off the
battle, could change its outcome.

DECEPTION

Stalin knew that he could definitely not count on the Allies at
this crucial juncture. Any doubt he may have had about that
would evaporate on June 13—two weeks before the German offensive—when Winston Churchill finally told Stalin that he
could expect no second front in 1943. "It would be no help to
Russia if we threw away a hundred thousand men in a disastrous
cross-channel attack such as would, in my opinion, certainly occur if we tried under present conditions and with forces too weak
to exploit any success that might be gained at very heavy cost. In
my view and that of all my expert military advisers, we should,
even if we got ashore, be driven into the sea as the Germans have
forces already in France superior to any we could put there this
year."[52]

This was not true: Germany had sent almost all competent
forces to the east, and Churchill knew it. The cracking of the
German Enigma code was now three years old, and the British
knew in detail almost everything that Hitler planned. Regardless, Churchill continued, again with deception: "Our information about German intentions is conflicting. On balance I think
Hitler will attack you again, probably in the Kursk Salient, and
that he will cut his losses in Italy. On the other hand, our intelligence reports show that the Japanese are urging him not to
make a third attack on Russia but to turn his forces against the
United States and Great Britain."[53]

By now, Stalin already knew about Hitler's plans. He must have considered Churchill's qualified warning strange at best. A week later, Churchill sent Stalin an even stranger message that did not even mention Kursk. Instead, Churchill said that Allied moves in North Africa had "been an important factor in causing Hitler to hesitate and to delay his plans for a large scale offensive against Russia this summer."[54]

By the time this disinformation reached Moscow, the Trepper playback, Gisela's family, and captured German prisoners were sending the Center detailed plans for the Kursk offensive. Churchill's deception simply could not be believed.

Stalin told Churchill that the British prime minister did "not fully understand my disappointment" in the revelation about the second front. "I must say: here is not simply the question of disappointment on the part of the Soviet Government, here is the question of its confidence in the Allies which is severely tried by the above happenings."[55]

Churchill was not impressed: "The reproaches which you now cast upon your Western Allies leave me unmoved."[56] And Churchill took credit for his North African policy having greatly helped Russia by increasing "the enemy's uncertainty as to where the blow will fall and what its weight will be." This, according to Churchill, would "lead to the delaying of Hitler's 3rd attack upon Russia, of which it seemed great preparations were in existence six weeks ago. It may even prove that you will not be heavily attacked this summer."[57]

Either British cryptographers had been uncharacteristically asleep or Winston Churchill was again prevaricating. But for what purpose?

Some thought that the Western Allies, in reneging on the second front and trying to misinform Stalin about Hitler's true intentions, were playing a dangerous game. Spanish foreign minister Jordana had earlier handed the British ambassador, Samuel Hoare, a note warning of the possible consequences of a lone Soviet victory over Germany: "If events develop in the future as they have up to now, it would be Russia which will penetrate deeply into German territory. And we ask the question: if this should occur, which is the greater danger not only for the Continent but for England herself, a Germany not totally defeated but with sufficient strength to serve as a rampart against Communism, a Germany hated by all her neighbors, which would deprive her of authority though she remained intact, or a Sovietized Germany which would certainly furnish Russia with the added strength of her war preparations, her engineers, her specialized workmen and technicians, which would enable Russia to extend herself with an empire without precedent from the Atlantic to the Pacific?"

Jordana warned, "Should Russia succeed in conquering Germany, there will be no one who can contain her." Then he said a truth that became brutally apparent only after the war: "If Germany did not exist, Europeans would have to invent her."[58]

ORDER OF BATTLE

On July 1, Hitler gave his final orders that the offensive would begin sometime between July 4 and July 6.[59] Within twenty-four hours, Werther managed to notify Moscow of Hitler's decision. To be on the safe side, the Stavka told its commanders at Kursk that the Germans would begin their battle sometime between July 3 and July 6.[60] Every troop was to be prepared.

"The Russians were aware of what was coming, and had converted Kursk into another Verdun," complained Gen. F. W. Mellenthin later.[61] "D day was finally fixed for 4 July—Independence Day of the United States, the beginning of the end for Germany."

The Red Army that now faced the Germans was different in tone, valor, and brains from the army that Hitler had first encountered. The Red Army was, first of all, less red. Instead of being seen as an extension of the Communist Party, now it was promoted as a nationalist force, shaped more upon German lines than Bolshevik. Some 122,000 political officers were now drafted into the front lines. No longer was their approval needed before an officer could direct operations.[62]

And the army that had lost so many men and so much materiel had replenished itself. In 1943, Russia produced 24,000 tanks, including 15,812 formidable T-34s. Germany had also increased production, but not as fast as Stalin. In 1943, Germany produced 17,000 tanks.[63] The Russians were also producing large quantities of SU-122 antitank guns, called "animal killers" for their potential ability to successfully attack the new German Tiger and Panther tanks. The Russians were also receiving vast amounts of materiel from America. Though America's inferior Sherman tank would make little impression on the Germans, the raw materials, light vehicles, and communication equipment were essential. Zhukov said that without lend-lease aid, Russia could not have continued the war.[64]

And the Red Army, despite an occasional knee jerk by Stalin to begin a senseless attack, was patient and prepared. The Russians stuffed seven whole armies into the Kursk salient. Behind those were four others held in reserve. More than 3,000 miles of trenches had been dug, 400,000 mines laid, 150 airfields built. In all, 1,336,000 men with 3,444 tanks and 19,000 pieces of artillery were ready for the Germans. A full 40 percent of the Red Army was in the salient, and 75 percent of its armored forces. This was the cream of the Red Army, bunched in one deadly bulge, with guns arranged to treat the German panzers to murderous cross fire.[65] Opposing these forces were 900,000 German troops with 2,700 tanks and 10,000 artillery pieces.

Military doctrine says that in most cases the attacker must have superior numbers in order to succeed. Some textbooks say that the advantage should be two to one. Here the attacker had an inferior force. Doctrine also called for the attacker to have strategic and tactical surprise. Here, because of the Russian spies, Germany had neither.

Although there was some preliminary skirmishing on July 4,[66] the Russians were sure that this did not amount to the great invasion. But things changed rapidly in the early-morning hours of July 5. At 2 A.M. a Russian officer told Zhukov that a captured Czech soldier had revealed that the long-anticipated attack was to begin in an hour. The officer asked: "What shall we do? Inform Supreme Headquarters or issue orders for the preliminary bombardment ourselves?"[67] Zhukov, controlling Red Army forces on the northern side of the salient, ordered the Red Army to begin at once one of the most intense artillery bombardments in the history of war. He did not first consult with Stalin, explaining that he could not "waste time."[68] Russian general Nikolai Vatutin had made a similar independent decision to open fire on the southern front.[69]

Things were happening in reverse. It was the army on the offensive that was supposed to fire artillery in the dark of night just before a major attack. Most major offensives in the twentieth century had followed this course. Not now. The Red Army fired into German lines with so much steel and cordite that even some German officers in the rear thought that the concussions meant only that some of their forces had started early. Someone, somehow, had miscalculated. But those closer to the receiving end of the Russian cannonade knew positively that the Russians knew where they were.

Zhukov called Stalin to tell him of his bold decision. Stalin approved. Zhukov later said of Stalin at this moment: "I got the impression that he was tense . . . In fact, all of us, despite our long-prepared defenses in depth, despite our powerful striking potential, were in a state of high excitement. It was night, but none of us felt like sleeping."[70]

German troops were read a message from the Führer: "Soldiers of the Reich! This day you are to take part in an offensive of such importance that the whole future of the war may depend on its outcome. More than anything else, your victory will show the whole world that resistance to the power of the German Army is hopeless."[71]

Werther immediately informed the Center that to "make sure of success the German high command is throwing in the greater part of the reserves belonging to Manstein's army group; these reserves are being brought up continually via Kharkov. The high command sees no danger to the right flank and the middle sector of Manstein's army group."[72]

For all its import and buildup, Kursk was not a long engagement. The decisive battle of the European theater of the Second World War was decided in days, not months. In the Pacific, the

Americans had already won their decisive battle at Midway Island in the span of a few lucky minutes when dive-bombers spotted the Japanese fleet through a break in the clouds. Both battles also owed their success to intelligence work: The Americans had cracked the Japanese code, and the Soviets had Werther.

There had never before been the armored firepower that was assembled at Kursk. And although the sheer weight of steel held that the Germans should never have started their attack and that, once started, it should have been immediately crushed, they put on a fierce fight. Manstein even contended afterward that the battle could have been won, though that assessment is in the minority. What is clear is that the new German tanks performed well. But in the hellish Russian cross fire from the prepared positions that Model had warned about, they could not prevail.

After the Russians christened the battle with their preemptive bombardment—what Zhukov called "the mighty symphony of the battle"[73]—the Germans were caught off guard. The German generals hardly mentioned this in the memoirs, for good reason. Zhukov said that the impromptu bombardment cost the Germans at least two crucial hours when the Wehrmacht's guns were supposed to command the field.

Wrote Zhukov: "The Germans' offensive, launched at 5:30 A.M., was not well organized or fully coordinated [suggesting that] they had taken heavy losses. Prisoners later reported that our softening-up bombardment had been unexpected, the German artillery had suffered greatly and that communications and observations and control systems had been disrupted almost everywhere."[74] Others maintain that the Germans began on schedule—3:30 A.M.—which befits a battle that was steered from the shadows.[75]

In the map room, the plan was simple. The 4th Panzer Army was to advance from the south and the 9th Panzer Army from the north. The pincers would meet somewhere east of Kursk, surrounding whatever Red Army forces were left in the salient.

The 4th Panzer Army was one of the most formidable forces ever created, consisting of the divisions SS Leibstandarte, SS Das

Reich, SS Totenkopf, SS Gross Deutschland, 3d Panzer, 6th Panzer, 7th Panzer, 11th Panzer, and 19th Panzer.[76] These nine divisions were side by side on a mere thirty-mile front. The 9th Army in the north was nearly as strong, with three panzer corps and two supporting corps of infantry.[77]

The Germans soon understood the hell they were entering. As the first wave of German tanks entered the salient, they discovered just how many mines had been laid there. Many of the older tanks soon lost their tracks and were target practice for the vastly superior Russian antitank guns. Because the Germans had been told to remain inside any tank whose guns still functioned, the crews were savaged. The Tigers proved that they could withstand most of what the Russians could offer, but they often ambled slowly ahead without supporting infantry.

Alan Clark argued that the whole operation was an abandonment of the traditional use of the panzers as highly mobile piercing spearheads. Instead, they were to lumber on in close support of the infantry. Of course, there was no chance of the panzers speeding through the Kursk salient, which Mellenthin called "the strongest fortress in the world."[78] But that was the point. There were many places in Russia where they could go with some success, but Kursk was not one of them. In fact, it was the worst possible place to send new Krupp steel.

The Russians had developed a new tactic known by the Germans as *pakfront*. An officer commanded ten antitank guns at a time, each aimed at an individual panzer. The minefields funneled the panzers into prearranged lines of fire, and the *pakfront* turned those lines into killing fields.

From the north, the Germans managed to advance some ten miles before Zhukov stopped them. Ninety Tiger tanks, called Ferdinands, specially designed by Professor Porsche, headed the German force. In other circumstances, they would have been the most powerful tank in the world. Their armor could not be matched, and their main gun was the largest anywhere. The problem was that their main gun was their only gun. Guderian had already said that the tank could not be used as it was now ordered to be used.

"The Ferdinand," Guderian wrote after the war, "had an 88 mm, L70 cannon in a fixed turret, as in an assault gun. Apart from this single, long barreled gun it possessed no other armament and so was valueless for fighting at close range."[79] The Russians proved Guderian right. Red Army infantry soon learned that they could crawl on the monsters with impunity, then disgorge gasoline into engine ventilation slats to kill the crews.[80] Used as spearheads in an open field, the Ferdinands could have been decisive. Had they been around two years before, maybe Moscow would have fallen. But in the tightly constrained venue of a fortress, they were dinosaurs.

In the south, there was better news for the Germans: Manstein's and Hoth's forces had driven the Russians behind their first defense lines. More progress was made on July 7, with Hoth pushing almost halfway to his objective. By the ninth, parts of Gross Deutschland had penetrated the main Russian defense line.[81] By the eleventh, a significant hole had been punched into Fortress Kursk. The next day, July 12, was the day of decision. Model was checked in the north, and the Germans were betting everything on the forces to the south. The Germans sent some nine hundred tanks headlong into a comparably equipped and offensively minded Soviet 5th Army.[82] At 6:30 A.M. the German air offensive began, leaving the town of Prokhorovka veiled in smoke and fire. Russian fighters appeared, and soon planes from both sides were being shot out of the sky. Then Russian artillery opened a barrage, and at 8:30 A.M.—using the code name Stalin—the Russian tanks advanced.[83] It was the largest tank engagement of the war. At the end of the day, seven hundred shattered tanks, roughly evenly divided, littered the battlefield. Thousands of men had been killed. It was a tactical draw but a strategic win for the Russians. The German advance had been stopped. The Russians were in control of the battlefield.

It became clear, said Mellenthin, "that the time table of the German attack had been completely upset. At the very beginning of the offensive, the piercing of the forward Russian lines, deeply and heavily mined as they were, had proved much more difficult than we anticipated. The terrific Russian counterattacks, with masses of men and materiel ruthlessly thrown in, were also an unpleasant surprise."[84]

Mellenthin complained that the Panthers that Hitler had wagered so much on had proven to be battlefield liabilities, easily set ablaze because of the poor design of their fuel system.

On July 13, Hitler was ready to give up. He ordered Manstein and Kluge to headquarters and said that the battle should be stopped. The Western Allies had invaded Sicily, and the Führer was afraid that Italy might be knocked out of the war. The Italians, Hitler complained, were not resisting. Kluge agreed, saying that the 9th Army was making no headway and was already withdrawing forces to meet a new Russian offensive near Orel. Manstein, however, disagreed: "To break off at this moment would be tantamount to throwing a victory away."[85] Hitler agreed that Manstein's force could continue fighting until it had smashed the enemy's armored reserves. But this did not happen, because more and more forces were needed to head off the Orel offensive.

Though fighting would continue until July 22, it was becoming clear to all that the battle of Kursk had been a monstrous mistake. Said Guderian: "By the failure of *Citadel* we had suffered a decisive defeat."[86]

Kursk had done what Stalingrad had not: It broke the back of the Wehrmacht. Never again would the Germans launch a major offensive on the eastern front.

Just before Kursk, Stalin had sent signals through Sweden that the Soviets were determined "not to fight for a day or even a minute—'ni odnu minitu'—longer than necessary on behalf of British and American interests."[87] According to one of Ribbentrop's men, Peter Kleist, Stalin wanted a Germany at peace and in economic cooperation with Russia. Ernst Kaltenbrunner, now head of the RSHA, severely questioned Kleist before accepting the approach as real. Ribbentrop even told Hitler of the contact, though Hitler had specifically forbidden such endeavors.[88] Hitler listened carefully and did not complain that his orders had been broken, but he insisted that they be followed in the future.

Ribbentrop did not obey; he sent Kleist once again to Stock-holm to find out more. Unfortunately for Germany, Russia had by then won at Kursk. The peace feeler was withdrawn.[89]

Now Stalin resolved to win the war, with or without trustwor-thy allies and the forever delayed second front. But the might of the Wehrmacht still haunted him. Could his country, poor in al-most every category when compared to the Western powers, ac-tually beat the Germans and have enough resources left to con-front London and Washington?

He turned again to Werther for an answer.

Notes

1 Mellenthin, p. 253.

2 Heinz Guderian, *Panzer Leader* (Washington, D.C.: Zenger Publishing Co., Inc., 1952), p. 295.

3 Ibid., p. 298.

4 Clark, p. 312.

5 Guderian, p. 295.

6 Manstein, p. 443.

7 Ibid., p. 445.

8 NAZ, p. 861.

9 Trepper, p. 250.

10 RG 319, Box 59, Vol. 1.

11 Ibid.

12 Report on the Schellenberg case, p. 44.

13 Ibid., p. 45.

14 Ibid.

15 Guderian, p. 300.

16 Ibid.

17 Ibid.

18 Ibid., p. 301.

19 Gisevius, p. 469.

20 Georgi K. Zhukov, *Marshall Zhukov's Greatest Battles* (New York: Harper & Row, 1969), pp. 209–10.

21 Reed and Fisher, p. 152.

22 NAZ, p. 861.

23 Ibid.

24 Ibid.

25 Ibid., p. 862.

26 Carell, p. 107.

27 Garlinski, p. 138; Carell, p. 102; Rado, p. 176.

28 Rado, p. 178.

29 CIA, pp. 177–78.

30 Guderian, p. 306.

31 Ibid., p. 307.

32 Ibid., p. 302.

33 Ibid., pp. 308–09.

34 Zhukov, *Greatest Battles,* p. 221.

35 Carell, p. 102.

36 Ibid.; Rado, p. 205.

37 Reed and Fisher, p. 163; Rado, p. 206.

38 Carell, p. 102; Rado, p. 207.

39 Zhukov, *Greatest Battles,* p. 215.

40 Carell, p. 102.

41 Clark, p. 327.

42 RG 319, Box 59.

43 Trepper, p. 251. The CIA's report confirmed that Moscow asked the Trepper network about gas on May 29, 1943. It maintained that the director's question was part of a successful use of psychological warfare against the Germans (CIA, p. 115).

44 Trepper, p. 251.

45 Ibid., pp. 251–52.

46 Ibid., p. 264.

47 Ibid.

48 CIA, p. 113.

49 Ibid.

50 Dallin, p. 173.

51 Ibid.

52 Message C-310 from Churchill to Roosevelt, per Kimball, Vol. 2.

53 Ibid.

54 Message C-322 from Churchill to Roosevelt, per Kimball, Vol. 2.

55 Message C-335 from Churchill to Roosevelt, per Kimball, Vol. 2.

56 Ibid.

57 Ibid.

58 Guderian, p. 286.

59 NAZ, p. 683.

60 Zhukov, *Greatest Battles,* p. 233.

61 Mellenthin, p. 264.

62 Richard Overy, *Russia's War* (New York: TV Books, 1997), p. 231.

63 Ibid., p. 236.

64 Ibid., p. 238.

65 Ibid., pp. 243–44.

66 The Germans give the afternoon of July 4 as the start of the battle. The Russians give the early-morning hours of July 5, the same date given by several historians of the period.

67 Zhukov, *Greatest Battles*, p. 233.

68 Ibid.

69 Gilbert, p. 441.

70 Zhukov, *Greatest Battles*, p. 234.

71 Clark, p. 329.

72 Rado, p. 222.

73 Zhukov, *Greatest Battles*, p. 234.

74 Ibid., p. 235.

75 Gilbert, p. 442.

76 Clark, p. 328.

77 Ibid.

78 Mellenthin, p. 264. See also Clark's analysis on p. 331.

79 Guderian, p. 299.

80 Clark, p. 333.

81 Ibid., p. 335.

82 NAZ, p. 864; Overy (p. 250) says that the Germans had 600 tanks engaged and the Russians had 850.

83 Overy, p. 250.

84 Mellenthin, p. 276.

85 Manstein, p. 449.

86 Guderian, p. 312.

87 Toland, p. 750.

88 Report on the Schellenberg case, p. 52.

89 Toland, p. 751.

Chapter Nine

CLAIRVOYANT

UNRELENTING

Although Germany could not win the war by anything that its men and steel produced, it was still possible that Stalin would find a way to lose or have victory bargained away. Stalin was determined to do neither. To win, the Soviet leader needed to know where the Germans were and where they were not. From Gisela's family in Switzerland came answers.

Werther was now at his best in his role as Soviet clairvoyant, capable not only of finding out important details about where the Gross Deutschland panzer battalion was but also discerning the strategic concepts about how the German High Command planned to conduct its defense. He knew that there was not a single, monolithic plan but a menagerie of conflicting concepts. Generals in the west wanted more forces there to thwart a feared Allied invasion; those in the southwest wanted more forces to protect the Italian theater; and those in the east thought that nothing short of maximum effort could now stop the Russian bear. And although Hitler issued orders and tried to synthesize all the conflicting potentialities, his generals still often took matters into their own hands.

But out of this fog came unusually precise information from Werther. He not only reported the conflicts and the often searing personality clashes behind them, but at times he even told Moscow exactly when Hitler entered a meeting room, when he left, and what was said in his absence. Nothing seemed beyond Werther's reach.

Such specific, detailed, and timely intelligence over an extended period of time is likely unprecedented in the history of war. For instance, as the Russian offensive sought to crush the

German southern armies after Kursk, Werther told Moscow Center: "The order to withdraw the base organizations in the southern sector can probably not be executed. A planned retreat is practically impossible because Red Army pressure is increasing, losses in the whole Donets salient are high, and the Soviet air force is stepping up its activities in the German rear . . . As of today the southern wing of the Donets front is in process of disbandment. South of Stalino and Makeyevka there is no line of defense prepared."[1] It was as if Werther had a secret hologram of Hitler's map room.

Sometimes, Werther not only gave Moscow the highest secrets of the Reich but went on to tell the Center how best to interpret them: "As of 15 September Manstein's army group can be regarded as beaten. In the period since 15 August it has lost half its equipment and heavy guns and 40 percent of its strength or a total of some 250,000 men."[2]

Werther's service was unrelenting. On September 24, he reported: "Wehrmacht high command has decided to pull its eastern front supply organization back to and behind the 'eastern rampart.' This partially fortified line is the so-called tank-buster line planned in January."[3] The next day, he told the Center: "In giving up Smolensk the Germans have lost their strongest focus or resistance on the Soviet-German front since Orel . . ."[4] On September 29, Werther reported: "Wehrmacht high command considers it possible that the Russian high command may very soon attack the Lake Ilmen–West Dvina and Kieve-Kremenchug lines in full force, piling on the tanks and mobile divisions, and that the attack may be pushed as far as the Gulf of Riga in the north and Odessa and the lower and middle Dniester in the south before winter sets in; in the central sector the Russians will probably economize on troops and weapons. The Wehrmacht high command regards this as the most dangerous plan of all as far as the German army in its present condition and situation is concerned. The Wehrmacht high command has rejected the proposal put forward by Kleist and Küchler and is determined for political reasons not to rush things . . ."[5]

Werther continued his services in October, telling Moscow: "The Germans are reckoning with very big war-material losses in the Vitebsk region. They have only the road to Polotsk for moving out their heavy stuff."[6]

DANGER TO THE ROTE DREI

As Werther waged his offensive against the Germans, the Germans began their own offensive against Werther. Certain forces still loyal to Germany, if not Hitler, intended to shut down Gisela's family and thereby silence Stalin's most important spy. Walter Schellenberg, the foreign intelligence head of the SS, received the first two decrypts of the Swiss network's wireless traffic with Moscow in December 1942 or early 1943.[7] The enormity of the treason must have been obvious to a man who knew firsthand the art of betrayal. Though he had made almost casual attempts to penetrate the network before, now there appeared to be fire in Schellenberg's efforts.[8]

His main attacks on the Swiss net began in the spring of 1943, though accounts differ about the exact timing of each. Apparently, the first came when a female Russian paratrooper code-named "Inge" landed in Germany with instructions to contact a member of Gisela's family. Her mission was to gather a wireless transmitter from Poliakova's Swiss underground. The man delivering the set was Hans Müller, brother of Anna Müller, a matronly veteran of Gisela's family. The Germans learned of the mission and arrested Inge, Hans Müller, and another Soviet agent. Soon, Anna received a letter from Hans asking her to come to Freiburg. A close relative, he said, was ill. In fact, the Gestapo had already executed Hans, and the letter was a fake.

Anna, somehow, did not suspect this. She unwisely traveled to Freiburg and was arrested. It is not certain what, if anything, the Germans got out of Anna, Inge, and Hans or, in fact, what use they made of the transmitter itself. What is clear is that soon after these events, German secret agents began zeroing in on one of the most successful spy rings in history.[9]

ROSA

There were so many attempts made to break the back of the Rote Drei that they seem more like shotgun blasts than well-aimed rifle shots. First blood was drawn from perhaps the Swiss net's weakest link—a young, high-spirited, and overly romantic radio operator named Margarete Bolli, code-named "Rosa." Margarete was twenty-one years old and a waitress when Rado first brought her into the network as a cutout and handler of routine messages between the spy ring's more important elements.[10] But Rado quickly decided that Margarete could move up in the organization to the material position of wireless operator. She would work as the third radio in the net, backing up Foote—who handled the bulk of the Werther material—and Edmond and Olga Hamel, a husband-and-wife team who had handled much of the rest. When the German Sonderkommandos picked up Rosa's signal, they knew that they had three Red targets in Switzerland, and they dubbed the network there as the Rote Drei, or Red Three.

It is not known what special attributes Bolli had that recommended her for secret work, but her physical attributes soon got the better of Rado. Breaking every rule of the dark trade, Rado not only began sleeping with Bolli but made no secret of keeping company with her at various bars and restaurants in Geneva.[11]

German secret agents were not slow studies when it came to affairs of the heart, and they soon sent one Hans Peters to try to steal away Bolli's affections. Peters—described in various accounts as a hairdresser, an SS officer, a Gestapo agent, and an Abwehr agent—managed his task spectacularly. Soon Margarete began cheating on Rado, sneaking away to an apartment for liaisons with Hans. The supposed spymaster Rado had no idea that his beautiful mistress had a new lover. Foote also had no suspicions, but in his case that is more understandable.[12]

While Rado remained happy and ignorant, Hans set about exploiting his conquest. He managed to win Margarete over so completely that she revealed everything that Hans asked, apparently without ever suspecting that a hairdresser didn't need to know about secret codes.[13] Then again, in Margarete's favor, she had not been schooled in the work of conspiracy. As with much that went wrong in the Swiss spy ring, it was Rado who was the bungler.

With Margarete, the Germans had the number three of the Rote Drei, and that was not bad. But until they had "Jim" Foote and, more importantly, Rachel Dübendorfer, they would not have the keys to Werther, the ostensible object of the search. Unluckily for the Swiss network, Hans Peters was an industrious spy who managed to partly surmount this problem.

As Hans extracted more and more about the current operations of the network, he began learning something of its past. And it was during one of those supposedly idle conversations about the past that Hans made a great discovery. Margarete told him about a time during her cutout phase when she had taken a message from Rado to Foote. It contained some important material that Rado wanted Foote to send to Moscow. While Foote and Margarete chatted, Foote was uncharacteristically careless, and he began to nervously shred some papers in his hands. He didn't stop until he realized, to his horror, that he had pretty much destroyed Rado's important message. As is often true, a simple, unpredictable error by someone not even on the battlefield had far-reaching consequences.

Realizing his stupid error, Foote desperately hauled the fragments of Rado's message out of the wastebasket and, believing that the situation demanded improvisation, enlisted Margarete's help to reassemble them.[14] The two largely succeeded, and Foote later sent the message to the Center. Unfortunately for the Rote Drei, Margarete Bolli had an excellent memory and was able to convey to Hans much of the text that she and Foote had pieced back together. With this, the Germans had wording from a preenciphered message that was later sent to Moscow in Foote's important secret code.

Soon, Berlin cryptographers started to compare some of the Morse code gibberish that they had recorded but had been unable to decipher to those parts of Rado's message. With this, they began to break Foote's code. American intelligence said simply that Margarete Bolli "was the means of providing German intelligence with its first important clue to Foote's cipher."[15] She had, in effect, given German cryptographers a crib sheet into the Red Army's most secret communications.

It was now that the Germans confirmed a leak in the high command and learned of his code name: Werther.

If Schellenberg had any reason to doubt the great damage that this source had caused, it was surely now wiped out. But he did not sound a general alarm. For reasons that remain unclear, neither Schellenberg nor his boss, Heinrich Himmler, informed Hitler of Werther's existence, nor did they tell anyone else in the OKW or OKH. This was to remain a closely held secret of the SS, and more particularly of Obergruppenführer Walter Schellenberg.

According to many accounts, Schellenberg arranged many meetings with his Swiss counterpart, Roger Masson, to discuss ways in which the Swiss police could help the Germans in decapitating the Rote Drei. Schellenberg never mentioned this in his postwar accounts. Instead, he said that his contacts with Masson were secret efforts to betray Hitler, not destroy the Führer's enemies.

Whatever Schellenberg's real goal, it is clear that the representative of the secret police could not appear to ignore the most important security risk to the Third Reich if he wanted to keep his job. By either volition or compulsion, Schellenberg's men continued to circle ever closer to their prey.

Rachel Dübendorfer began to worry about Nazi penetration when she heard that a Red Army courier named Maurice, most probably one Maurice Aenis-Haenslin, had been captured by the Gestapo. Maurice in 1941 had been one of Dübendorfer's connections with Henri Robinson in France, and Dübendorfer saw only trouble in his arrest.[16] Rado reported to Moscow: "Sissy fears that the Gestapo will thus come across her trail. Maurice knows Sissy's true name. I have initiated discreet inquiries and shall report further."[17]

Soon, an unknown man made a series of telephone calls to Rachel's house, asking for "Mr. Dübendorfer."[18] The man refused to give his name but said that he had been asked to call by "a gentleman from Lausanne, Mr. Foote."[19] Dübendorfer knew Foote only through his code name, Jim, so the introduction meant little. But the rest of the presentation meant a lot. There was no "Mr. Dübendorfer." Rachel's lover was Paul Boettcher.

Moscow was alarmed but not fully convinced that its operation was in peril. Alexander Foote put an end to this fantasy.

ORANGE BOX

Dübendorfer had not been mistaken. The Germans had captured the courier Maurice and through their often-successful methods had learned that he was supposed to personally deliver money to Foote. Naturally, the Germans did not miss the opportunity to send one of their own in the courier's place to help ferret out the Swiss organization.[20] Unfortunately for the Germans, their agent was not as adept as Hans Peters.

The Americans said that the meeting between the false courier and Foote took place in April 1943. Rado said that there were actually two meetings in late March or early April. For his part, Foote recalled that the critical meeting was in June. Despite these discrepancies, Foote's and Rado's accounts of what happened are near carbon copies. Foote said that the Center told him that the meeting with the courier was to be simple and quick. He was to exchange code words, hand over the money, and be off. There was to be no conversation.

Foote and Maurice met at the Botanical Gardens in Geneva—in Foote's terms, a designated "place of conspiracy." Everything appeared normal at first. But after Foote handed over the money and prepared to leave, the courier hesitated, then pulled out a large book wrapped in bright orange paper and told Foote that inside there were three ciphered messages of prime importance. They must, the courier said, be sent to the Center immediately.[21]

It did not take the instincts of a master spy to realize that this was unusual. The orange paper could only call attention to an exchange that was supposed to be secret. As Foote thought more about it, he realized that carrying a brightly colored object that could be spotted easily might actually be the intent of his courier. Spotters would have little trouble tailing a man carrying an orange box. But such spotters, Foote accurately deduced, would not be on his side.

Sensing the setup, Foote tried to hide the package beneath his coat. He could have done much more. Discarding the orange box straightaway, perhaps even slapping the courier in the face for his indiscretion, would not have been a bad idea. Failing this, Foote could have gone to a safe house or Bern or anywhere else until he was absolutely certain that he wasn't being followed. But he didn't. He later explained that he made his way home to Lausanne by "a round-about route" and took certain other unstated evasive actions.[22]

Foote was usually an adroit practitioner of these small conspiracies. But his decision here was wrong. The Germans had him in their cross hairs and successfully followed him home. But for all he did that was wrong, Foote did at least manage to deduce that there was a problem. He had no intention of sending the ciphered messages, realizing that if they were as phony as the courier, "they would serve as admirable pointers towards identifying my transmitter."[23] Instead, he told the Center of his suspicions.

At the Center, Foote's suspicions rang crystal clear. Combined with Dübendorfer's warning about Maurice and the mysterious caller for "Mr. Dübendorfer," the Center knew that it faced grave danger.[24] The Germans seemed only a step away from Lucy, and if they got her, they would surely get Werther. As far as the Center was concerned, everyone else in the net could run to ground, at least temporarily, while the Center came up with some way to keep the Germans off the trail of its source in the German High Command. The Center told Foote that the courier was a Gestapo agent and that German agents had "managed to tail you to your flat and find out your name." The director told Foote to remove all intelligence-related items from his apartment, hide his transmitter elsewhere for use at another time, and temporarily break off connections with Rado. "If you are interrogated by the Swiss police," the Center told Foote, "deny everything categorically."[25] In the meantime, Foote was to have no contact with Rado.

On June 4 Rado was given similar orders with regard to Dübendorfer. The Center told him to break connection to Dübendorfer "completely" but not before he could "convince" Rachel to turn over her sources to another uncompromised agent. The Center told Rado to try anything. "Tell her," it suggested, "that it will be for only three months."[26] If Rado, Foote, and most importantly Dübendorfer were out of the picture, the Werther operation could continue.

There was one big problem. Dübendorfer would have none of it; she would not give up her spies. The Center grew frustrated. Poliakova personally wrote to Rachel in Rachel's private code on July 8, repeating the instructions to turn over her network.

But it was to no avail. Dübendorfer, who herself had pressed many of the alarms, now grew to believe that the courier problem and the mystery phone calls were not the work of Germans but of her own masters.

On the same day that Poliakova sent the message to Dübendorfer, Rado sent the Center Dübendorfer's reply to their pleadings: "Sissy and her men do not believe the story has anything to do with Maurice and the Gestapo. They believe that the man who asked about them came from the Center and just handled himself clumsily. They assume that the Center wants in this way to take away the Taylor [Lucy] group,* and in such a manner that I too shall know nothing about it."[27]

The Center reproached Dübendorfer. In an August 16 message beginning "Dear Sissy," not authored by Poliakova, the Center told Dübendorfer: "We, the Center, which has its people everywhere and can determine what is happening in other countries and around you, have told you clearly and explicitly that we have hard evidence that the Gestapo knows that you work for us and will try to uncover your connections into Germany. You, however, deny this possibility and interpret it as an attempt to take the Taylor [Lucy] group away from you. You must understand, inasmuch as you assume this position, that you know nothing of the danger which threatens you and Taylor's people, especially those in Germany [that is, Werther]. Your behavior is

---

*The "Taylor group" refers to Christian Schneider, who was a cutout between Dübendorfer and Rado. To help the reader, mention of largely extraneous members of Gisela's family has been minimized wherever possible.

frivolous and irresponsible. We demand that you recognize the seriousness of the situation and place full confidence in our statements."[28]

Dübendorfer did not care. If the Center wanted Lucy and Werther, it would have to go through her. At this point, Rado more or less threw up his arms and told the Center in September that Dübendorfer had constructed an impregnable wall around Lucy and Werther and there was nothing much that he or the Center could do about it. He confessed that he had "no direct connection with this group"[29] and said that Rachel had even refused to send a letter that he had composed to Lucy because she (Rachel) viewed it "as an attempt by the Center or by me to set up a direct contact with the Lucy group."[30] Rachel's lover, Paul Boettcher, was no kinder to Rado. Rado complained to the Center that Boettcher had "boasted in such a way that I had a hard time controlling myself. He refuses to come to Geneva for meetings . . . Again I beg you to release me from further contact with Paul."[31] The resident director was getting no respect.

HER RULES

With no alternative, the Center realized that it would have to play by Dübendorfer's rules. With the Germans knowing about Dübendorfer, she or, indeed, the whole apparatus could be rolled up at any time. But there was no need to send everybody else to ground if Dübendorfer stayed out in the open. Foote was recalled to service, and Rado was told to get some starch in his back. Between now (August) and whenever the Germans were going to attack, Werther was to be bled dry.

It was a cold but clear decision. The Red Army was planning to shift the rules. Instead of breaking off its offensive for the inevitable debilitating Russian winter, it planned to carry on the offensive relentlessly. As much as ever, the Red Army now needed the day-to-day German plans that only Werther could deliver.* If

---

*That information continued to be detailed and to cover all fronts. For instance, on August 7, Werther told the Center: "a) Richthofen is still in Italy but in view of events and in consequence of a fresh directive from

that meant the inevitable destruction of the Swiss network and
the lives of its agents, it was worth it. Every day that Werther operated, countless numbers of Germans would die. American intelligence after the war accurately determined that the Center's
"attitude was that the supply of the 'Lucy' material must be maintained at all costs . . ."[32]

But while the Center waited for the right-hand blow of the
Gestapo, a danger that it didn't anticipate rapidly approached.
The Center did not believe that the Swiss would act against its
agents, because now the Red Army was winning on the battlefield and German prospects had greatly dimmed. The Swiss, who
had managed to remain neutral even when Hitler was ascendant, would not now act as his agent. Besides, if anyone were to
act, it would be the Germans; they had the most to lose and certainly had the power to do whatever they pleased in Switzerland.
Hitler, after all, was a man who acted boldly.

What the Center did not know was the pressure that Schellenberg, for whatever reason, was putting on Masson to do Germany's work. The Center also did not know that Hitler had not
been told what his security services were learning about Gisela's
family.

The first hint that the Swiss were preparing an attack came in
October. Swiss lieutenant Maurice Treyer had located the ad-

---

the Wehrmacht high command he has not yet replaced Kesselring as
commander of the 2nd air fleet . . . b) The Wehrmacht high command
has decided to maintain the present combat strength of the 2nd air
fleet on the Italian airfields by means of reinforcements . . . c) The
Wehrmacht high command has allowed Laval to organize French regiments against the danger of Italy's defecting . . . d) The Wehrmacht
high command informed Badoglio on 29 July that it reserved to itself
every possible means of preventing the Allies from gaining a foothold
in Italy or Italian-occupied areas. . . . e) Göring visited Italy on behalf
of the Wehrmacht high command on 29 July and apparently met
Badoglio." (From Rado, p. 237.)

dresses of the two Geneva transmitters: the Hamels' residence at
192 Route de Florissant and Margarete Bolli's residence at 8 rue
Henri Mussard.[33] After someone from the "electricity board"
showed up unexpectedly at Bolli's apartment to check connections, she panicked. In Rado's account, Bolli told Rado's wife
that there was a security breach. Rado and Bolli met the next day
at a small Geneva restaurant. She was, Rado later said, "in a terrible state of nerves, staring wildly at everyone who came in or
went out the door."[34] Rado said that he told Margarete to take a
Sunday train to her parents' house in Basel. Instead, Margarete
went to the flat of Hans Peters. Rado later complained that the
"girl" had "deceived" him.[35] "She was undoubtedly afraid I would
not let her go on working for the group if I discovered she was
having an affair with a German hairdresser. She was right about
that at least," the defeated lover moaned.

The arrests came quickly. As many as seventy Swiss police with
dogs surrounded the Hamels' residence. A few slipped quietly
inside. Only minutes after midnight on October 13,* the police
flung open the door to the upstairs room and found Olga, in a
nightgown, tapping away on a transmitter. Police with drawn re-
volvers flooded the room. Olga did not even have time to tap out
a brief emergency warning to the Center.

As the Hamels were being led away to Bois-Mermet prison, another police party broke into Bolli's apartment, but she was not
there. The police, however, knew exactly were to look next. Bolli
was arrested in the same early-morning hours, *in flagrante delicto,*

---

*Rado and Foote recalled the arrests coming one right after the other,
although Foote said that the date was October 8 and Rado said it was
October 13. Most accounts of the Rote Drei agree that the correct date
was October 13. However, the CIA in 1979 said that the Hamels' arrests
came on October 8 and Bolli's on October 13, meaning that there were
five days separating the operations. Earlier American intelligence reports merely give October as the date of the arrests. These small discrepancies are frustrating to readers but especially to writers. In this account the commonly accepted date of October 13 is used for both
arrests.

with Hans Peters. Peters was briefly detained, but after the Swiss learned who he was, he was released.

Rado knew of neither operation. But on the same day as the attack, he had what he thought was important information for Moscow from Werther. Foote, who was loaded down with transmissions after his return to the fold, could not handle all the traffic. Moreover, the Hamels in Geneva were closer than Foote in Lausanne. So Rado set out to see the Hamels.

The messages that Rado carried from Werther were direct and simple. "The German high command estimates the Soviet troops attacking Vitebsk, Orsha, and Gorki at five army corps . . . ," the German spy warned in one.[36] In another, he told the Center: "The Germans have found out that there are large Russian Armored and other units in the Gorodok-Nevel sector."[37] Still another message from Werther, dated October 11, said: "The Wehrmacht high command also regards as lost the defensive sector between Zaporozhye and the Crimea."[38]

These were vital facts to get to Moscow, but it should not have been the resident director who delivered them. Using a cutout was the typical tradecraft. Rado later explained that he usually used his wife, Helene, for these operations, but this day she was feeling slightly ill. So Rado decided to do it himself. Alone and potentially exposed, Rado arrived at the Hamels' flat that afternoon.

Sensing no danger, he walked up and rang the doorbell. There was no answer. Puzzled, Rado lingered about for a while, looking in windows, then scurried to a nearby telephone booth and called the Hamels. Again, no answer. Had the Swiss police been the least bit wise, they would have left some watchers at the Hamels' apartment to see who might want to contact these Soviet spies. Rado would have then been arrested and the apparatus closed. It would have been just punishment for the resident director for not sending a cutout, then hanging around after the Hamels did not answer his ring and generally for acting stupidly. But the Swiss had not been so sapient, and Rado made it home untouched. That evening he opened a copy of the *Tribune de Geneve* and read that a major Soviet spy network had been raided.[39] Unnerved, he broke another Red Army rule of conspiracy. He called Foote on the telephone with the thinly coded message that "Edmond had been taken ill suddenly and was in hospital."[40]

As befits matters of intelligence operations, there are variations in the stories. Foote, for instance, recalled reading the same edition of the *Tribune de Geneve* but said that it was five days earlier. He also recalled somewhat differently the message. Rado, he said, told him that he would "be sorry to hear that Edouard [Edmond's code name] is much worse and the doctor has been called in. He decided after consultation that the only thing to do was to take him to hospital."[41] Despite the discrepancies, the consequences were the same. Rado went to see Foote— the same day in Rado's version, the next day in Foote's. Rado had never before done this, and it was a blatant violation of procedure. Perhaps the situation called for it (Rado's version), or it was another stupid act by Rado (Foote's version). But the Swiss police and their German backups were asleep anyway, and the meeting went undetected.

What Rado and Foote agreed on is that they both notified Moscow that Swiss police had closed two of the three Red Army transmitters in Switzerland. Foote's station was the last on-line. The Center, acting on the principles it developed after Dübendorfer's defiance, said to hell with caution; Foote was to continue to send the Werther material despite the risk. Rado was told to make every effort to recruit backup transmitters from the local Communist Party to fill in after Foote was arrested.[42]

Foote was game. The man who, as Sonia'a agent, had been willing to risk his life to assassinate Adolf Hitler agreed to risk his life again for the Center. He would keep his transmitter open and running for hours a day and for days on end until the inevitable happened.

Rado was not of like mind, being "frantic with worry and anxiety," said Foote.[43] And for good reason. Rado did not tell the Center that a blunder he had made would lead police inevitably to his front door. The groundwork had been laid more than a year earlier, in September 1942, when police in a routine search of the

Hamels' flat had found a transmitter under a floorboard. Asked to explain why he had a secret transmitter, Edmond had told the police that he was a professional radio mechanic who had built the device for receiving shortwave broadcasts, but because it looked so much like a transmitter, he decided to hide it in case anyone came searching. The police apparently believed his story, for they did not confiscate the transmitter and in the next thirteen months made no further attempts to shut it down.[44]

Edmond's quick wits led Rado to a wrong conclusion. Feeling that the Hamels had been more or less vetted by the Swiss police, Rado decided that their flat was the perfect place to hide almost anything. So, breaking every rule of tradecraft, Rado deposited with the Hamels for safekeeping highly incriminating documents, including financial records of the network, messages that Rado had sent, and, worse, copies of encoded versions of those same messages. With these, the Swiss and Germans had a good chance of decrypting many messages sent in Rado's code. But Rado's negligence went further. "As if this were not sufficient," Foote later complained, "he had been idiotic enough to leave a copy of his code book there, and this, too, fell into the hands of the police."[45]

Although Rado doesn't say so directly, he must have been weighing the consequences of his missteps. Would the Swiss police deport him to Russia if he were caught? And how would he be received in Moscow—a hero of the Soviet Union or a bungler who destroyed the Red Army's most valuable net? Whatever he was thinking, it's clear that Rado, unlike Foote, did not intend to fight to the last bullet for Moscow. Instead, he did something that took the breath away of the conspiracy pros at the Center. Rado told Moscow that his radio network was collapsing, his own arrest was imminent, and desperate solutions were needed. He proposed seeking the protection of the British legation, reasoning that because Russia and Britain were allies, the British would welcome him into their arms and bestow on him not only their diplomatic umbrella but their transmitters as well. Through such a plan, the Center would be assured of a continued supply of Werther material.

Certainly the British would have welcomed the Russian spy into their arms, and maybe even indulged his use of their transmitters, but the resulting intelligence could never be trusted by Joseph Stalin or, in fact, by those even less given to suspicion. Rado would be giving the British, who already suspected that Russia would soon replace Germany as the primary enemy in Europe, the blueprint of Soviet underground operations. No one thinking clearly would ever imagine Stalin or any other Russian agreeing to such a plan.

The Center responded immediately, telling Rado: "Your suggestion that you hide with the British and continue to work from there is absolutely unacceptable. In that case, your network would lose all independence . . . We are now in a greater need than ever of cooperation with the Lucy group. We ask you, dear Dora, to be calm . . ."[46] Rado then informed the Center that he had actually made preliminary contact with the British attaché through a cutout code-named "Salter."

The Center fired back a salvo that was the intelligence equivalent of a Katyusha rocket attack. The Center denounced Rado's "unprecedented breach of discipline" and said that it would find a way to keep the Werther group alive, but until that happened Rado had a duty to maintain contact with Dübendorfer. "You must take immediate steps somehow to undo this unfortunate action and to keep it quiet. At the same time, take care of Jim's [Foote's] security so that the most important information from Lucy can be sent through him."[47] In a later dispatch, the Center underlined its intention just in case the jittery Rado somehow failed to comprehend the obvious. "We must make use of Lucy at this time, when she is so very precious to us, or we will lose her not only now but also in the future."[48]

HIDING

But Rado was not calmed. He made one more pitch for his harebrained British plan, arguing that the Lucy group wouldn't work without pay and that pay had been interrupted. Going through the British legation would solve this problem. The British, after all, would be able to get money to the group.

The director was dumbfounded. The reasons for Dora's persistence, the Center said, was "totally incomprehensible" and apparently the product of some British SIS endeavor that had "no understanding of the importance of this historic moment to the common cause of the allied nations."[49] Then, in a follow-up, the Center told Rado: "Tell Lucy in our name to be calm, the transmissions of his information to us is assured and that his group will most certainly continue to be paid, and at the rate he demands. We are prepared to pay a rich reward for his information."[50]

Instead of maintaining contact with Lucy and calming Foote, Rado went into hiding. He did not, as the Center had asked, bother putting Foote in contact with Dübendorfer so that Dübendorfer would have a way of getting her messages to Moscow, a blunder that would have far-reaching impact not only on this war but the Cold War that followed. Instead, he told Foote that he would emerge from his hiding spots long enough to take in Dübendorfer's messages, which he would then send to Foote. The resident director would be a simple cutout, and not a very good one, at that.

Rado did his best not to come out of hiding at all. Foote was convinced that Rado's real motive was to keep Dübendorfer and Foote from getting together and comparing notes. "Rado had been indenting on me for large sums of money to pay 'Sissy' and her agents, but had been keeping a large proportion of this money for himself," Foote charged. "This discrepancy would immediately come out when we met, as it did a year later."[51]

Foote kept transmitting; he was receiving occasional Lucy information from the underground Rado. But Foote soon learned from a prison source that the interrogators had told the Hamels that they knew of another Red Army transmitter working in Lausanne. Foote immediately told the Center that he was about to be unmasked. The Center told the intrepid Foote that he "must risk everything and continue to transmit."[52] Rado and Foote carried on their irregular liaisons at their "place of conspiracy." But after Foote said that he thought he spotted surveillance when the two met at the Parc d'Eaux Vives in Geneva, what little fortitude Rado possessed evaporated. Said Foote after the war, "This little incident put the finishing touch to Rado's fears. From that time on it was impossible to lure him out of his hidey-hole." To be sure, Foote also noted that Rado had been under intense pressure for years. "I prefer to remember him at the height of his power," Foote said, "as the genial cartographer to the world at large, and the successful spymaster to the favoured few, rather than as the hunted rat of his last Swiss days . . ."[53]

While Rado hid, Foote began planning how to bribe the friendly prison guard and get Bolli and the Hamels set free. But there was no time. At 1:15 A.M. on November 20, an ax crashed into Foote's front door. The door, however, refused to give way. Foote had a few moments to try to save what he could. He disabled his transmitter, poured lighter fluid on the few papers he had, ignited them, then awaited his capture.[54] The last transmission from the Swiss net was over.

Under interrogation, Foote stunned his captors. He pointed out that if it was true that he was a Red agent, the Soviet Union would look upon his arrest as an act of aggression. But he insisted that he not be released for a long time, so that his masters wouldn't draw the conclusion that he had been "turned." He told the Swiss that he "infinitely" preferred "a few years in a Swiss prison to a few minutes up against a Russian wall."[55]

Rado's first reaction to Foote's arrest was to change his hiding place. A friend put up Rado and his wife in a small room. Fearing that they would be discovered by domestic servants working nearby, Rado and his wife sat all day, not making a move. "Looking back on the long months we spent in that tiny room," Rado wrote later, "it amazes me how Helene and I ever found the patience to bear our voluntary imprisonment, and in particular the ordeal of immobility it imposed."[56]

What Rado did not do was take any chances. He did not contact Dübendorfer, who was amassing Werther material in volumes; he did not try to recruit a new wireless operator from the Communist Party; and he did not try to find cutouts. The resident director was director incognito.

Dübendorfer did not know that Foote had been arrested. All she knew was that Rado had disappeared and no one was collecting the Lucy information. Dübendorfer grew desperate, knowing of its value to the Red Army cause. Why had the Center lost interest?

Dübendorfer was not a woman to suffer lightly the inanities of her superiors. And she had no intention of going into hiding. By December,[57] with no Soviet agent having attempted to contact her, she finally decided to break the rules of the game. In plain-language code, she began communicating with Hermina Rabinowitch, an employee of the International Labor Organization (ILO) in Montreal, who had served as a cutout in Gisela's family. She was probably not the best person to take on this most important task—the Americans described her as "morbidly introvert [sic] and emotionally unstable"[58]—but so paralyzed was the Swiss network through Rado's negligence that this was the only person to whom Dübendorfer knew to turn. They had worked together at the ILO in Switzerland before the war. Dübendorfer told Rabinowitch to give the Soviet embassy in Ottawa a message saying that the Lucy ring was still operating but desperately needed money if it were to continue to do so. Rabinowitch headed to the embassy, where she was met by the Russian counselor Tounkin, who knew nothing about Sissy or Lucy or even Rabinowitch herself. He brushed her off as a strange woman playing unknown games.[59]

Ironically, as Dübendorfer was desperately trying to reach Moscow, Moscow was desperately trying to reach Dübendorfer. It did not know that the entire Swiss transmission network had been uprooted or that Rado, who could have at least tried to find a new transmitter, was unwilling to risk any movement at all. In December, just as Rabinowitch approached Tounkin, the Center sent a message to the disappeared Rado: "Tell Lucy he should not worry about payments; we will certainly pay our debt not later than January. We request him to continue giving us most important information."[60] When no messages came from the net, Moscow became more alarmed, convinced that Lucy had stopped work because of the funding problem. The Center decided to appeal to moral, not merely pecuniary, values that Rössler (Lucy) may or may not have possessed. The Center told Rado—who, of course, never received the message—to "please tell Lucy that he and his group will receive large payment as soon as possible. He should wait patiently and should not waste time and work at this important hour of the last battle against our common enemy."[61]

Unknown to the Center, the Lucy-Werther network had not shut down, and material was still streaming into Dübendorfer's hands. For her part, Dübendorfer was infuriated that the embassy had turned a cold shoulder to Rabinowitch. What was the Center thinking? Dübendorfer had strategic information from Werther and no one, it seemed to her, seemed to care. Dübendorfer shot off another "clear-code" message through the compromised ILO diplomatic bag.[62]

The letter, intercepted by Western intelligence, is today quite transparent: "We live in the former apartment and are working as previously in the old firm. Some two weeks ago Sisi sent you a telegram. Tell us how did your journey to Gisel's parents turn out? My health is excellent. Albert is sick and will probably leave his profession for a long time, he is laid up in bed. Relations with Lucy are good, she is a very good woman. Gisel's family is for some reason no longer interested in her, although up to this time there was support. Lucy's situation has improved. Sisi's position is sad. Please inform Gisel's parents that they must remit 6,700 dollars. The sum must be handed over through you. There are no other possibilities. The Gisels must bear these expenses. Advise me about Aleksander where is he. —Rachel."

Obviously "Sisi" and "Rachel" refer to Dübendorfer, also known as Sissy. "Albert" was one of the code names used by Rado. "Gisel's family" is Gisela's family. And "Lucy" is Lucy, also known as Rudolf Rössler. That his position has "improved" meant that he was clearly still receiving the Werther material. "Gisel's parents," presumably Gisela's superiors, certainly could understand the bottom line: Send the $6,700.

Rabinowitch, who later testified that her first encounter with Tounkin at the embassy had been "unpleasant,"[63] chose to mail this message to the embassy instead of delivering it in person. Unfortunately for Dübendorfer and Red Army intelligence, this message made it into the hands of agent Vitali Pavlov, a member of the increasingly aggressive Foreign Intelligence department of the NKVD, the predecessor of the KGB. In Moscow, NKVD officials told Pavlov that this was a Red Army matter that he should drop, which he did.[64]

Rachel Dübendorfer was not deterred. She wrote to Rabinowitch on April 14, 1944, that Rabinowitch should "inform Gisel's family that she should advize Znamensky 19 [the address of Red Army headquarters in Moscow] that Sisi is alive and works as of old with Lucy. Lucy wanted to change personnel, but funds ran out. Albert [Rado] is sick and is not interested in business. For the work of Sisi, Gisel's family must transfer 10,000 dollars."[65]

This message, by mentioning Znamensky 19, got attention. Pavlov passed it on to his GRU counterpart, who got it to the director. Poliakova immediately started plans to reconnect the precious source and get her the money she was asking for. She wrote to Rabinowitch[66]:

Dear Hermina:
   Thank you very much indeed for your care in our affairs and we hope that you will help in the future. It is important for us to send a letter to Geneva to Sisi. Can you send this letter with a reliable man whom you trust? All expenses will be paid. Please let us know about your proposals in this connection as soon as possible. Please inform us about delivery of your service mail to Geneva and why are you sure that it is not censored? Please wire to Rachel or Alexander that Gisel's parents are interested about the health of Sisi and Paul and that they will help them. We ask you to forward $10,000 to that watch company according to Sisy's instructions. Make arrangements with our representatives about forwarding of this sum of money to the U.S.A. All your personal expenses will be paid.
   With best regards,
   Gisle

The money was almost instantly transferred to New York to the Heilbein Watch Company, which was to have transferred it to

Switzerland. But it was too late. The Swiss arrested Dübendorfer on April 19, only days after her last letter to Rabinowitch. Rössler was arrested in May.

In a critique of the Swiss spy ring after the war, American intelligence said that its collapse in late 1943 came about because of four weaknesses: "A. that Rado lacked personality and courage and never had complete control over his organization. B. that Dübendorfer, who was responsible for the most important source of intelligence, Lucy [Rudolf Rössler], distrusted Rado and through him the Center itself, suspecting them of attempts to cut her out with Lucy. She therefore disobeyed orders and disregarded security warnings. C. that the operators for the service, such as Bolli, Hamel and Foote himself, were inexperienced in undercover work and therefore showed bad security. D. that the members of the organization in general placed too much reliance on the protection afforded by neutral territory and on the complacence or inactivity of the Swiss authorities."[67]

The Americans also called the Center on the carpet for believing that Swiss action against the Red agents was "incomprehensible" and going so far "as to ascribe it to the machinations of the British Secret Service."[68] The Americans reported that Center masters "were reasonably energetic in the provision of money and material and they gave sound security warnings from their own point of view. But on the whole they showed an academic attitude, treating the Swiss service as a smoothly running, businesslike organization, which it never was, and making little allowance for field problems and the personalities of its agents. Perhaps Poliakova herself overlooking how much circumstances might have changed in Switzerland since she had worked there was responsible for this attitude."[69]

But even the Americans could not overlook what this sometimes bizarre collection of personalities had accomplished, noting, "It was only in the summer of 1944, when the network was already in dissolution, the Germans gained a full understanding of the damage done to them, particularly by the Lucy source."[70]

Notes

1 Rado, pp. 229–30.

2 Ibid., p. 242.

3 Ibid.

4 Ibid., p. 243.

5 Ibid., p. 244.

6 Ibid., p. 245.

7 Garlinski, p. 141.

8 See Garlinski, p. 142, for a narrative about the supposed German spies "Lorenz" and "Laura" and the supposed French journalist "Yves Rameau." Garlinski argues that all three were Schellenberg agents who had tried to puncture the net before 1943.

9 RG 319, Box 59.

10 Garlinski, p. 144.

11 RG 319, Box 59.

12 Ibid.

13 RG 319, Box 60.

14 *Der Spiegel,* April 15, 1953.

15 RG 319, Box 60.

16 Ibid.

17 CIA, p. 178.

18 The exact dating is confused. Rado (on p. 193) says that the calls started on June 26. But a page later, he says that he notified the Center of the calls on May 10, which means that he was clairvoyant. The Red Orchestra files say that the calls came in April, which the author judges to be correct. In the second mention of dates, Rado says that the calls came ten days before May 10, which is consistent with the late-April American assessment.

19 Rado, p. 193.

20 RG 319, Box 60.

21 See Foote, p. 112, or Rado, p. 191.

22 Foote, p. 112.

23 Ibid.

24 RG 319, Box 60.

25 Rado, p. 193.

26 CIA, p. 179.

27 Ibid., p. 180.

28 Ibid.

29 Ibid., p. 181.

30 Ibid.

31 Ibid.

32 RG 319, Box 60.

33 Garlinski, p. 153.

34 Rado, p. 245.

35 Ibid., p. 246.

36 Ibid., p. 250.

37 Ibid.

38 Ibid., p. 251.

39 This is Rado's own description; Rado, pp. 249–52.

40 Garlinski, p. 155.

41 Foote, p. 120.

42 Ibid., p. 121.

43 Ibid.

44 RG 319, Box 60.

45 Foote, p. 121.

46 Reed and Fisher, pp. 182–83.

47 Ibid., p. 184.

48 Ibid., pp. 184–85.

49 Ibid., p. 185.

50 Ibid., p. 186.

51 Foote, p. 122.

52 Ibid., p. 124.

53 Ibid., p. 125.

54 Ibid., p. 126.

55 Ibid., p. 129.

56 Rado, pp. 275–76.

57 RG 319, Box 60, Vol. 6.

58 Ibid.

59 Dallin, p. 224.

60 Ibid., pp. 197–98.

61 Ibid., p. 198.

62 RG 319, Box 60, Vol. 6.

63 Dallin, p. 224.
64 Ibid., p. 225.
65 Ibid.
66 Foote, p. 270.
67 RG 319, Box 60.
68 Ibid.
69 Ibid.
70 Ibid.

Chapter Ten

GESTAPO MÜLLER

SECRET AGENDAS

As the Swiss police tracked down and at least temporarily closed the Rote Drei, other dramas in the secret war unfolded. One of the most enigmatic involved Gen. Walter Schellenberg, head of Foreign Intelligence at the Reich Main Security Office. It is clear that Schellenberg intrigued with Himmler throughout the war to find contacts in the West with whom to negotiate. But it is also clear that, at crucial times, it was Schellenberg himself who disrupted those efforts. He never joined in the main conspiracy but instead was instrumental in shutting it down. In no instance was this more obvious than in Schellenberg's activities during and immediately after Kursk.

Before the battle, Schellenberg later told investigators, he had several meetings with a German lawyer, Dr. Carl Langbehn. Schellenberg said that he had heard of Langbehn through Himmler's osteopath, Felix Kersten, and thought perhaps that he—Schellenberg—and Langbehn had common interests. During the meetings, Langbehn slowly revealed himself to be a fellow traveler in the conservative Goerdeler-Beck conspiracy. Finally, Langbehn arrived at the bottom line: There was a plan to get rid of Adolf Hitler. Could Schellenberg help?

Of course, Schellenberg did not report this back to Hitler but turned instead to his always-conniving boss, Heinrich Himmler. Schellenberg said that he arranged for Langbehn to meet with Himmler. Langbehn and Himmler, Schellenberg said, should decide Hitler's fate.[1]

Perhaps Schellenberg didn't know it, but Himmler was already well acquainted with Langbehn, although only on a personal level. The two were neighbors, and their daughters were schoolmates. Himmler, according to Schellenberg, at first resisted meeting with the anti-Hitler conspirator, thinking that it was not yet time to attack Germany's main problem head-on. But Himmler began to change his mind after the Kursk debacle, when Germany's future seemed obvious and his own quite dubious. If he could save himself by eliminating Hitler, he would do so.

Himmler had his chief of staff, Obergruppenführer Karl Wolff, set up a meeting with Langbehn, Johannes Popitz (Prussian minister of finance), and another plotter against Hitler.[2] It was Popitz who had the strongest ties to the conspiracy, and he took the lead at the August 26 conference, outlining the plan for revolution in a soothing and understated way. Instead of having Hitler killed, which was now the certain requirement of any such scheme, Popitz talked of relieving the Führer of some of his burdens and having another strong man—someone such as, yes, Himmler—assume power.

The plan was attractive to the *Reichsleiter,* but it suffered the same problem as all previous plots—the inconvenience of the Second World War. Before there could be a palace coup, the West would have to agree to the structure of a new German government. And the West, at least in the guise of Churchill, had rebuffed all previous plans to replace Hitler with any German government whatsoever. It was now unfathomable that the British, who had shunned such honorable men as Beck and Halder, would agree to a government run by Himmler, an executor of all that was dark in Germany.

But Himmler did not see this clearly. Though there is no record of what Himmler said after Popitz made his pitch, actions show that he was at least momentarily seduced. Immediately after the meeting, Langbehn had traveling papers, arranged by Schellenberg.[3] Within days, the amateur intriguer was in Berne to meet with British and American intelligence officers about plans to overthrow Hitler.

It would have been better for Langbehn had he limited his adventures to meeting with the principal Western powers, but he didn't. He revealed the plot to other Allied countries and even to neutrals. One of these groups—the suspect party is the Free French—encoded a message to London reading: "Himmler's

lawyer confirms the hopelessness of Germany's military and political situation and has arrived to put out peace-feelers."[4] The
message was immediately and separately decoded by the Abwehr
and Schellenberg's SD.

The two agencies reacted quite differently. Admiral Canaris,
head of the Abwehr and friend to the conspirators, warned
Popitz that there was trouble ahead. Schellenberg, on the other
hand, ordered Langbehn's arrest the moment he returned to
German soil.[5] Schellenberg, interviewed extensively by Western
intelligence after the war, forgot to mention this point, as he forgot to mention many other troubling details of his command.

It is not obvious why Schellenberg acted against Langbehn,
because by doing so he placed Himmler and, by extension, himself in jeopardy. But Schellenberg did do this, even informing
Himmler's natural enemies—Müller and Bormann—of the affair. Alan Clark has argued that Schellenberg wanted to use the
Langbehn episode as a hole card against his superior, insurance
against the possibility that Himmler might someday turn on him.
That certainly was possible, but only a stone-cold gambler would
have chanced this against the leader of the SS. It must be asked
that if Schellenberg was up to such a dangerous game as betraying Himmler, was he so audacious as to have had other games
and motives throughout? Perhaps Schellenberg's continued
"peace contacts" with the West and the German conspiracy were
an illusion hiding a deeper agenda.

Though Schellenberg orchestrated many peace contacts with
the West during the war, these contacts accomplished little.
Worse, by arresting Langbehn, Schellenberg put an end to one
line between the West and the German conspirators. From these
effects, one might posit a cause: Schellenberg intended to derail
the effort.

Whatever the reason, the game was now up for Himmler's
friend. At the *Reichleiter*'s request, Langbehn was tried in secret.
However, to keep up appearances and cut down on rumors,
Himmler still handpicked an audience to dutifully nod agreement with the prosecutor's arguments. Convicted, Langbehn
was held for a while, then tortured to death, having his testicles
ripped off as he took his last few breaths.[6]

UNDETERRED

If the Langbehn affair ended in near disaster for Himmler, it left him undeterred in his efforts to seek out the West. His chief agent, again, was Schellenberg, who said that in late 1943 he met with an American businessman named Hewitt, who was on a fact-finding mission for President Roosevelt. Hewitt was nervous about the Red Army. Said the report: "Schellenberg went to visit Hewitt at the latter's hotel in Stockholm and opened discussions quite frankly on the general situation. Hewitt's views, briefly summarised, consisted in the transfer of as many Wehrmacht troops as possible to the East in order to stem the Russians and at the same time the conclusion of a compromise peace with the Western Powers. Hewitt admitted at once that he had no authority to make proposals but he suggested that he would return by air to the U.S.A. for instructions and if his plan met with approval he would endeavor to return to Lisbon for further discussions."

If he got approval, Hewitt was to place an ad in the Stockholm *Tidningen* in February 1944, reading: "For sale, valuable gold fish aquarium for 1,524 Kr." The ad never ran, and Schellenberg told interrogators that he later learned that the proposal was looked upon with disfavor in Washington.[7]

Schellenberg also met with Swedish banker Jakob Wallenberg shortly after meeting Hewitt.[8] Wallenberg, thought Schellenberg, was a man who could communicate with the British about a separate peace. These attempts were certainly not isolated. In fact, Himmler let Schellenberg and company meet with almost any person who might stoke peace efforts with the West.

Schellenberg and Himmler weren't the only ones thinking about the possibility of a change in strategy. At the Quebec Conference, Gen. George Marshall wondered aloud whether the Soviet Union would use the Red Army to spread Communism throughout Europe. He also "wondered if the Germans might prefer the entry of Anglo-American forces to an overwhelming Russian victory."[9]

These were dangerous times for Joseph Stalin. If Himmler succeeded in his efforts, it could be the end of Russia's victory. But before Stalin could act, he would have to know what was afoot. And it was at this point that the *funkspiel* paid its largest dividend to the Soviet dictator.

CHANGING OF THE GUARD

The double-dealing of Himmler and Schellenberg was more than matched by Trepper's triple game being played out in France. Since its beginnings in December 1942, the game had steadily intensified. No demand for information seemed too extreme for the director in Moscow.

Until Kursk, Trepper had been "controlled" by Giering,[10] a simple man with a peasant's cunning. Giering never fully believed that Trepper was cooperating in the playback, nor did he believe that Berlin was sending the Red Army—and through him, after all, a decent man—the Reich's secrets. Giering saw himself as a policeman in over his head. He was also in 1943 diagnosed with throat cancer, a disease that steadily drained him. Trepper helped him sooth his pain with cognac. In his cups, Giering even talked about his family to this Red Army spy. This was not the only mistake that Giering made. As caution about Trepper abated, the Soviet spy was able in the early-morning hours to write out a detailed analysis of the situation on a small roll of paper that he secreted in his room. He had only to figure out a way to deliver the message. Giering helped. The Kommando had been unable to establish contact with a certain Soviet agent named Juliette Moussier, a main link to the French Communist Party. According to American intelligence, Trepper convinced Giering that he, Trepper, should make the contact with Juliette.[11] In another version, Trepper convinced Giering that the task should be given to his personal assistant, Hillel Katz. However the contact was made, Trepper's secretly written messages were delivered to Juliette, who was ordered to send them to Moscow, then disappear.[12]

By all accounts, Moscow was warned of the German game but didn't seem to care. The game continued.

In the middle of the Kursk battle, Heinz Pannwitz replaced the ailing Giering as head of the Sonderkommando in France. Trepper described Pannwitz as "young, fat, with a round pink face and keen eyes hidden behind thick glasses, and elegantly dressed, with bourgeois mannerisms. He was calm and excited by turns. He gave the general impression of a slippery ball, difficult to grasp."[13] Elsewhere, Trepper described Pannwitz as a "little man, who looked like an accountant for some modest firm . . ."[14] In some versions of events, Trepper was more wary of the old lazy-eyed cop Giering than the new young inquisitor. But Trepper said that he took his new warden seriously. Whereas Giering had broken a few legs and sent some real spies to their end, Pannwitz had mass murder in his background.

Pannwitz was only thirty-two years old when he joined the Nazi criminal police in 1933. Though he had originally wanted to be a priest, Pannwitz soon gravitated toward the Nazi center of power. Trepper would write: "The young wolf approached the King of Beasts."[15] The beast that Trepper had in mind was SS general Reinhard Heydrich, a brilliant but deadly man and one of the architects of the final solution, the genocide of the European Jews. Heydrich was the number-two SS leader after Himmler and was the man who organized the Wannsee Conference, where the final solution was planned.

After Heydrich was ambushed in Prague on May 27, 1942, Hitler assigned Pannwitz the task of bringing those responsible to justice. Pannwitz, in fact, managed to kill the two assassins and five accomplices behind the assassination, but he was inelegant enough that at least 1,300* innocent Czechs, including every adult male in the village of Lidice, were also killed. The village, accused of hiding the assassins, was then bulldozed and blasted out of existence.[16] Though Pannwitz may not have personally given the order, his name became synonymous with repression. By his actions, he stirred up Czech nationalism and resistance, thus earning him equivocal scores on the Nazi open-book test on terror. He was not fully rehabilitated until his assignment to take over the "great game" in France.

---

*This is a conservative figure. Others place the total at more than 3,000.

Pannwitz, still only thirty-two years old, arrived in Paris full of fury. As a direct assistant to Heinrich Müller, known in most of the world as "Gestapo Müller," Pannwitz told Trepper that Giering had been a slow study; he had not managed to push the game beyond purely military aspects and into the ultimate realm of political relations between the Third Reich and the Soviet Union. He, Pannwitz, was the man to do this. Pannwitz, said Trepper, "played the part of a gentleman who dealt with politics at only the highest level. This was his chance, and he was arriving in the nick of time."[17] The Eastern front was dissolving, whereas for some reason the Western Allies were spending their resources attacking Sicily.

Pannwitz told Trepper that "he had an ambitious plan to send the Center an emissary who would inform Moscow that a substantial group of German military personnel wanted to discuss a separate peace with the Soviet Union. This special envoy would take documents with him that gave evidence of this attitude, but he would also carry proof to the contrary, testifying that in other German circles the same solution was being sought with the west."[18] One way or another, Trepper thought, the plan was really intended to break the anti-Nazi alliance.

Himmler, who was in fact trying every means to bring on discussions with the West, objected to the Russian approach for fear that it might work. But Pannwitz, who was serving other masters, persisted. He tried to arrange a meeting in Paris with a Center representative. Meanwhile, he made sure that the *funkspiel* notified Moscow of Dr. Langbehn's past maneuverings in Switzerland.[19]

Pannwitz helped ward off one of the greatest dangers to the Soviet Union: exposure of the Swiss ring and its agent Werther. Schellenberg came to Paris to try to learn everything that the "grand chef" knew about the Swiss ring, which by now Schellenberg realized was Germany's most mortal enemy. With stakes this high, any loyal SS officer would have given Schellenberg every assistance. Instead, Trepper reported, "Pannwitz made it quite clear to me that I was by no means obligated to tell [Schellenberg] what I knew."[20] Trepper followed the advice, and the Werther connection continued.

In August 1943, Pannwitz appeared to be winning in the great game. Moscow told Trepper that it was sending an agent to meet him. The Germans, reported the CIA, "were greatly intrigued by this prospect."[21] High-level talks with the Russians about a separate peace seemed close at hand.

But before Pannwitz and those who controlled the operation could complete their plans for discussions with Moscow, Trepper escaped. His plans had been in place for some time. After learning that the Germans had cracked the French Communist Party's code, he knew that he must act soon. His warnings to Moscow had been transmitted in this code, and it was only a matter of time before his triple cross became known.[22] Trepper also might not have known the true value of the information that the Germans were sending Moscow in his name. He bolted, when the Center would have preferred that he stay.

Trepper had softened up the Germans from the beginning by giving them the impression that he was in total agreement with their game. After all, he had betrayed his own network and his best friends. Then he convinced the Germans that he should be able to move around Paris occasionally, lest his absence be noted by Moscow's many spies. The Germans allowed this, but only under close undercover surveillance. Gradually, Trepper won the confidence of his most intimate guard, Willy Berg. Described as "short, squat, with a plump face and strong hands that could hit hard," Berg was said to have carried "his fifty years heavily."[23]

Trepper reported: "I sensed from the very beginning of my association with Berg that I would be able to make use of him. I realized, quickly, that he was vulnerable, that the assistant to the head of the Sonderkommando was a very unhappy man whose personal life had been a long series of disappointments. Two of his children had died of diphtheria during the war, and the third had died in an air raid. His wife, unable to endure this series of blows, tried to commit suicide and was confined to a mental hospital. Psychologically, Berg was in a very weakened state."[24]

It was Berg who allowed Trepper to have pencil and paper (on the pretext of Trepper's perfecting his German), which Trepper used to write his message to the Center. And it was Berg who frequently "watched" Trepper on his occasional extracurricular wanderings on the Rue des Saussaies in Paris. Trepper slowly and steadily gained Berg's trust. On September 16, 1943, he betrayed it.

Trepper had sympathized with Berg's health problems and told him that he would take him to the Pharmacie Bailly at 15 Rue de Rome for a remedy. Trepper knew that there was a back door to the pharmacy, and he slipped away through it while Berg waited out front. Trepper dissolved into the Parisian dusk. After a secret German dragnet failed to produce the "grand chef," the Sonderkommando was reduced to putting out wanted posters. It was all to no avail. Trepper could not be found.

Surely, Trepper reasoned, the Center would now learn of all his suspicions and impressions of the *funkspiel,* even if his message sent by Juliette had somehow not gone through. By his sudden disappearance, followed quickly by the wanted posters, the Center would at a minimum realize that its trusted agent had for some time been known to the Germans. And at that point, surely, any trust the Center had in the *funkspiel* would evaporate.

This was not winning logic. Neither the Germans nor the Center let on that anything was amiss. The Germans continued to gather military and diplomatic secrets, and Pannwitz continued to receive them. The only difference was that Pannwitz could no longer use the Trepper cover. Instead, he switched to sending the most sensitive intelligence through Victor Sukulov, the "petit chef," and his transmitter, known as "Mars."

The message that Sukulov sent was identical with the one that Trepper had been sending: Some leaders at the highest ranks in Germany still wanted a separate peace with Russia. This alone seemed to satisfy Moscow. The Center told Sukulov, code-named "Kent," that this line must be kept open at all costs. Trepper, Sukulov was warned, could no longer be trusted.

In January 1944, there came the biggest payoff of the great game. Sukulov sent Stalin the transcript of a top-secret communication that had been intercepted and decoded by the German secret services. It was from a neutral ambassador stationed in London and addressed to the diplomat's country. The message warned that the West was "disturbed by the rapid advance of the Red Army and that a secret meeting to discuss the situation had been arranged . . ."[25]

The warning startled the Kremlin, which lost little time in responding. On January 17, 1944, under the headline "Rumors in Cairo," *Pravda* let the West know that Soviet leadership was aware of some of the double games being played. Though the report distorted the content of the note sent over the *funkspiel*, thereby protecting its source, it did not miss the meaning. The report said that its Cairo correspondent had learned of dealings on the Iberian Peninsula between Ribbentrop and "British personalities" concerning a separate peace. "It is supposed that the meeting was not without results," said *Pravda*.[26]

The British, noting that *Pravda* did not have a Cairo correspondent, nonetheless sent reassurances to Stalin that no double-dealings were under way. The United States did the same. Stalin had checked the efforts by Himmler and Schellenberg to make a separate peace in the West.*

For Sukulov and Pannwitz, this victory was merely an intermediate step. The goal of the *funkspiel*—a new Russo-Soviet covenant—had not changed. This was so important that nothing else, including personal safety, much mattered. Even after the Anglo-British landings in Normandy in June 1944, the Center

---

*David Dallin has argued that this message was sent on to Moscow in an effort to strain relations among the Allies and was, therefore, one of the few victories of the *funkspiel*. The argument had one flaw: One usually does not deceive by telling the truth. And this most important message to Stalin contained a fundamental truth: There were many active, subterranean maneuverings between Himmler's men and the West bent on doing exactly what Stalin feared most. Whether any political leader in the West ever considered a separate peace at this late point is not known, but it is transparent that the Germans did, and that some men in the West, for whatever reason, were listening. The Bormann warning, therefore, consisted of political intelligence of the highest rank, not a deception. And far from producing a rift in the alliance, the information was used by Stalin to prevent a rupture, thereby preserving a Soviet victory.

and the Germans insisted that both sides keep up their wireless liaison. Nothing was to get in the way. Even when the Allies were about to enter Paris, Pannwitz and Sukulov continued the Great Game, retreating to the Alsace, then to the Black Forest, then to Bregenz am Bodensee.[27] As the Anglos got closer to the Rhein, the game only intensified.

The fall of Paris and most of France did not deter Pannwitz and Sukulov from keeping up their back channel to the Kremlin. The game worked as before, with Bormann supplying the intelligence and the Mars transmitter sending it to Moscow. But Sukulov and Pannwitz could not stay in liberated France, nor could they repair to Germany proper. They had to keep up the appearances of an illegal network operating on the fringes. Despite the chaos that was engulfing Europe, they managed to do this until the end.

Finally, on May 3, 1945, French police discovered their hideout in a mountain hut near Bludenz.[28] By then, Hitler was dead, the war all but over, and the great game of no apparent use. Yet, when arrested, Pannwitz and Sukulov still had their transmitter. The *funkspiel* had never ceased.

Sukulov was unfazed by his new predicament. He plunged forward, announcing proudly that he was a Russian intelligence agent. If the police needed proof, he provided it, handing the gendarmes cables from the Center.[29] Further, he introduced SS commander Pannwitz and others in the group as members of the German resistance.[30] For his part, Pannwitz agreed. He was, the French were told, part of a sensitive intelligence operation in the service of France's confederate, the Soviet Union. Pannwitz and Sukulov were taken to Paris for questioning. There, they insisted upon making contact with the Soviet legation. Sukulov even demanded that he be allowed to keep and use his transmitter.[31]

The two did something else that would prove their bona fides beyond question. They told the Allies that as soon as possible— and the emphasis was clearly that the sooner the better—they wanted to be sent to Moscow. After German capitulation, the French obliged. Pannwitz and Sukulov boarded a plane headed for the heart of the Soviet Union on June 7, 1945. According to Trepper, Pannwitz arrived with his secretary, a radio operator, fifteen suitcases, and a list of German agents operating in Soviet territory. From all appearances, he expected to be named a hero of the Soviet Union.

Backing and Protection

From this behavior, the American CIA drew the logical conclusion, though it chose to phrase it in a curious bit of passive voice: "He [Pannwitz] is said to have been a convinced believer, as were many other RSHA officials, in the necessity for a compromise agreement with Russia."[32]

The agency's inference is inescapable. If the Sonderkommando head had truly been engaged in an effort to destroy the winning alliance, he would have been expected near the end of the war to follow the common practice of shedding his SS uniform and blending into the shadows. At the least, he would have tried to avoid incarceration by the country he supposedly betrayed most. Even absent specific crimes, SS officers tended to fare badly once in Russian hands. The Butcher of Prague and betrayer of the Red Army, if that was what he was, would never have willingly let the henchmen of Lavrenti Beria loose at his throat. Yet Pannwitz did.

The reasoning applies as well to Sukulov. If he had actually participated in treachery against the Soviet Union, he would not have conducted himself so brashly once captured by the French. His goal would have been to dissipate into the ether, not call attention to himself. Sukulov would have known that, as a traitor, his life expectancy back in the Soviet Union approached zero. But it was Sukulov who first insisted on returning to Moscow.

In fact, had either Pannwitz or Sukulov worked against the Soviet Union on behalf of Germany, there is no reason why they allowed themselves to be captured by the French much less be surrendered to the Russians. They would have reinvented themselves months before, when everyone knew, save Adolf Hitler, that the collapse of Germany was inevitable. They would not have stayed around only to broadcast Nazi lies.

Their actions can be explained only by seeing them as true believers in the Russian cause.

In the 1960s, French writer Gilles Perrault tracked down Pannwitz. Perrault's first question was why an SS *Hauptsturmführer* would willingly go to Moscow. Pannwitz was evasive. "I may have gone because I felt I could be of use to Germany one last time. Equally, I may have gone because I had been in touch with them, quite genuinely, for a long time past. In my view it's better to leave the issue undecided . . ."[33]

But it cannot be undecided. The first option was not a possibility at all, for the Germany that had employed Pannwitz barely existed at the time of his capture and had vanished completely by the time he traveled to Moscow. Pannwitz could not have served Nazi Germany if he wanted to, and no new Germany had been formed. It is Pannwitz's second alternative that prevails. He traveled to Moscow, as did Sukulov, because he had "genuinely" been in her service all along.

Though Pannwitz and Sukulov may have thought that they were heroes of the Soviet Union for the risks they took, neither mistook himself for a prime mover. They were vital, centrally placed pawns, but that was all.

Although Perrault made little progress in convincing Pannwitz to talk openly about the *funkspiel,* he did manage to catch a few inadvertent slips. One of the most important was simple and direct: "I never ran the show," Pannwitz said. "It wasn't on my initiative that we began to make sincere contact with the Russians. What was I, when all is said and done? Just a link between Moscow and a group of people in Berlin. I would never have got involved if I hadn't received backing and protection."[34]

GESTAPO MÜLLER

Heinrich Müller, head of the German secret police and the German torture chambers, was always a better Stalinist than a Nazi. He was a special type of policeman who, according to one who knew him well, "took the Russian secret police as his model."[35] He was not an early—and therefore more trustworthy—Nazi; he obtained his party card only in 1939, six years after Hitler won power. But he was an advocate of state power.

Schellenberg, that other advocate of state power, was his enemy; as such, his statements about Müller should be viewed with some caution. But they are so fundamental that they must be considered, and at length.

In his memoirs, Schellenberg discussed a strange conversation that he had with Müller in early 1943, as the *funkspiel* was beginning its broadcasts. In a meeting arranged to discuss foreign-based police attachés, Müller switched the conversation to a discussion of the Schulze-Boysen and Harnack arm of the Rote Kapelle. Müller was fascinated by the power of the philosophy that drove such men to treason.

According to Schellenberg's recollection, set down some thirteen years later, Gestapo Müller continued: "You will agree, I suppose, that from your own experience, the Soviet influence in Western Europe does not exist among the working classes alone—that it's also gained a hold among educated people. I see in this an inevitable historical development of our era, particularly when you consider the spiritual 'anarchy' of our Western culture, by which I mean to include the ideology of the Third Reich. National Socialism is nothing more than a sort of dung on this spiritual desert. In contrast to this, one sees that in Russia a unified and really uncompromising spiritual and biological force is developing. The Communists' global aim of spiritual and material revolution offers a sort of positive electrical charge to Western negativism."[36]

Schellenberg reports that he was dumbstruck: "Here was the man who had conducted the most ruthless and brutal struggle against Communism in all its various forms, the man who, in his investigation of *Rote Kapelle*, had left no stone unturned to uncover the last ramifications of that conspiracy. What a change here!"[37] Schellenberg said that Müller went on to discuss their class differences. Schellenberg was a lawyer of ranking class; Müller was from poor parents and had worked as a detective, clawing himself to the top of his profession. Perhaps that was why the two did not get along. Then Müller contrasted Schellenberg to Schulze-Boysen and Harnack—people of Schellenberg's class but with ideological convictions. "They

were pure intellectuals," Müller mused, "progressive revolu-
tionaries, always looking for a final solution; they never got
bogged down in half measures. And they died still believing in
that solution. There are too many compromised in National
Socialism for it to offer a faith like that; but spiritual Communism can. It's got a consistent attitude toward life, which is lacking among most of our Western intellectuals, excepting perhaps some of the SS . . . If we lose this war, it won't be because
of any deficiencies in our war potential; it will be because of the
spiritual incapacity of our leaders. We haven't got any real leaders—we do have a Leader, the Führer—but that is the beginning and the end of it. Take the mob immediately below him,
and what have you got? You've got them all squabbling among
themselves night and day, either for the Führer's favors or
about their own authority. He must have seen this long ago,
and for some reason that's incomprehensible to me he seems
to be exploiting this state of affairs in order to rule. That's
where his greatest failure lies . . . I can't help it, but I am forced
more and more to the conclusion that Stalin does these things
better . . . He's immeasurably superior to the leaders of the
Western nations, and if I had anything to say in the matter we'd
reach an agreement with him as quickly as possible."[38]

To try to lighten the conversation, Schellenberg said: "All
right, Comrade Müller, let's all start saying 'Heil Stalin!' right
now—and our little father Müller will become head of the
NKVD." Müller looked back with a "malevolent glint in his eyes,"
saying, "That would be fine. And you'd really be [in] for the high
jump, you and your die-hard bourgeois friends."[39]

Schellenberg grew so suspicious that he secretly surveilled the
funkspiel and discovered that in 1944 Müller "was using 'turned'
radio operators to make real and sincere contact with the Russians."[40] He told Kaltenbrunner, who didn't believe him. Schellenberg said that he would keep his evidence so that someday
the "people should know that the head of the Gestapo had
worked for the Russians."[41]

Schellenberg's investigation lasted until the end of the war.
He told an assistant that when the Red Army surrounded Berlin,

Müller slipped away to his foxhole and from there continued "radio communication with the Russians."[42]

It can be assumed that Müller was sending dispatches to the Pannwitz-Sukulov transmitter, for they were the only ones left standing at the end of the war. But it should not be assumed that they were the only ones with whom Müller had communicated. In the critical years of 1943 and 1944, the *funkspiel*, as Trepper discovered, was merely a means to confirm information already at the Center from another source. And there is no doubt today that the other source was Werther. From Müller's handling of the *funkspiel* and the statements and writing of Schellenberg, it is clear that he had the motive and the opportunity to handle such secret transmissions.

But Müller was in no position to actually gain the top-secret information that came directly from the Führer's conference table. First, Müller was not a participant at these meetings and was not briefed on military matters. Second, the military information that he received officially for use by the *funkspiel* never included the type of firsthand intelligence that Werther gained. However damaging the playback information was to Germany, it still had to be passed through military headquarters, then to Rundstedt for approval. Though the generals complained, they did not rebel, which they surely would have if asked to relay the type of information that made its way to Rössler and Gisela's family. Simply, the information that Müller passed through the *funkspiel* was an order of magnitude less important than the Werther messages. Werther provided real, contemporaneous battle information on plans and intentions. The *funkspiel* gave information about troop movements that was much more delayed. Though Müller is likely the answer to the question of how Werther got his intelligence so quickly to Gisela's family—who except for a half dozen men wouldn't dare question the actions of the Gestapo chief—the information reaching Switzerland had to come from a source much closer to the high command than even Müller.

Though Müller was a Communist sympathizer who betrayed the Third Reich through the *funkspiel*, he was not Werther. And while Müller was busy confirming broad brushes of the Werther material, the spy himself had kept active and continued to operate despite a major crackdown.

WERTHER RETURNS

By mid-1944, the battle had so turned against the Germans that the Swiss had no intention of keeping jailed the Soviet spies whom they had just arrested, and they certainly were not going to ill-treat them. The Rote Drei was, after all, a collection of agents who did not work against Switzerland but for the powers that seemed destined to win the Second World War. The Swiss were now far more concerned about pleasing the Allies than Adolf Hitler.

The first to be freed were the Hamels; they were released on bail in July. The Swiss released Foote, Rössler, and Dübendorfer in September.[43] Shortly thereafter, Rado, who had never been arrested and knew nothing of the fate of his comrades, summoned enough bravery to slip out of the picture altogether. Instead of contacting his flock, he and his wife crossed the border to mostly liberated France.[44]

Without their boss and with no contact with the Center, the apparatchiks of the Swiss net were adrift. Foote fell back to old tradecraft, periodically checking his "places of conspiracy" in case someone like-minded showed up. One day, Rachel Dübendorfer appeared, and Foote introduced himself; for the first time, these two stalwart Red Army operatives met face-to-face.

Foote was shocked by what Rachel revealed. As she had been trying to tell the Center before her arrest, she was still in contact with Lucy. And Lucy—the now-released Rössler—was still getting Werther material from the belly of Hitler's crumbling empire. To Foote, this was astonishing and almost unbelievable. After the Claus von Stauffenberg assassination attempt on Hitler's life on July 20, 1944, the entire German resistance had been wiped out. At least, that's what the world thought. Now Dübendorfer was saying that Werther not only survived but was operating unscathed. It was too much. Foote wanted to see for himself.

Dübendorfer, Foote, and the mysterious Lucy arranged to

meet at the Restaurant Bolognese in Zurich. Foote and Dübendorfer arrived first. Neither had seen Lucy before, and their expectations were high for the "agent who had his lines so deep
into the innermost secrets of Hitler."[45]

Foote was unprepared for reality. Moments later, a "quiet,
nondescript little man suddenly slipped into a chair at our table
and sat down. It was 'Lucy' himself. Anyone less like the spy of
fiction it would be hard to imagine. Consequently he was exactly
what was wanted for an agent in real life. Undistinguished looking, of medium height, aged about fifty, with his mild eyes blink-
ing behind glasses, he looked exactly like almost anyone to be
found in any suburban train anywhere in the world."[46]

Lucy said that in the ten months since the Rote Drei ring had
collapsed, he had continued to receive his precious material
from the Third Reich. But no one had come to gather it. Even
after the great purge of July 20, Werther himself was intact.
"Lucy," Foote reported, "was most anxious for communication to
be re-established so that he could send his material to the Center regularly."[47] The purge, Foote said, had "obviously merely
embarrassed and temporarily inconvenienced [Lucy] rather
than removed his sources."[48]

These three people, whose lives were so intertwined and yet so
walled off by tradecraft, now knew that they had one last duty to
perform for Moscow. With Rado gone and no transmitter available, there were no resources in Switzerland with which to contact Moscow. If Moscow was to get the intelligence, the intelligence had to get to Paris. From there, the newly operating Soviet
legation could handle matters. So in November, using his valid
British passport, Foote passed into France carrying almost a
year's worth of secret messages.

Foote was soon at the legation. After some initial confusion,
his packet of information from Werther was accepted and sent to
Moscow. Foote wanted to get back to Switzerland and restart the
network, a plan that Moscow initially approved but then revised.
Rado had also made his way to the legation, and apparently the
two men's stories about the fate of the Swiss network greatly differed. Moscow decided that Rado and Foote should return to

Moscow so that the Center could figure out in its own time what really happened. After that, if the war was still going, Foote would return to Switzerland.

But that was not to happen. With the material sent to Moscow in November, Werther had performed his last duty for Gisela's family. He was never heard from again.

But by now he had left behind enough evidence to uncover his identity.

Notes

1 Report on the Schellenberg case, p. 35.

2 Clark, p. 347.

3 Report on the Schellenberg case, p. 36.

4 Clark, p. 348.

5 Ibid., p. 349.

6 Ibid., p. 350.

7 Report on the Schellenberg case, pp. 59–60.

8 Ibid., p. 57.

9 Papers Relating to the Foreign Relations of the United States, 1943 (Washington, D.C.: Government Printing Office, 1950), pp. 910–11.

10 Unless otherwise footnoted, the information on Pannwitz is derived primarily from Trepper.

11 RG 319, Box 60.

12 Trepper, p. 194.

13 Ibid., p. 261.

14 Ibid., pp. 263–64.

15 Ibid., p. 262.

16 Toland, p. 713.

17 Trepper, p. 264.

18 Ibid., p. 265.

19 Ibid., p. 267.

20 Ibid.

21 CIA, p. 115.

22 Ibid., p. 109.

23 Trepper, p. 210.

24 Ibid., p. 211.

25 Dallin, pp. 173–74.

26 Ibid., p. 174.

27 CIA, p. 121.

28 Ibid., p. 128.

29 Ibid.

30 Gilles Perrault, *The Red Orchestra* (New York: Simon & Schuster, 1969), p. 449.

31 Ibid.

32 CIA, p. 121.

33 Perrault, p. 468.

34 Ibid., p. 481.

35 Wilhelm Hoettl, *The Secret Front* (London: Weidenfeld and Nicolson, 1953), p. 58, as quoted in Perrault, p. 453.

36 Schellenberg, *Hitler's Secret Service*, p. 315.

37 Ibid.

38 Ibid., pp. 316–17.

39 Ibid., pp. 317–18.

40 Perrault, p. 458.

41 Ibid., p. 459.

42 Ibid., p. 460.

43 CIA, p. 167.

44 Rado, p. 285.

45 Foote, p. 134.

46 Ibid.

47 Foote, p. 134.

48 Ibid. p. 79.

Chapter Eleven
Endgame

The Bunker

He finally knew that he had failed absolutely. Five years of war had produced 50 million corpses but no victory for the Third Reich. The Red Army was less than two hundred yards from the Führerbunker, and no amount of make-believe could mask the concussion of its artillery. Outside, a mere three thousand men were trying to preserve German rule in the streets around the Reichschancellery. For a people so utterly beaten, the resistance was remarkable. But the man for whom they fought was now at last a fatalist. He and Germany had lost. He took his new bride into his living quarters and gave her a capsule of cyanide. Eva Braun, in a black dress, slumped onto a sofa and died. Next, Adolf Hitler, wearing the Iron Cross that he had won during the First World War, picked up his Walther pistol, pushed the barrel into his mouth, and pulled the trigger.*

Outside waited a short, burly man known to a handful in Germany and to almost no one else. He was the man who had controlled the visitors and information that Hitler received, the Fürher's shadow whose brutal orders and insidious influence had done more to destroy Germany than anyone else, save Hitler himself. Upon hearing the shot, Martin Bormann raced into Hitler's room. Hitler had collapsed onto a table. Behind him was a painting of Frederick the Great. In front, on the table, was a

---

*The description of Hitler's end comes mainly from two sources: John Toland, *The Last 100 Days* (New York: Random House, 1966), and H. R. Trevor-Roper, *The Last Days of Hitler* (New York: Macmillan, 1947).

photo of Hitler's mother, Klara. There was the sting of cyanide in the air and the smell of gunpowder.

The Third Reich had ended.

For some reason known to no one else, Bormann hoisted Eva, who had in life detested him, and tried to carry her out of the bunker to a point where Hitler had decreed that he and Eva should be cremated.

Although those remaining would still honor even the dead Hitler's orders, Bormann's station was no more. An instant before Hitler died, Martin Bormann was the second-most powerful man in the Reich. Now he was not. Hitler's chauffeur, Erich Kempka, sickened by the sight of Bormann holding Eva, physically blocked the *reichsleiter*'s way. Wordlessly, Bormann surrendered the body, and Kempka took it up the remaining steps.

Martin Bormann seemed to accept his demotion, or at least he didn't let it get in the way of more important matters. While Joseph Goebbels and his wife prepared to kill their six children and themselves, and most others in the bunker toyed with similar ideas, Bormann planned his escape. The day after Hitler died, Bormann and a few others slipped out of the bunker. They headed north along a subway line beneath the Friedrichstrasse and arrived at the Friedrichstrasse station, about two hundred miles south of the river Spree.* Bormann, Arthur Axmann, and Ludwig Stumpfegger, Hitler's surgeon, followed German tanks across the river, but a Russian shell hit one of the tanks and Axmann was wounded. Nevertheless, the three headed north and east to the Lehrter station. Bormann and Stumpfegger decided to go east. Axmann went west but encountered Russian forces, so he retreated. He later recounted that he happened upon the dead bodies of Bormann and Stumpfegger, lying on their backs. There were no signs of violence.

---

*Officials in 1998 said they had determined that remains discovered in 1972 near the spot where Axmann said he saw the bodies were Bormann's.

The world did not trust this account. And when no bodies were found, Martin Bormann became the object of the most massive manhunt in history.[1]

After Bormann vanished, his reputation grew. The person earlier perceived in the West as the self-effacing secretary to the Führer soon became the most wanted man in Europe. Nazi chieftains, who were by nature reluctant to blame the Führer for Germany's many crimes, freely blamed Bormann. Hans Frank, the Nazi Gauleiter of Poland who had helped let the blood of millions, described Bormann as the "arch-scoundrel." Count Lutz von Krosigk, the Nazi minister of finance, labeled Bormann the "evil spirit" and—a term that soon became synonymous with Bormann—"the Brown Eminence."

Those more cynical were just as damning. Reichsmarschall Hermann Göring, asked if he felt that Bormann was dead, replied: "If I had my say about it, I hope he is frying in hell. But I don't know." Göring's anger was well placed. Bormann had been as valuable to Russia as fifty Red Army divisions.

His value to Stalin began early. In 1941, when Germany could have used millions of Ukrainian nationalists to defeat Soviet rule, Bormann decided that they deserved only "enslavement and depopulation." Said Bormann: "The Slavs are to work for us. In so far as we do not need them, they may die."[2] Faced with the choice of genocide by the Germans or political domination by the Soviets, the Ukrainians chose to live, and by doing so ruined German hopes for an easy conquest.

The Jews of Eastern Europe didn't have this choice. As they came under German domination, it was Martin Bormann who issued the orders that made him, in the words of the Nuremberg prosecutor, "a prime mover in the program of starvation, degradation, spoliation, and extermination of the Jews."[3] Bormann created a whole German industry of death, one that used precious resources and detracted from the war effort. "It was the Defendant Bormann," said the prosecutors, "who was charged by Hitler with the transmission and implementation of the Führer's orders for the liquidation of the so-called Jewish problem."[4]

Bormann went so far as to actually shield the Führer from the grim details of the Holocaust. In April 1943, Himmler came to him with an interim report that 1.27 million Jews had been liquidated. Bormann insisted that the terms *liquidation* and *special treatment* be eliminated before Hitler saw the document. Himmler was to report instead that 1.45 million Jews had been deported to the east and 1.27 million had been "processed through the camps."[5] Months later Bormann handed the document back to Himmler, telling him that, even with the corrections, the Führer "did not wish to receive the report."[6] Bormann also forbade the *reichsleiters* from talking to Hitler about the Final Solution. The Nuremberg prosecutors summed up Bormann's role succinctly: "He was, in truth, an evil archangel to the Lucifer of Hitler."[7]

Bormann's role with the Ukrainians and the Jews was only part of his devastating effect on the Third Reich. Albert Speer had a thousand grievances against the deputy Führer. In charge of war production, Speer wanted to force the Germans to total war after the Russian invasion began. He was defeated by Bormann. Speer later complained to secret American interrogators at Nuremberg that even after Stalingrad, Bormann refused to mobilize for total war.

"The people," Speer said in secret, "were in favor of total war at a much earlier date and they were prepared to sacrifice everything in order to avoid a total defeat."[8] Instead, Bormann backed Fritz Sauckel, an opponent of total war, for the key position of plenipotentiary for the Allocation of Labor. The Allies, Speer thought, should have declared Bormann a hero of the Soviet Union.

The problem was not that Bormann was under Hitler's influence, but that Hitler was increasingly under Bormann's. Hitler, Speer said, "gave Bormann authority to handle, in Hitler's name, matters which were outside the Party sphere. It enabled him to pass on any order of Hitler's in any field. He made wide use of this privilege."[9]

By 1945, Bormann seemed to some to be as much in control as the Führer. And it was then, with Germany's defeat certain, that Bormann suddenly became a belated proponent of the total war that he had so resisted when it could have done the Reich some good. From the *Führerbunker,* under Bormann's pen, came orders that Germany would either win or be "turned into a desert."

"Bormann's influence," Speer concluded, "was a national disaster."[10]

As the scope of Bormann's influence became clear at Nuremberg, old Nazis began to wonder which master the Führer's deputy really served. Speer noted: "It seemed to me as if he had been impressed by the career of Stalin, who had also begun his career as secretary to his leader, Lenin."[11]

Others took more direct aim. Martin Bormann, they suspected, was the ultimate mole, the double agent at the highest reaches who had gone undetected because of his ruthless willingness to kill identified, though defenseless, enemies of the Third Reich. The ultimate mole with the ultimate cover. Gottlob Berger, SS general and head of Himmler's Main Office, noting that Bormann had "done the greatest harm of anybody in all those [war] years," insisted at Nuremberg that Bormann was a Soviet mole. "This judgment concerning Bormann," Berger said, "will, I think, be confirmed in the course of the next years."

Otto Ohlendorf, the erudite SS general who supervised the deaths of 90,000 Jews and others on the eastern front, also concluded at Nuremberg that Bormann was a Russian spy. How else, he wanted to know, could one explain Bormann's strategic benefit to Germany's enemies? "It was a proven fact that Bormann was working for the Kremlin in 1943," Ohlendorf said.[12] Even Bormann's own defense attorney, Dr. Friedrich Bergold, indicated Bormann's likely political proclivity when he told the Nuremberg jury that his client was "probably dead or being held by the Russian occupation authorities."[13] Paul Leverkuehn, an assistant to Admiral Canaris, head of German military intelligence, said that Canaris became "extremely worried about the situation revealed by the discovery of the Red Orchestra, being convinced that the network stretched into Hitler's own H.Q. and possibly to his deputy, Martin Bormann."[14] The head of the Abwehr was given to label Bormann the "Brown Bolshevik."[15] Newspapers in

Germany and Hungary began investigating. The *Echo der Woche* in Germany had this front-page headline: "Martin Bormann: Stalin's Gauleiter?"[16] The Americans took the article seriously and believed that a letter written to the newspaper in response actually came from Bormann.[17]

The tribunal spent little time on the Soviet agent accusation, what with the Russians sitting as judges and Europe trying to come to terms with a Red Army that seemed more inclined to encamp than go home. But American agents—first those of the OSS and later the army and the CIA—were under no such political constraints. They conducted an extensive, clandestine probe of Bormann's possible ties to the Kremlin.

From a variety of sources came suggestions that Bormann had been Stalin's most deadly spy. Investigators tracked down one of Bormann's mistresses, Marie Rubach Spangenberg, and were surprised to find that she was a member of the German Communist underground—not exactly the type to fraternize with the secretary to the Führer.[18] Charlotte Pollex, a friend of Frau Spangenberg, described the actress as "small, slim, blond, and with an amazing attraction for men for one who was not particularly beautiful."[19] Yet she also confirmed that Spangenberg was "active in the KPD."[20] Americans soon learned from an informant who was with the Rote Kapelle that a German professor named Werner Cleff "was one of Bormann's Soviet contact men."[21] A high-ranking Catholic priest reported to an American subagent "that Martin Bormann had been working together with the Russians and the German Communists for a considerable time before the end of the war. At the time when the Russians moved into Berlin, Martin Bormann presented certain credentials to high ranking Russian Officers and was taken to Moscow."[22] The American 970th Counter Intelligence Corps Detatchment told headquarters that it had "in the past received information hinting at the possibility of Bormann being in Russian hands, and such is held as being credible."[23] In 1949, American military intelligence revealed that "a reliable source" reported that "Martin Bormann has recently been appointed head of the Rote Kapelle in Germany per orders of the Cominform."[24]

The British also picked up Bormann's scent and told the American liaison officer in Heidelberg that its agents had learned that Bormann was in Moscow on March 1, 1948.[25] As did many such reports of the time, the British one said that Bormann was still active in the Communist Party and was leading activities in the West. He was even believed to have revisited Germany.[26] When U.S. intelligence learned that the Associated Press in September 1948 had information that "Martin Bormann is alive and in Russian hands," it asked for a quiet investigation because "such publicity could have injurious aspect on present international negotiations."[27] The report went on to say that the top American jurors at Nuremberg, including Justice Jackson, "have expressed great interest in these press reports."[28]

The Americans also learned that Bormann had direct ties to Switzerland, where, of course, Rudolf Rössler was based. Several reports said that Bormann owned a house and an apartment in Bodensee, where he vacationed.[29]

Most of the reports on Bormann and his alleged ties to the Kremlin were buried deep inside American intelligence archives. The man on the street in Berlin typically had not heard of Bormann, and because Bormann had disappeared there wasn't great substance to his image. Though a few well-placed witnesses spoke openly at Nuremberg of his treachery, Justice Jackson showed no inclination to actually investigate. Canaris's suspicions were not announced; Schellenberg steered clear of the entire issue of the Red Orchestra; and no one asked Ohlendorf or anyone else why Bormann was thought to be in Stalin's service.

The reason was probably no more complicated than that the notion did not fit the times. Who in the late 1940s—with American forces mostly returned home while the stain of the Red Army was soaking in throughout Eastern Europe—wanted to say that the man most responsible for the Holocaust after Hitler was really an agent of Joseph Stalin? No one. The issue would have consumed the Nuremberg trial, turning it from a morality set piece about Nazism into something opaque and dangerous. Just as the NKVD massacre of the Polish officer corps at the Katyn Forest was swept under the rug and blamed on the Germans, anything that involved Bormann beyond his persona as a Nazi war criminal was dismissed. The moral formula was simple: There were good Germans and there were Nazis. Even the Red tint of the July 20 bombing of Hitler was lost in the overwhelming propaganda that the plotters were German heroes who wanted only to stop a vicious tyrant, not aid one just as bad.

As early as 1949, accounts of the Lucy ring began appearing after French journalists interviewed Foote. "'Lucy,'" he told them, "was able rapidly to obtain intelligence of the highest secrecy. Between the time when the German General Staff made a decision and the time when the Center was informed of it, there elapsed scarcely 24 hours—that is to say, hardly more than the time needed to code and decode the message in question. In order to act so quickly, Lucy must be able to maintain contact with the German high command."[30] General Halder concurred. He declared in dismay to *Der Spiegel:* "Almost every offensive operation of ours was betrayed to the enemy even before it appeared on my desk." Although this was fascinating, it did not matter to the German psyche. There was a collective will that nothing was going to nurture any nascent would-be Hitler with a new "stab-in-the-back" theory such as those that grew out of 1918. German dishonor must be without excuse.

A quarter of a century later, the psychology of guilt that the Germans had so well earned still prevented an analysis of Werther and his role in Germany's defeat. On September 11, 1971, the German newspaper *Die Welt* printed an excerpt of the memoirs of Gen. Reinhard Gehlen. Until 1945, Gehlen had been head of German Foreign Armies East. After the war, Gehlen took charge of West Germany's foreign intelligence operations in the east and from 1956 to 1968 was head of the BND, the West German secret service. He was considered one of the sharpest spymasters in the world, and what he said demanded consideration and respect. But in this case, what he said stunned Germany into disbelief. Martin Bormann, Gehlen said, had been a Soviet spy. And Bormann had lived for a time after the war in the Soviet Union. There—it was finally in the open.

Ohlendorf, Canaris, and Schellenberg were now joined by a Cold War hero.

But Gehlen's revelations stopped there. Just before the excerpt appeared, and amid rumors of its contents, Horst Ehmke, minister in the federal chancellery, warned Gehlen that he could not release any state secrets. Gehlen agreed that he would not.[31] In the excitement that followed, with demands that he reveal his proof, Gehlen stayed quiet. He never answered any questions on the first part of his disclosure—that Martin Bormann had been a Soviet agent. Even when the editors of *Die Welt* begged him for more insight, the spymaster declined.

On the second assertion—that Bormann had lived in Moscow after the war—Gehlen was only slightly more helpful. Though he refused to testify under oath, he told an investigating magistrate that one of his agents had spotted Bormann in a Russian newsreel that panned a broad audience. This was hardly satisfactory, and it did not constitute proof. But it was all that could be had from Gehlen. He refused to further commit himself. The magazine reported that Gehlen was unresponsive, and its own reporters could not confirm his Bormann revelation. The story died about as fast as it had begun, with Germany's guilty conscience more or less intact.

The world should have known that Gehlen had not dredged the Bormann-as-spy notion out of nothingness. He had to have had a reason to choose this assertion as the anchor of his memoirs. But in the context of the time, even if Gehlen had revealed his sources, it is quite possible that they would have been dismissed. In 1971, the Western intellectual elite was still blaming Himmler for the Katyn massacre. And although Khrushchev had disclosed Stalin's crimes at the 1956 party congress, in the West he still had strong defenders. This was the Vietnam era, and Russia was portrayed as the protector of small states, whereas the West in the guise of the United States was the oppressor. The mood was not fertile for uncovering Soviet crimes. Instead, demanding unilateral disarmament was in vogue. On most college campuses, the military was seen as inherently evil, and military intelligence—which Gehlen exemplified—was universally condemned as an oxymoron. Gehlen's revelations simply had no constituency. Except, of course, in the hidden files.

The CIA in a subtle way got into the middle of the Bormann question in the 1970s. The question was not whether the convicted Nazi war criminal was a spy, but where on earth he was. The agency studied three possibilities. It found the simplest answer to be the most likely. Bormann had probably been killed and buried near a bridge in central Berlin in May 1945. The second possibility—that Bormann was living in South America—the agency found less convincing. The South American sightings had been numerous, but all attempts to confirm them had failed. The agency, with great assets throughout South America, had concluded that most of the sightings were well meaning but faulty.

The CIA offered a third choice: that somehow Bormann was snug inside the Soviet Union. But the agency discounted this notion, though it gave it equal weight with the others. Lost to most was a simple question: How could American intelligence waste any time even considering this possibility? The answer is straightforward. The CIA was considering the possibility of Bormann's presence in Moscow for the same reasons that Gehlen had: American intelligence had information that Bormann had worked as a Soviet spy. Therefore, why not look for him in Russia?

Untangling the web surrounding the identity of Werther was not furthered by certain charlatans who populated the field of espionage historians. French writers Accoce and Quet, for instance, simply fabricated their findings in their 1966 study of the Swiss spy ring. They said that they had uncovered what they called the ten sources for the Werther material but, to protect the living relatives from possible neo-Nazi retribution, would identify the Werther team only through abbreviations of their real names.[32] The writers had boxed themselves in, however. In order to be convincing, Accoce and Quet had to have their abbreviations closely match some real people. And they did, which produced an uproar. Though the dead cannot sue for libel, their relatives can be indignant, and they were. Wanting to clear the names of their ancestors, the relatives clamored for proof. Worse, historians began to pick away at the story. Accoce and

Quet finally acknowledged that they had lied in their book. The whole story was phony. There were no ten traitors, nor did the writers know if a collection of spies had adopted the name Werther. The authors had allowed themselves the license to guess at the identities of the anti-Hitler alliance, then concoct a story of how it all worked during the war. Their retraction should have been the end of it, but unfortunately, even as late as 1996, some historians were still quoting from Accoce and Quet as though they had told the truth.[33]

But for all the harm they did to the field, Accoce and Quet did capture the spirit of the day. Their ten German agents were not cutthroat betrayers of Germany but were really German patriots trying to rid the Continent of a great and evil force. They imagined the heroes as quixotic anti-Nazis. They did not imagine them as Heinrich Müller or Martin Bormann. That would have been unthinkable.

Finally, still another spymaster would join Canaris, Gehlen, and the others in believing that Bormann was not what he appeared to be. In 1975, four years after Gehlen's bombshell, Leopold Trepper wrote the French version of his book, *Le Grand Jeu*. He admitted that while he was in the custody of Giering and Pannwitz, he "could not make out the ultimate objective of this 'great game.'"[34] He was suspicious that it was designed to somehow break the Grand Alliance and insisted that he was justified in abandoning it when he made his escape. But during the years he had to think about it in Soviet jail cells, his notions evolved. Said Trepper: "From mid-1943 on, the outcome of the war was no longer in doubt. At that point, the Nazi leaders oriented the great game toward a real quest for a separate peace—with the west, for Himmler, though in the case of Bormann, who supervised the whole affair, this is less certain."[35]

There was no reason why Trepper should have left out an obvious question. If Bormann, through Gestapo Müller, was sending true Nazi secrets to the Center—and of this there is no doubt—then why not posit the same chain of command in the secrets going to Switzerland? It is a question that no one asked. But the answer is now clear.

DEDUCTION AND PROOF

The Werther messages are the key. They limit to three people those who physically could have been Werther. And a closer examination limits the number to one.

First, though, it is necessary to dispense with two theories that have retained some currency over time. One holds that the Werther source in the German High Command didn't exist at all. Instead, the British, having broken the German codes, funneled the intelligence to Russia through a back channel in order to disguise its real origin. The other theory maintains that the part of the German resistance that was always seen as Western oriented actually went over to the other side. Those suspected of belonging to this group include Hans Bernd Gisevius, Carl Friederich Goerdeler, and Hans Oster, whom the CIA believed to be the best candidate for Werther.

The theory that the Werther material came from the British is an irresistible hypothesis. The British had, as authors Reed and Fisher point out, broken many of the German codes. They knew sometimes within hours what orders had been sent to German submarines, divisions, and fighter squadrons. Though the penetration was not perfect—there were times when a new "key" was sent to the operators of the German Enigma coding devices and the British were for days, and even months, in the dark—for the most part the British knew about German military decisions. Most historians now agree that were it not for the British cracking of the Enigma cipher, the Battle of the Atlantic could have gone in Hitler's favor. Reed and Fisher and many others have made the logical but flawed leap that the British shared this information with Moscow by sending it through Foote's transmitter in Switzerland. That theory is based on happenstance. The British knew of German High Command orders (presumably including those sent to the eastern front), and about the same time Moscow knew them as well. Therefore, the theory goes, the British were responsible for Moscow's good fortune. Why the need to camouflage the operation by creating Werther? This is the supposed answer: Stalin would never have believed any direct intelligence from Great Britain, and the British would have never risked Ultra, the name they used for the breaking of the German code, by telling Stalin anything about it. Therefore the British created Werther. Though the theory has no evidence behind it, it does constitute a logical notion. Proponents, unfortunately, do not seek to prove even the most basic cause and effect sequence that must hold if the theory can even be considered— that information was received in Great Britain before it was seen in Moscow. Many of the messages exist for comparison, but the effort has not been made. And maybe this is just as well, for the theory falls on its face in at least two areas.

First, even if Great Britain had certain information, it would never have sent it to Stalin.

In the darkest hours of Stalingrad, when it appeared that Russia could be forced out of the war or defeated altogether, the British had great motivation to help Moscow. But after the Paulus surrender of Stalingrad and the United States' strength was building exponentially, Great Britain had no reason to support a quick victory by the Red Army. Western leaders were creating atom bombs, in part to dissuade Stalin's grand ambitions. They would not turn around and help those same ambitions by letting Stalin beat Hitler at too low a cost. Certainly after the German debacle at Kursk, Great Britain's self-interest rested far more in delaying Stalin's advance westward than in quickening it. Yet it was the period from the Russian counterattack at Stalingrad to well after Kursk that Werther performed his greatest services.

The second reason to discard the British-did-it notion is decisive. Enigma and Werther supplied far different types of data. Enigma decrypted orders sent from headquarters to commanders. Such orders are simple and direct. They do not discuss the personalities of those making the orders or the debate that preceded them. Tactical in nature, they are not strategic concepts having little need to be sent to field commanders.

Werther's information was different. Much of it came in response to specific questions by the Center: what troops in one sector were going to another, what ones were to remain in reserve, and so on. Enigma had no way to quiz the Wehrmacht. It could only listen passively. Werther was proactive. The number of times that Werther was ordered to answer specific questions is clear from previous chapters. For instance, on May 6, 1943, the Center sent the Rado net this message: "Tell 'Lucy' that we are not only interested in decisions made by the OKW in this matter, but also in all the discussions of the General Staff and OKW."[36] The Center later asked Lucy to immediately explain the "financial and material means (that) have been set aside by OKW for the construction of the Ostwall? (And) how is the construction board organized?"[37]

Werther kept an ear open for subtleties in the high command debates, even noting what was said when the Führer was in the room and when he was not. In April 1943, Werther told the Center: "The conference opened under Göring's chairmanship without Hitler, then Hitler arrived and also took part. The conference revealed the existence of fundamental differences of opinion between Göring on one hand and Halder on the other [Halder had been invited to attend in an advisory capacity] . . .

"Göring was supported by Dönitz, Keitel, Manstein, List, Zeitzler, Fromm, Milch, and Jeschonnek, all of whom were present at the conference. Kluge, Kuchler, and Rundstedt . . . were not invited to take part."[38]

None of these details would have been transmitted in a coded message to field commanders. Commanders need decisions, not debate.

There are also examples—although only on paper and not in code—of where commands were sent from headquarters to the field. In such cases, the British Enigma machines would have been useless. But a man inside the Führer conference would have known. At some critical moments, Werther knew such things. As noted earlier, before the battle of Kursk, Hitler ordered that the plans not be broadcast. Instead, they were reduced to thirteen paper copies. Hitler ordered that no duplicates be made and that no one outside the conference should know the entire scope of the plan. Despite this restriction, Werther was able to send this plan to the Center overnight.[39]

F. W. Winterbotham, the first man to reveal Enigma and the breaking of the German codes, underscored their limitations.

One may or may not learn of the orders, but divining what was behind them was far more difficult. In talking about the preparations for the cross-Channel invasion, Winterbotham said: "During the spring of 1944 the Germans made what was to be probably the most important decision of all those affecting the Allies and the Overlord plans. The decision arose from a clash of views between Hitler, Rundstedt, Rommel, Guderian, and Schweppenburg, who commanded a group of four panzer divisions that made up the panzer reserve stationed near Paris. In view of the importance of this whole affair, I think it would be of interest to give the full facts of what went on, as we learned them from documents captured after the war, then show how much we learned from Ultra at the time."[40]

Winterbotham goes on to explain—all from captured documents—the give and take of negotiations among Hitler, Guderian, and Rommel. Rommel wanted to attack the beachhead with everything Germany could muster, whereas Guderian wanted to hold back and pick a weak point to counter the invasion. Hitler wavered. None of this, says Winterbotham, was known through code breaking. It became known only after the war.

Yet this is exactly the type of information that Werther was able to gather. It is clear, then, that however attractive the idea is that the British were the source of the Werther material, the notion fails when tested against actual messages sent to and from Moscow.

The CIA provides a second theory about Werther. In a 1979 study, the agency suggested that formerly pro-western German resistance was the likely source of many of Rudolf Rössler's sources, including Werther. The CIA said: "Despite the printed assertions to the contrary, Rudolf Rössler did divulge the identity of his sources, or at least of some of them. Three and a half years before his death, he provided identifying information about four of his chief sources to a trusted friend. They were, said 'Lucy,' (1) a German major—whom he did not name—who had been the chief of the Abwehr before Admiral Wilhelm Canaris assumed command; (2) Hans Bernd Gisevius; (3) Carl Goerdeler; and (4) 'General Boelitz, deceased.'"[41]

The agency did not reveal the source of this information. But it did draw conclusions. It figured that Rössler had confused things. The major in the Abwehr had not come before Canaris, but after. And he had never been head of the organization. The person whom Rössler indirectly fingered was Hans Oster, according to the CIA. Oster, the agency said, "became convinced that the plots to eradicate the Nazis through the internal interventions of the German armed forces would fail because of the wavering of the German generals. He warned the West because he recognized that Hitler could not be brought down inside the Reich until he had been defeated on the battlefields."[42]

The CIA summarized its evidence: "We have Werther, Teddy, Olga, and Anna as Lucy's principal sources and as the principal sources in the Rote Drei network. We have Oster, Gisevius, Goerdeler and Boelitz identified by Rössler as having been among his sources during World War II. We have no basis for matching true and cover names, although Oster seems the likeliest candidate for Werther."[43]

For all its massive ability to gather intelligence, the CIA in its analysis made a disastrous chronological error. The agency thought that Oster could have been the Werther source because he remained the number-two official in the Abwehr "until his discharge . . . on 31 March 1944."[44] Unfortunately, it was a year earlier that Oster's ring came crashing down. Himmler and Schellenberg had suspected Oster of betrayal as early as the winter of 1942, when Himmler began tapping his telephone, opening his letters, and shadowing his movements.[45] In April 5, 1943, the SD had gathered enough evidence to arrest Dohnanyi. Oster made his ill-conceived attempt to hide incriminating documents and was relieved of his command a few hours later. For the German resistance, said Gisevius, "The worst blow . . . was the destruction of the Oster circle, which took place in April, 1943."[46] Oster was placed under house arrest, then in June 1943 was sent to "leadership reserve."[47] In December 1943, Oster was forbidden any contact with the Abwehr. He was officially relieved of service, as the CIA noted, in March 1944, but for a full year he had played no role in Abwehr affairs.[48]

During the time when Oster was, according to the CIA, performing his greatest feats for the Russians, he was being surveilled by the SS, placed under house arrest, banished, then totally cut off from any communication with the Abwehr. This is hardly a person whom the Center could call upon to interrogate the high command. Besides, Werther kept sending Rössler intelligence until September 1944, which would have been difficult for Oster because he was by then in a concentration camp.

Further, even if Oster wanted to supply the Russians with Germany's greatest secrets, and even if he somehow managed to subvert the massive impediments encumbering him, he was never in a Führer conference. The same problem that defeats the British-did-it theory defeats the Oster theory. Oster, for a time, had access to military orders, but he had no access to military discussions. He may have learned of the discussions from someone who was involved in them, but that doesn't help the CIA's analysis. In that case, Oster could have been a conduit for information but not the originator. The person on the inside was still the key. Werther was still unidentified.

Reading the flawed CIA analysis makes it clear why Oster was granted the starring role. Somehow, information was flowing from the high command to Rössler within hours. A courier would have been too slow; therefore, an electronic means was necessary. The CIA noted, "Oster had the entire communications network of the Abwehr at his disposal . . ."[49] That the CIA failed to note exactly when Oster's command of the network ceased is inexcusable. But the logic that electronic means must have been used to contact Switzerland is unshakable. Some secret service organization with great latitude in the Third Reich must have been involved. It is natural that the CIA looked to the Abwehr as that organization. It was, after all, closely connected with the German resistance, and it had the latest communication equipment.

But there was another organization that sprang not from the bourgeois roots of the Abwehr but from proletarian roots. The Gestapo also had lines of communication. The Americans never considered that.

ELIMINATION

Who could Werther have been? Whoever he was, he must have fit these criteria: He operated freely in the German High Command from June 1941 to October 1944; he had secure communication links to the outside; and he knew the total picture. Oster and the British have been ruled out as suspects. Who remains?

As glamorous as high-stakes spying might seem, much of the work—at least in the twentieth century—revolved around lowly code clerks. Indeed, a Russian operative in the German High Command's encoding office could have provided much of the information that Werther gained. But a code clerk would have had the same limitations as the British with Enigma, and much less talent at analysis. He would have seen only orders sent, not the debate that preceded them. And he would have worked only one of three shifts a day, so he could not have been the source of Werther's global findings. Finally, a code clerk would have been hard pressed to find a clandestine method of sending Stalin the secrets of the Reich.

By necessity, then, Werther was in the power structure of the Third Reich; he was at the meetings about which he reported. As such, he must have been someone improbable, who from all appearances was at least a German patriot, if not a devout Nazi.

Who were these people? Because this was Hitler's war, the decisions that mattered were almost always made by him. The OKW (Wehrmacht), OKH (Army), or OKL (Luftwaffe) might have designed masterful plans on the staff level, but until they were vetted at a Führer conference, nothing could come of them. General Warlimont lamented after the war that had Hitler simply remained in Berlin he would have been forced to have a more global understanding of the war. Instead, "over the course of three years 'Wolfsschanze' was turned into a 'fortress'; the barbwire fences and the minefields became thicker and the concrete blocks stuck up like superstructures of old-style cruisers; in addition underground rooms and passages of an unknown extent were constructed beneath the Berghof, whither Hitler still went for sometimes shorter, sometimes longer periods."[50]

Most of the planning for Barbarossa was done by OKH, but it was constantly under Hitler's supervision. In the beginning, Brauchitsch was the OKH commander and Halder his chief of staff. Brauchitsch can be eliminated as a Werther candidate because Hitler sacked him on December 19, 1941, the day that Hitler assumed personal command of the armed forces. Halder, who was truly involved in the resistance, would lose his post, too, before Werther's major damage was done. General Gerhard Engel remarked in his diary in September 1942 that the Führer "trusts none of the generals . . . he would promote a major to a general and make him chief of staff, if he only knew such a man. Nothing seems to suit him and he curses himself for having gone to war with such poor generals."[51] On September 24, Halder was gone. "You and I have been suffering from nerves," said Hitler. "Half of my exhaustion is due to you. It is not worth going on."[52] General Kurt Zeitzler was appointed in his place. Zeitzler was a durable rubber stamp for Hitler, but he did not have the respect of the field commanders. Ailing, he was removed from power the day after the July 20 bombing. Werther's information continued to be sent to Lucy after this date, which rules out Zeitzler as a suspect.

Guderian was another man who toyed with the resistance, but the calendar also rules him out. Hitler had dismissed Guderian as a panzer commander on December 20, 1941, when the German generals wanted to flee the Moscow front. Guderian was not invited back to the seat of power until February 28, 1943, when Hitler made him inspector general of the armored troops. Much of the important intelligence that passed from Werther to the Center came when Guderian was out of the picture.

Manstein came on the scene too late to have been the provider of the early Werther material. In fact, not one of the key field commanders—among them Kluge, Bock, Kleist, Reichenau, and Rundstedt—was in a position to know the whole picture that Werther commanded. They were always either in a specialized theater of war or out of the picture altogether.

Göring is not a possible choice either. He generally did not attend many of the Führer conferences but stayed somewhat aloof in his kingdom of the Luftwaffe. The navy operated almost completely in its own realm and was largely divorced from the concerns of the eastern front. Admirals Raeder and Dönitz knew only a fraction of what Werther did.

Naturally, because Dübendorfer had reported that the Werther source was in the OKW, the source may have been there. The chief of the high command was Keitel, and the operations chief was Jodl. The chief suspect in the OKW should be Jodl, for he was the one designated to attend Führer conferences, whereas Keitel and Warlimont, chief of the national defense section, usually stayed behind.[53] Warlimont often felt completely left out.[54] Could Keitel or Jodl theoretically have been Werther? Yes. They held their positions from the beginning of the Werther traffic to its end. But their subsequent actions made it almost impossible to believe that they were culpable. Both went to the gallows at Nuremberg. Had one of them actually been a secret benefactor of the Allies, it seems that he would have raised his hand and said, "Wait one minute, please."

Who is left? Let us eliminate Hitler, not only for the obvious reasons but because some discussions that Werther described were conducted outside of even his presence. After that, we are left with a barren field. Although some outside source, such as the old anti-Hitler general Georg Thomas, perhaps could have cobbled together enough information from rumors and side conversations to account for a few of the Werther messages, no one beyond the inner circle could have accounted for all of them. But this deduction produces a null result: In a state where treason was everywhere, it seems that not a single individual attended all of the requisite meetings to have gathered all of the Werther intelligence.

But, of course, someone did.

It is natural then to look for the fly on the wall, a secret microphone that betrayed the Third Reich. In this case, though, the secret microphone was not as small as a fly. In fact, Bormann's stenographers had been an open wound in the headquarters ever since they arrived on September 12, 1942—the approximate time that, according to the CIA, the Werther messages began. Even before the stenographers, Bormann had ordered Koeppen and Heim to take secret notes of the Führer conferences. There is no reason to suppose that Foote was wrong when he said that Werther had made his appearance much earlier than the CIA believed. Hitler's shadow and confidant, Martin Bormann, had set up the perfect system. He could request information directly from the Führer if need be, and demand it from others with the full power of the Führer at other times.

But mostly, Bormann could work unnoticed as a Russian operative. He was not at the Führer conferences, so even when Hitler began to suspect that there was an inner-circle traitor, he apparently never suspected his own secretary. And if anyone in the leadership ever suspected Bormann—and many did—there was from 1942 until the end no ability to tell Hitler, at least not without Bormann's knowledge. Bormann was the keeper of the gate. Outside of the military conferences and Hitler's private table talks, the only people with direct contact with the Führer were Speer, Goebbels, and Himmler.[55] Even then, Goebbels gave way to the powerful secretary, preferring to communicate with Hitler through "Führer Informations" sent through Bormann.[56] Himmler no doubt had suspicions, because his assistant, Schellenberg, certainly did. But the man who was too cowed by Bormann even to present the Führer with accurate accounts of the Holocaust was maybe not the man to challenge the Führer's shadow. Besides, Himmler was compromised in so much treason that he could not cast the first stone.

Speer, whose IQ tested as the brightest of the major defendants at Nuremberg, had no death wish. But he was not a coward. He consulted with Goebbels about the Bormann problem. With Goebbels's backing, Speer flew to the Obersalzberg in May 1943 to confer with Göring, who had lately been content to run his own kingdom, letting *Führerpolitics* alone. "I told him," Speer later told American investigators, "if it was not too late already, he would have to become active on a considerable scale again. It was necessary to create a league against Bormann since otherwise Hitler would ultimately be completely isolated . . .

"Göring agreed with everything, and on the following day he conferred with Goebbels who had followed me to the Obersalzberg for this purpose. After that, Funk, Goebbels, Göring, and myself had another meeting in Berlin at which Göring promised once more to defend his position more energetically with our assistance. Göring, however, was by then already in a state of lethargy and apathy, and he lacked the courage to carry out this intention."[57] Goebbels soon defected and "began to link up with Bormann."[58] Without powerful allies, Speer would have been crushed in a confrontation with Bormann. So he avoided one.

ARCHANGEL

Usually a case is solved when a detective proves a suspect's motive, opportunity, and means of committing the crime. With Bormann, the stenographers and his own fidelity to Hitler provided the opportunity. Although as Hitler's shadow, Bormann had no individual means of transmitting the intelligence to anyone in Switzerland, the Gestapo did. And Bormann and Gestapo Müller had worked well together during the *funkspiel.* The playback of the great game showed that the two had links to Moscow and were betraying the Third Reich.

But what was Bormann's motive?

Speer, one of the most sapient observers of the Third Reich, had mentioned that Bormann had great respect for Stalin.[59] Speer also told American interrogators that when Hitler finally said in 1944 that he would abandon state socialism, "Bormann was very much displeased with this speech."[60] This is a key clue.

The record is clear that Bormann believed in socialism as a youth, and nationalist socialism later. So did Hitler. Speer told interrogators: "It is certainly a fact that Hitler had the serious intention of raising the living standard of the workers. This was his principal post-war aim, besides his building projects. After the war, undoubtedly a radical line would have been taken against the 'idle capitalist' living on his profits. The working men of all classes would probably have benefited at his expense."[61] If Hitler's shadow had the same aim, it would not matter much who actually won the war—the racist socialist Stalin or the racist socialist Hitler.

It was not unnatural for men in Hitler's Third Reich to begin to see in Russia a more natural ally than they saw in the West. July 20 had been all about such a shift in geopolitical vision. Even the boss himself had begun to have doubts. That Great Britain was Germany's only natural ally had been a bedrock of Hitler's beliefs since 1923. But twenty years later, his ideas had not exactly paid dividends. Hitler was faced with manufacturing Germany's second loss of a world war in a quarter century. The west had rebuffed all overtures. The British never seemed to appreciate his courtesy at Dunkirk or the great strategic gift he had given Great Britain by attacking Russia. Instead, Great Britain and America at Casablanca had said that nothing short of unconditional surrender would be accepted. To Hitler, that could only mean that these natural German allies wanted to blot Germany off the map.

Maybe Hitler had allowed himself to say to insiders that perhaps he had been wrong. Maybe his enemy was not Jewish bolshevism but Jewish capitalism. Hitler told Mussolini that the coalition opposing the Axis was unnatural. "It involved two different worlds. One could rather imagine a German-Russian coalition than one between the egotistical capitalism of England and America and egotistical Bolshevism or anti-capitalism. Both sides were still dominated by imperialism but one in which the imperialist tendencies were opposed to and clashed with each other."[62] The strategic break point, Hitler said, would come over oil when either the Russians or the Anglos tried to "get their hands on the Persian Gulf."[63] Hitler made it clear that the Anglos he envisioned in this final showdown would not fly the Union Jack. America was replacing Great Britain as a world superpower. Roosevelt, Hitler said, was swindling Great Britain into "giving away its substance."[64]

Hitler had always admired Stalin, just as Stalin always admired Hitler. We should expect nothing less of the evil archangel. The *funkspiel* clearly shows that Bormann wanted to set up direct negotiations with the Russians to arrange an alliance. That alone is proof of motive.

All the suspicions concerning Bormann by the spymasters over the years were valid. The pieces of the puzzle fit together. In Martin Borman, we have found Werther

Notes

1 Chuck Anesi, www.brainlink.com/~Anesi/bormann.html.

2 IMT, Vol. 5, p. 332.

3 Ibid., p. 319.

4 Ibid., p. 318.

5 Jochen von Lang, *The Secretary* (New York: Random House, 1979), p. 234.

6 Ibid., pp. 234–35.

7 IMT, Vol. 5, p. 334.

8 RG 226, XL 17234.

9 Ibid.

10 Ibid., Report 19, Part 1, on Speer examination.

11 RG 226, XL 17234.

12 XE003212, RG 319, IRR, Box 269.

13 Associated Press, May 28, 1947.

14 Perrault, p. 458.

15 Ibid.

16 XE003213, RG 319, IRR, Box 269.

17 Ibid.

18 Ibid.

19 Ibid.

20 Ibid.

21 Ibid.

22 Ibid.

23 Ibid., letter dated September 25, 1947.

24 RG 319, Box 59, Vol. 1.

25 XE003213, RG 319, Box 269, Vol. 3. For other Bormann sightings in Moscow, see documents in Vol. 3, Part 1.

26. This is another report from the British listed in Vol. 3, Part 1.

27 XE003213, RG 319, IRR, Box 269, Vol. 3.

28 Ibid.

29 XE003213, RG 319, Box 269, Vol. 3, Part 2.

30 RG 319, Box 60, Vol. 1.

31 Heinz Hohne and Hermann Zolling, *The General Was a Spy* (New York: Coward, McCann & Geoghegan, Inc., 1972), p. xix.

32 See Pierre Accoce and Pierre Quet, *La Guerre a été Gagnee en Suisse* (Paris: Librairie Academique, 1966); Nigel West, *A Thread of Deceit: Espionage Myths of World War II* (New York: Dell Books, 1985), p. 66.

33 See Tarrant, chapters 37–39.

34 Trepper, p. 178.

35 Ibid., 319.

36 RG 319, Box 59.

37 Ibid.

38 Rado, p. 178.

39 Read and Fisher, p. 152.

40 Winterbotham, p. 183.

41 CIA, p. 185.

42 Ibid., p. 186.

43 Ibid., p. 193.

44 Ibid., p. 187.

45 Gisevius, p. 474.

46 Ibid., p. 473.

47 Peter Hoffmann, *History of the German Resistance 1933–1945* (Cambridge, Mass.: The MIT Press, 1977), p. 294.

48 Ibid.

49 CIA, p. 188.

50 Warlimont, pp. 177–78.

51 Toland, p. 719.

52 Ibid.

53 Warlimont, p. 184.

54 Ibid., p. 176.

55 RG 226, XL 17234.

56 Ibid.

57 Ibid.

58 Ibid.

59 Ibid.

60 Ibid.

61 Ibid.

62 NAZ, p. 868.

63 Ibid.

64 Ibid.

EPILOGUE

As Adolf Hitler prepared to take his life on April 30, 1945, his thoughts turned to the two people who most mattered to him—Eva Braun and Martin Bormann. In his will, Hitler wrote:

As I did not consider that I could take responsibility, during the years of struggle, of contracting a marriage, I have now decided, before the closing of my earthly career, to take as my wife that girl who, after many years of faithful friendship, entered, of her own free will, the practically besieged town in order to share her destiny with me. At her own desire she goes as my wife with me into death. It will compensate us for what we both lost through my work in the service of my people.

What I possess belongs—in so far as it has any value—to the Party. Should this no longer exist, to the State; should the State also be destroyed, no further decision of mine is necessary.

My paintings, in the collections which I have bought in the course of years, have never been collected for private purposes, but only for the extension of a gallery in my home town of Linz on Donau.

It is my most sincere wish that this bequest may be duly executed. "I nominate as my Executor my most faithful Party comrade, Martin Bormann.

He is given full legal authority to make all decisions.

He is permitted to take out everything that has a sentimental value or is necessary for the maintenance of a modest simple life, for my brothers and sisters, also above all for the mother of my wife and my faithful co-workers who are well known to him, principally my old Secretaries Frau Winter etc. who have for many years aided me by their work.

I myself and my wife—in order to escape the disgrace of deposition or capitulation—choose death. It is our wish to be burnt immediately on the spot where I have carried out the greatest part of my daily work in the course of a twelve years' service to my people.

Given in Berlin, 29th April 1945, 4:00 A.M.

[Signed] A. Hitler

[Witnesses]
Dr. Joseph Goebbels
Martin Bormann
Colonel Nicholaus von Below[1]

The Führer's wish was carried out as much as possible. The bodies of Hitler and his new bride were laid down outside the *Führerbunker* and doused with gasoline. But there was not enough on hand to do the job to proper German standards. The corpses were blackened but not destroyed. Hitler and Eva would be exhumed and reburied several times before the German dictator's skull was finally in the hands of Josef Stalin.

It is now clear that Bormann did not long outlast his master. In 1972 a construction crew unearthed two skeletons near the spot where Axmann said he had seen the bodies of Bormann and Dr. Stumpfegger. Dental records suggested that the bones of the shorter skeleton were, in fact, the remains of Martin Bormann. A year later, the German federal prosecutor's office ruled that the Führer's secretary died near the Weidenbammer Bridge sometime between 1:30 A.M. and 2:30 A.M. on May 2, 1945.

Naturally, this did not sit well with those who insisted that Bormann somehow had made it to South America where he hatched diabolical plots to conquer the world in the name of his old boss, Hitler. Such a notion was dealt a severe setback in 1998 when DNA expert Wolfgang Eisenmenger compared genetic samples from Bormann's relatives with samples from the skeleton. His conclusion: The remains were Bormann's.

Of course, even this will not satisfy some who are dead set on a Bormann survived the war theory. For instance, they can argue that the remains found near the Weidenbammer Bridge in 1972 were not necessarily buried there in 1945. It could be, for instance, a Russian or Nazi trick. Bormann, the thinking might proceed, did cooperate with the Soviets for several years after the war or, down a different line, did hatch a Nazi plot from South America. But after his death, say in 1972, the Russians or the South American Nazis had him buried at a place that would conveniently fit Axmann's story. By this cunning stroke, Bormann's movements following May 2, 1945, would be erased.

This is possible, but far-fetched. If Bormann had made it into Stalin's hands, for instance, the Soviet leader would have undoubtedly erased his trail straight away. Stalin was not sentimental over those who had helped the Russian side, much preferring to see them dead or locked away. The South American theory has similar problems, not the least of which would be logistical. Burying Bormann in Berlin in 1972 would have been problematic.

Instead, it is best to settle for the easiest explanation: Martin Bormann, during the final convulsion of the European theater of the Second World War, was killed on May 2, 1945, taking his secrets to the grave. He may have been felled by a German or Russian bullet. Or he could have taken his own life. This much is sure: We will never know.

There is no such assurance that his partner in the *funkspiel* died at any such appropriate time. Heinrich "Gestapo" Müller simply vanished, leaving behind no skeletons or reports of grand escapes. The man who faithfully carried out Bormann's orders for the Holocaust might as well have been made of ether. Sure, there have been periodic sightings of the secret police czar in South America, but even at that, the sightings of Müller have been less frequent than South American sightings of Hitler and Bormann, and no more credible. Heinrich Müller may be the most notorious war criminal ever to escape justice.

Heinz Pannwitz arrived in Moscow in 1945 with Victor Sukulov. He carried with him several pieces of luggage and acted as though he should be treated as a Hero of the Soviet Union. He had, after all, allowed the Director in Moscow to contact the German resistance. Instead, Pannwitz was sentenced to twenty-five years in a Soviet work camp. After Stalin died in 1954, Pannwitz was released. He made it back to West Germany where he told the American CIA that he did not go to Moscow because he was a Soviet spy, but because he feared the Soviets less than he feared the United States.[2] Others warned the agency that he was still acting as a Russian spy. Regardless, he did occasional work for West German intelligence.

Sukulov was also imprisoned after arriving in Moscow, being released in 1956. He is reported to have lived out his life in Leningrad under the name Gurevitch.

"Le Grand Chef," Leopold Trepper, suffered gravely while in Stalin's prisons. After the dictator's death, Trepper also emerged from the gulag. He made it to freedom in 1957 when he arrived in Warsaw. He wrote memoirs, visited Auschwitz, and lived to be seventy-seven. He died in 1982, still bitter about Stalin and his system.

THE ROTE DREI

By most accounts, Alexander Rado wanted to defect to the British after he bolted from the spy plane in Cairo.* But the British repatriated him to the Russians on July 29, 1945. Like the others, Rado was imprisoned in the Soviet Union until after Stalin's death. He eventually made it back to Hungary where he took up his old profession of cartography and wrote a book in 1971 about the Rote Drei. He is reported to have died in the early 1980s.

Alexander Foote, the would-be Hitler assassin and Rote Drei wireless man, avoided Stalin's reflexive urge to punish those who had most helped him win the war. After the Director and Maria Poliakova vouched for his truthfulness and assured superiors that he was not responsible for 100,000 Red Army deaths on the approaches to Kharkov, Foote was given a new identity as Albert Müller and was asked to work for the KGB in Argentina. His target: the United States. In 1947, shortly after he crossed into West Berlin to begin this mission, he surrendered to British officials and dis-

---

* See Chapter 1.

gorged the sensational story of Gisela's family. He was by then hopelessly disillusioned with the Soviet cause and wanted to help the West as best he could.

The British did not welcome Foote with a warm embrace. He was debriefed at length, but only offered a clerk's job in the Ministry of Agriculture and Fisheries. He hoped his book, the now-famous *Handbook for Spies*, would propel him out of poverty, but it was not to be. He drank heavily and was hospitalized.[3] He died a bitter man on August 1, 1956, at the age of fifty-one.

Rudolf Roessler, code-named Lucy, survived his stint in the Swiss prison system in 1944 and emerged ready to work again. Although he had the most sensational story of all—maybe even knowledge of the identity of Werther—he chose to keep it to himself. Where Trepper, Rado, and Foote sold their stories for gain, Roessler did not. During the war, the Russians had assumed that Lucy was in the game only for his economic interest. But Roessler's refusal to cash in when the cashing in could have been substantial shows that something else was afoot.

Two years after the war, Roessler again became a spy, this time for the communist Czech intelligence service. In March 1953, Swiss authorities arrested Roessler for espionage and he spent another year in prison. He weathered it well.

Although the CIA later said that Roessler discussed some of his German war contacts with someone the agency has so far not identified, Roessler never tied these contacts to his famous spies: Olga, Anna, Teddy and, of course, Werther.

Roessler died on December 17, 1958, taking Werther's identity, if in fact he knew it, with him.

The fate of Rachel Dübendorfer, Roessler's master, is less certain. She returned to Moscow and was undoubtedly arrested. By trying to reconnect to her Swiss network, Dübendorfer had exposed Hermina Rabinowitch to American scrutiny. This, with the help of defector Igor Gouzenko, led American spies to break part of the Soviet code. Dübendorfer could not have been rewarded for this. But, whatever else, she survived Stalin.

Rachel Dübendorfer died in East Germany in 1973.

Maria Poliakova, the young, beautiful, Jewish spy that as much as

anyone else brought down Adolf Hitler, also survived the war. Foote
remarked that in 1946, Maria was reported to have fallen ill. To
Foote, this meant only one thing—she had been tainted by the
Gouzenko affair and had been taken aside by one of Stalin's execu-
tioners. This was logical, but incorrect.

No one so far has told how Maria survived when in 1937 her father
and brother were exposed as "spies" against Stalin and executed. She,
like hundreds of others, was recalled that year. But unlike those hundreds, she prospered, being promoted from captain to major in the
GRU, controlling the European theater of the 4th Department's
technical intelligence division. She controlled Werther and other assets of the Swiss net throughout the war.

The CIA reports that Maria remained an instructor in military intelligence until at least 1953. What she did after that is unclear. But
in 1990—at the age of eighty—Maria wrote a small piece in the Soviet publication called the *Military Historical Journal.* It concerned a
mission she undertook inside Germany after the war began, but
does not touch upon Werther or other aspects of Gisela's family.

The mystery of Maria Poliakova has yet to be solved. How did she
survive in a profession that left most others arrested or dead? What
secrets did she alone hold? How was she able to spare Foote's life?
Why was she not punished after Foote defected to the British?

There is much to the Poliakova story that has yet to be told.
Someday we may learn how she became Russia's lead undercover
agent in Germany at the age of twenty-six. We may learn how she
protected Dübendorfer from reprisals after Dübendorfer refused
Stalin's order that she turn over her agent network to another Red
Army spy. And we may find how this cosmopolitan, Jewish spy survived an anti-Semitic system that distrusted all things foreign.

But for now we are left with an incomplete picture of one of the
most important and least known figures of the twentieth century.

Notes

1 This account is from the Internet site: "historyplace.com/worldwar2/holocaust/h-death.htm"

2 Studies Relating to Foreign Intelligence, CIA: 1973. RG 263, St. 190, Row 25, Comp. 7, Shelf 2, Box 1. National Archives. Most of the epilogue descriptions derive from this formerly secret file.

3 Read and Fisher, p. 225.

BIBLIOGRAPHY

Note: RG = U.S. National Archives Record Group and archivist's coordinate.

Unpublished American Documents.

Bently, Elizabeth. American Intelligence Reports. RG 319, Boxes 17 and 18.

Biographies of War Criminals. RG 319, Box 6.

Bohle, Ernst Wilhelm. OSS Interview Report. RG 226, XL 19614.

Bormann, Martin. American Intelligence Records. RG 319, Boxes 269 and 270, and Box 25A.

The Case of the Rote Kapelle. RG 319, Boxes 59 and 60.

CIA's secret 1973 Report on the Rote Kapelle. RG 263, Stack 190, Row 25, Comp 7, Shelf 2, Box 1.

Dietrich, Otto. Interim Report on Interrogation. RG 319, Box 39A.

Foote, Alexander. "Revelations of a Soviet Agent in Switzerland." Translated from the *Gazette de Lausanne,* March 28, 1949. RG 319, Box 60.

German Order of Battle. RG 319, Boxes 5 and 6.

Halder, Franz. Interviewed as part of the U.S. Strategic Bombing Survey, APO 413. RG 226, XL 137995.

Haushofer, Karl. OSS interview. RG 266, XL 22853.

———. Report of Interrogation. RG 226, XL 11080.

Hitler's War Conference, November 10, 1937. RG 226, Roll 112.

Jodl, Gen. Alfred. Interviewed as part of the U.S. Strategic Bombing Survey, APO 413.

Lee, Raymond. Report of the U.S. Military Attaché, November 28, 1941. RG 319, Box 83.

The Political and Social Background of the 20 July Incident. RG 226, XL 17383.

Report on Soviet, German, Japanese Relations, State Department Archives. RG 59, 740011, Roll 1153.

Ribbentrop, Joachim von. Interrogation Report, Special Detention Center "ASECAN." RG 319, Box 8.

Rudolf Hess documents. RG 238, Entry 51, Box 180.

Schellenberg, Walter Friedrich. Final Interrogation Report. RG 165.

Speer, Albert. Interrogation Report by the Combined Intelligence Objectives Subcommittee. RG 319, Box 8.

———. Interrogation Report by the U.S. Group Control Council. RG 226, XL 17234.

Unpublished Documents, Russian Archives

Black Bertha files, the KGB's file on the Rudolf Hess affair reviewed by this author at the Lubyanka in Moscow.

Published Works

Andrew, Christopher. *The Making of the British Intelligence Community.* London: William Heinemann, 1985.

Andrew, Christopher, and Oleg Gordievsky. *KGB: The Inside Story.* New York: HarperCollins, 1990.

Best, Payne S. *The Venlo Incident.* London: Hutchinson, 1950.

Borovik, Genrikh. *The Philby Files: The Secret Life of Master Spy Kim Philby.* Edited by Phillip Knightley. Boston: Little, Brown and Company, 1994.

Bullock, Alan. *Hitler: A Study in Tyranny.* New York: Harper & Row, 1964.

Cadogan, Alexander. *The Diaries of Sir Alexander Cadogan.* New York: Putnam, 1971.

Carell, Paul. *Scorched Earth: The Russian German War, 1943–1944.* Boston: Little, Brown and Company, 1970.

Cave Brown, Anthony. *Bodyguard of Lies.* New York: Harper & Row, 1975.

———. *"C": The Secret Life of Sir Stewart Graham Menzies.* New York: Macmillan Publishing Company, 1987.

Churchill, Winston S. *The Gathering Storm*. Boston: Houghton-Mifflin, 1948.

———. *The Grand Alliance*. Boston: Houghton-Mifflin, 1950.

———. *The Hinge of Fate*. Boston: Houghton-Mifflin, 1950.

———. *Their Finest Hour*. Boston: Houghton-Mifflin, 1949.

CIA. *The Rote Kapelle: The CIA's History of Soviet Intelligence and Espionage Networks in Western Europe, 1936–1945*. Washington, D.C.: University Publications of America, 1979.

Ciano, Galeazzo. *The Ciano Diaries*. London: William Heinemann, 1946.

Clark, Alan. *Barbarossa: The Russian German Conflict, 1941–1945*. New York: William Morrow, 1965.

Colville, John. *The Fringes of Power*. New York: Norton, 1985.

Conquest, Robert. *The Great Terror*. New York: Oxford University Press, 1990.

Conot, Robert E. *Justice at Nuremberg*. New York: Harper & Row, 1983.

Costello, John. *Ten Days to Destiny*. New York: William Morrow, 1991.

Dallin, David. *Soviet Espionage*. New Haven: Yale University Press, 1955.

Deutsch, Harold. *Conspiracy Against Hitler in the Twilight War*. Minneapolis: University of Minnesota Press, 1968.

Documents on German Foreign Policy: 1918–1945. Series C, Vols. 1–6, and Series D, Vols. 1–13. Washington, D.C.: Government Printing Office, 1957–64.

Eden, Anthony. *Memoirs: The Reckoning*. Boston: Houghton-Mifflin, 1965.

Foote, Alexander. *Handbook for Spies*. London: Museum Press Limited, 1964.

Fugate, Brian. *Operation Barbarossa*. Novato, Calif.: Presidio Press, 1984.

Garlinski, Jozef. *The Swiss Corridor*. London: J. M. Dent & Sons, Ltd., 1981.

Gilbert, Martin. *The Second World War*. New York: Holt, 1989.

Gisevius, Hans Bernd. *To the Bitter End*. Boston: Houghton-Mifflin, 1947.

Goebbels, Joseph. *The Goebbels Diaries: 1939–1941.* Translated and edited by Fred Taylor. New York: Putnam, 1983.

Goralski, Robert, ed. *World War II Almanac: 1931–1945.* New York: Putnam, 1981.

Guderian, Heinz. *Panzer Leader.* Washington, D.C.: Zenger Publishing Company, Inc., 1952.

Halder, Franz. *The Halder War Diary: 1939–1942.* Edited by Charles Burdick and Hans-Adolf Jacobsen. Novato, Calif.: Presidio Press, 1988.

Hassell, Ulrich von. *The von Hassell Diaries.* Garden City, N.Y.: Doubleday, 1947.

Hilberg, Raul. *The Destruction of the European Jews.* New York: Octagon Books, 1978.

Hinsley, F. H. *British Intelligence in the Second World War.* Vol. 1. London: H. M. Stationery Office, 1979.

Hitler, Adolf. *Hitler's Secret Conversations.* Compiled by Martin Bormann. Translated by Norman Cameron and R. H. Stevens. New York: Farrar, Straus and Young, 1953.

———. *Mein Kampf.* Translated by Ralph Manheim. Boston: Houghton-Mifflin, 1943.

———. *My New Order.* Edited by Raoul de Roussy de Sales. New York: Reynal & Hitchcock, 1941.

———. *Speeches of Adolf Hitler: April 1922–August 1939.* Edited by Norman H. Baynes. New York: Howard Fertig, 1969.

Hoettl, Wilhelm. *The Secret Front.* London: Weidenfeld and Nicolson, 1953.

Hoffmann, Peter. *History of the German Resistance 1933–1945.* Cambridge, Mass.: The MIT Press, 1977.

Hohne, Heinz, and Hermann Zolling. *The General Was a Spy.* New York: Coward, McCann & Geoghegan, Inc., 1972.

Hoyt, Edwin. *The Battle for Stalingrad.* New York: Tom Doherty Associates, 1993.

Irving, David. *Hitler's War.* New York: Avon Books, 1990.

Keitel, Wilhelm. *Memoirs of Field Marshall Keitel: 1940–1945.* Translated by David Irving. Edited by Walter Gorlitz. London: William Kimber, 1965.

Kersten, Felix. *The Kersten Memoirs: 1940–1945.* Translated by

Constantine Fitzgibbon and James Oliver. New York: Macmillan, 1957.

Khrushchev, Nikita. *Khrushchev Remembers: The Last Testament.* Translated and edited by Strobe Talbott. New York: Little, Brown and Company, 1974.

Kilzer, Louis C. *Churchill's Deception.* New York: Simon & Schuster, 1994.

Kimball, Warren F., ed. *Churchill and Roosevelt: The Complete Correspondence.* Vols. 1 & 2. Princeton: Princeton University Press, 1984.

Klemperer, Klemens von. *German Resistance Against Hitler.* Oxford: Clarendon Press, 1992.

Lang, Jochen von. *The Secretary.* New York: Random House, 1979.

Lee, Raymond E. *The London Journal of General Raymond E. Lee: 1940–1941.* Boston: Little, Brown and Company, 1971.

Lessor, James. *The Uninvited Envoy.* New York: McGraw-Hill, 1963.

Lukacs, John. *The Duel.* New York: Ticknor & Fields, 1991.

Manstein, Erich von. *Lost Victories.* Chicago: Henry Regnery Company, 1958.

Masterman, J. C. *The Double Cross System.* New Haven: Yale University Press, 1972.

Mellenthin, F. W. von. *Panzer Battles.* New York: Ballantine Books, 1984.

Noakes, J., and G. Pridham. *Nazism, A History in Documents and Eyewitness Accounts: Foreign Policy, War and Racial Extermination.* New York: Schocken Books, 1988.

———.*Nazism, A History in Documents and Eyewitness Accounts: The Nazi Party, State and Society.* New York: Schocken Books, 1983.

Overy, Richard. *Russia's War.* New York: TV Books, 1997.

Perrault, Gilles. *The Red Orchestra.* New York: Simon & Schuster, 1969.

Prange, Gordon. *Target Tokyo.* New York: McGraw-Hill, 1985.

Rado, Sandor. *Codename Dora.* London: Abelard-Schuman, Ltd., 1976.

Radzinsky, Edvard. *Stalin.* New York: Doubleday, 1996.

Reed, Anthony, and David Fisher. *Operation Lucy*. London: Hodder & Stoughton, 1980.

Rosenberg, Alfred. *Memoirs of Alfred Rosenberg*. Translated by Eric Posselt. Chicago: Ziff-Davis, 1949.

Schellenberg, Walter. *Hitler's Secret Service*. New York: Jove Publications, Inc., 1977.

Schmidt, Paul. *Hitler's Interpreter*. London: William Heinemann, 1951.

Speer, Albert. *Inside the Third Reich*. Translated by Richard and Clara Winston. New York: Macmillan, 1970.

Sudoplatov, Pavel, and Anatoli Sudoplatov. *Special Tasks*. Boston: Little, Brown and Company, 1994.

Tarrant, V. E. *The Red Orchestra*. New York: John Wiley & Sons, Inc. 1995.

Taylor, A. J. P. *The Origins of the Second World War*. New York: Atheneum, 1983.

Toland, John. *Adolf Hitler*. Garden City, N.Y.: Doubleday, 1976.

Trepper, Leopold. *The Great Game*. New York: McGraw-Hill, 1977.

Trevor-Roper, H. R. *The Last Days of Hitler*. New York: Macmillan, 1947.

Trial of German Major War Criminals: Proceedings of the International Military Tribunal Sitting at Nuremberg, Germany, Vols. 1–23. London: H. M. Stationery Office, 1945–1951.

Volkogonov, Dmitri. *Stalin: Triumph and Tragedy*. London: George Weidenfeld & Nicolson, 1996.

Warlimont, Walter. *Inside Hitler's Headquarters, 1939–45*. New York: Frederick A Praeger, 1964.

Winterbotham, F. W. *The Ultra Secret*. New York: Dell, 1974.

———. *Secret and Personal*. London: William Kimber, 1969.

Zhukov, Georgi. *The Memoirs of Marshal Zhukov*. New York: Delacorte Press, 1971.

Zhukov, Georgi K. *Marshall Zhukov's Greatest Battles*. New York: Harper & Row, 1969.

INDEX